Karl Pearson

The Chances of Death

And Other Studies in Evolution

Karl Pearson

The Chances of Death
And Other Studies in Evolution

ISBN/EAN: 9783337404970

Printed in Europe, USA, Canada, Australia, Japan

Cover: Foto ©Lupo / pixelio.de

More available books at **www.hansebooks.com**

THE CHANCES OF DEATH

AND

OTHER STUDIES IN EVOLUTION

BY

KARL PEARSON, M.A., F.R.S.

PROFESSOR OF APPLIED MATHEMATICS IN UNIVERSITY COLLEGE, LONDON,
AND FORMERLY FELLOW OF KING'S COLLEGE, CAMBRIDGE

WITH ILLUSTRATIONS

IN TWO VOLUMES

VOL. I

EDWARD ARNOLD

Publisher to the India Office

LONDON   NEW YORK
37 BEDFORD STREET   70 FIFTH AVENUE

1897

PREFACE

THE Essays and Lectures contained in these volumes have either been written, or else very carefully re-written, within the past six years. Of the twelve essays, five—"The Scientific Aspect of Monte Carlo Roulette," "Socialism and Natural Selection," "Politics and Science," "Woman and Labour," and "Reaction!" have already appeared in print. The first four were originally published in the *Fortnightly Review*, and for permission to reprint them, as well as the paper contained in the Appendix, I have to cordially thank Messrs. Chapman and Hall. The fifth paper was published as a pamphlet in October, 1895. Of the remaining seven essays, two—namely, "The Chances of Death" and "Woman as Witch"—have been delivered as lectures; two others—namely, "Kindred Group-Marriage" and "The German Passion-Play"—contain material on which papers were read or lectures delivered a good many years ago; the remaining three, "Reproductive Selection," "Variation in Man and Woman," and "Ashiepattle," are new, except in so far as some of the results of the first two have been communicated in a very different form to the Royal Society. I have to thank the Council of that Society for permission to reproduce the plate showing the resolution of the mortality curve in the paper on "The Chances of Death." The volumes, as a whole, contain what the author considers of most value on the more popular side of his work as lecturer and essayist since the publication of his *Ethic of Freethought*.

To some readers a few words of explanation on the apparent want of unity in the contents of this book may seem desirable. In the first place, the author believes this heterogeneity will be found more in the titles of the several essays than in their contents. There must always be a unity, interesting at least to the psychologist, if not to the general reader, when a mind with its opinions and methods of investigation reasonably matured approaches even very diverse problems. But the author would be unwilling to admit that this is the sole unity of his essays. He believes that the sympathetic reader will find in one and all the essays the fundamental note of the author's thought, namely: the endeavour to see all phenomena, physical and social, as a connected growth, and describe them as such in the briefest formula possible. Without asserting that evolution can explain anything, but accepting it as a most invaluable formula for describing the sequences of phenomena as we have experience of them, the rationalist has at present a quite impregnable stronghold against reactionaries of every type. He is not called upon to show that evolution explains the universe; he may content himself with the simple challenge to his critics to produce any other formula so useful in describing our experience of the concatenation of phenomena —any other formula which so markedly economises thought, or, differently expressed, which so amply fulfils the purport of science. From this standpoint the reader will find the fourth, fifth, and sixth essays, and the Appendix, are endeavours to defend modern science from recent attacks on the part of the pseudo-scientific, the political, and the theological critic. The remaining essays deal with evolution from either the statistical or the historical standpoint. Into the former, or statistical category fall the first, third, and eighth essays. In this also may be included the second essay, on "The Scientific Aspect of Monte Carlo Roulette." It originally formed one of a series of popular lectures on chance, of which others on tossing, whist, guessing, etc., may some day be published, and which were especially designed to introduce the audience to those theorems in probability, without a knowledge of which it is impossible nowadays to appreciate the arguments for and against the Darwinian theory of evolution. The essay, on its first publication, appealed to a wider audience than might have been anticipated, and the author still receives communications from all sorts of devotees of Monte Carlo.[1] He can only hope they may seek for the reprint in this volume, and that a study of probability will lead them to its more social applications.

Into the second category of essays dealing with the historical aspect of evolution fall the seventh and the last four papers in this series. "Woman as Witch" and "Ashiepattle" are only slight sketches drawn from a much greater mass of collected material, and on this account, perhaps, the reader will be more ready to pardon their imperfections than in the case of the longer and more elaborate studies on "Kindred Group-Marriage" and the "German Passion-Play." These essays, in substantially their present form, the author, according to a well-known recommendation, has put aside for periods of ten and twelve years respectively. Re-writing them during the last few years, he has suffered from the great disadvantage of having no time to thoroughly study the more recent literature dealing

---

[1] One of his latest correspondents reports great successes attending the betting on a disproportionate number of intermittences ! Would the Casino authorities be persuaded of the imperfections of their tables if a majority of the frequenters took to laying on a superabundance of intermittences ?

with their topics. This will no doubt offer a wide field to specialists to point out the enormity of the blunders committed. At the same time, the renewed study of these papers has convinced the writer that much in them is probably correct, and that, if what is correct be well known to the select few, it has certainly not yet made itself a part of current thought. The idea that mediæval western Christianity was a product neither of Jewish nor Greek minds, but of the Teutonic folk-spirit, is certainly not general, and yet it illustrates one of the most important axioms of comparative religion, *e.g.* that neither the propounder nor the dogma, but the convert, makes a religion what it is. The principle that the noblest characteristics of man must have developed from animal instincts under the pressure of natural selection may be commonly accepted in theory, but a study of the Aryan words for kinship and sex shows in an almost startling manner this evolution in progress.

Beyond the one chief helper to whom the author dedicates this book, he has to express his keen sense of gratitude to Mr. Francis Galton, F.R.S., Professor W. F. R. Weldon, F.R.S., Professor George Thane, Mr. G. U. Yule, Miss Alice Lee, and Dr. R. J. Ryle for friendly assistance in a variety of ways.

KARL PEARSON.

December 1896.

CONTENTS OF VOLUME I

	PAGE
1. THE CHANCES OF DEATH	1
2. THE SCIENTIFIC ASPECT OF MONTE CARLO ROULETTE	42
3. REPRODUCTIVE SELECTION	63
4. SOCIALISM AND NATURAL SELECTION	103
5. POLITICS AND SCIENCE	140
6. REACTION! A CRITICISM OF MR. BALFOUR'S ATTACK ON RATIONALISM	173
7. WOMAN AND LABOUR	226
8. VARIATION IN MAN AND WOMAN	256
APPENDIX—SECTARIAN CRITICISM	379

ILLUSTRATIONS IN VOLUME I

	PAGE
THE BRIDGE OF LIFE	*Frontispiece*
HEIDELBERG BLOCK-BOOK	4
GROSS-BASEL DANCE OF DEATH	5
HOLBEIN'S DANCES OF DEATH	9
GAMES OF CHANCE	13
FREQUENCY CURVE	16
CEPHALIC INDEX OF LONG-HEADED POPULATION IN ROW-GRAVES	20
DISTRIBUTION OF ENTERIC FEVER CASES	22
FREQUENCY OF TARGET HITS	23
ENGLISH MALE MORTALITY	*to face* 26
SCARLET FEVER AND DIPHTHERIA	33
ROULETTE DIAGRAM	46
CURVE OF FERTILITY IN MAN—ANGLO-SAXONS	71
CURVE OF FERTILITY IN MAN—DANES	87
DIAGRAM OF EQUAL RANGE FREQUENCIES	275
UNITED STATES RECRUITS	277
CEPHALIC INDEX OF BAVARIANS	279
TYPICAL SKULLS	288
MALE AND FEMALE VARIATION	373

ERRATA

Vol. I

P. 169, footnote, for *throu* read *through*.

For footnote, p. 283, read, "The probable error of a coefficient of variation is approximately $\cdot 6745 \times \dfrac{1}{\sqrt{2n}}$ of its value," etc.

THE CHANCES OF DEATH[1]

'I see a bridge,' said I, 'standing in the midst of the time.' 'The bridge thou seest,' said he, 'is Human Life; consider it attentively.' . . . 'But tell me farther,' said he, 'what thou discoverest on it.' 'I see multitudes of people passing over it,' said I, 'and a black cloud hanging on each end of it.' As I looked more attentively, I saw several of the passengers dropping through the bridge into the great tide that flowed underneath it.—*Vision of Mirza.*

THERE is an old German proverb: "Death has no calendar," which taken in conjunction with our English, "Death is no respecter of persons," strongly marks the folk-conception of Death as of one who obeys no rule of time, or of place, or of age, or of sex, or of household. This idea of Death as the lawless one, the one who strikes at random, arose early in mediæval tradition, and is represented in the well-known Dances of Death, from the primitive block-book to the finished designs of Holbein. Parallel with this notion of the random character of Death's aim, has run in the mind of the folk a vague idea of Chance as that which obeys no rule and defies all measure and prediction. The two conceptions cross one another in the mediæval representa-

[1] Delivered as a lecture before the Leeds Philosophical and Literary Society, January, 1895.

tion of Death seizing the gambler's dice-box and casting the dice with him for his life.[1]

Almost the earliest mediæval conception of Chance is associated with the idea of dice—the origin of the word itself is very possibly related to the *falling* of the dice from their box,—and certainly the first attempts at a theory of Chance arose from the general interest in gambling with dice. It is indeed in a fifteenth century commentary on the lines of Dante—

> When from their game of dice men separate,
> He, who hath lost, remains in sadness fix'd,
> Revolving in his mind, what luckless throws
> He cast—

that we find the first attempt to rise above the folk-conception of Chance as the chaotic, to the modern notion of Chance as obedience to law. Let us bear these points in mind, the association of Death and Chance, the notion of both as chaotic in their action, and their embodiment in a great artistic ideal—the Dance of Death—which gave so much colouring to mediæval thought and life. We find this sombre notion everywhere — on the church walls, on the bridges, in the engravings and broadsides, but as well in the sermons, the poetry, and the very turn of folk-sentiment.[2] That the reader may realise more clearly

---

[1] DEATH TO THE GAMBLER.

> Kom her, spilgur, ietz ist dein zil,
> Muest mitt mir thon ein seltzamss spiel ;
> Wan du schon hast drey beste thauss,
> Gwinst nichts damitt, daz spil ist auss.
>   *Fücssener Todtentanz.*

[2] Even medals or coins were stamped with the death's head upon them as mementoes of times of plague and death.

PLATE I.

HEIDELBERG BLOCK-BOOK.

PLATE II.

GROSS-BASEL.

the significance of the old Dance of Death, I will place before him the development of the artistic side of the mediæval idea of death during the space of more than a century.

The earliest Dance of Death, of which fragments are still preserved to us, appears to be that on the wall of the cloister of a former nunnery at Klingenthal, near Klein-Basel. The cloister has long been used as a barn, and but for the pious pencil of a good old master-baker of Basel, who copied the Dance in 1773, but little would have been preserved to our day. The language and costume of the designs suggest the first quarter of the fourteenth century; but they have certainly been renewed twice, if not more often—once towards the end of the fifteenth, and once in the beginning of the sixteenth century. In 1480 the nuns of Klingenthal were dispersed, and probably in this year the Dominicans reproduced the nuns' Dance on the wall of the cemetery of their own church in Gross-Basel. This is the dance of death so famous through several centuries. I give in facsimile the pictures of Empress and Cripple in the Gross-Basel Dance as reproduced by Massmann from the drawings of the old master-baker. That the monks copied the nuns' Dance is as clear from the baker's drawings as that Holbein was afterwards influenced by the Gross-Basel Dance. As both the Basel Dances have only reached us after several restorations, I add a reproduction of the Empress and Cripple from a block-book in the Heidelberg Library, scarcely later than 1450, and belonging to the very infancy of woodcutting. During the fifteenth century we find Dances of Death at Lübeck, Luzern, Bern, Strasburg, and other towns, painted in public places, and at the end of this century and during the whole of the next, many woodcuts, engravings, and other forms of representation were published. The artistic value of the Dance of Death has been usually supposed to culminate in the Holbein cuts published first at Lyons in 1538 (see our figures, reproducing the Empress and the Old Man), but throughout the sixteenth, and even in the seventeenth century, we still find vigorous productions dealing with the same central idea, and illustrating how widespread and deeply-rooted this traditional representation of the random action of death remained for more than four centuries. Nor was this folk-idea of death—even if it arose in a time when men were face to face with the terrible mortality of the plague, and heard almost daily the shriek of the wounded and the cry of the condemned—without a healthy lesson for later ages. It taught in public places and in symbols, which the mass of the people could interpret, features of human life common to all classes and to all ages. The shadow of death, more strongly even than blood or nation, maketh mankind akin; it arouses sympathy and understanding, which surmount all the barriers of caste and station. The old Dances of Death supplied what fails so much in our modern life—an artistic representation appealing to all classes of at least one experience common to the whole of humanity.

Standing in 1875 on the well-known wooden bridge at Luzern, with its pictures of the Dance of Death, it struck me that something might be done to resuscitate the mediæval conception of the relation between Death

PLATE III.

HOLBEIN.

and Chance, and to express it in a more modern scientific form. It is only within the last year that I have reached such a generalisation of the theory of Chance, that I have been able to work out my idea of 1875, and my aim in this essay is to place before the reader a modern conception of the Dance of Death. To achieve this, however, I must ask the reader first to follow me in the statement of one or two general principles of the theory of Chance, and some apparently dry statistics derived from the Census and Registrar - General's returns.

In the first place, we have to recognise that our conception of Chance is now utterly different from that of yore. Where we cannot predict, where we do not find order and regularity, there we should now assert (as in the case of the Monte Carlo roulette returns) that something else than Chance is at work. What we are to understand by a chance distribution is one in accordance with law, and one the nature of which can for all practical purposes be closely predicted. Let me exemplify this by some experiments on throwing dice, the particular game of Chance in which our ancestors were so interested. Twelve dice were thrown together 26,306 times,[1] and on each occasion the number of dice having 5 or 6 pips on their upper faces was recorded. Reduced to a diagram we at once see a certain order in the distribution. The most frequent occurrence —6100 odd times—is 4 fives and sixes in the throw of 12 dice. We may term that occurrence, which happens *not necessarily a majority of times*, but more frequently

[1] I owe these returns to the kindness of Professor W. F. R. Weldon, F.R.S.

than any other the "mode." The "mode" in this case is 4 dice in the 12 thrown with 5 or 6 pips. Now the reader will notice on examining the diagram that the frequency of other casts does not distribute itself symmetrically round the "mode." For instance, casts of 2 and casts of 6 both deviate by 2 from the mode 4, but their frequencies are in the ratio of about 16·5 to 14·15. The whole system of frequencies, however, forms a fairly smooth polygon, which conveys at once the notion of law and regularity in chance distributions.

Now, suppose we were to consider every possible combination of the faces which could be thrown with our 12 dice, and count up in all these possible combinations the number of those with no fives or sixes, then the number of those with one five or six, then with two, three, four, etc., fives or sixes, and suppose we then distributed our actual total of 26,306 throws according to the frequency of these various possible combinations.[1] I will not enter into the mathematics of it, but the result is indicated on the diagram by the dotted line. We see that the two lines are in very close agreement.[2] We may therefore conclude that all the combinations mathematically possible in tossing 12 dice together do actually occur in their due proportions when we throw 12 dice several thousand times. This is not a result which we have any right to assume beforehand; that the mathematically *possible* actually does occur in

---

[1] Those who are acquainted with the elementary theory of Chance will know that it is expressed by $26,306 \times (\frac{2}{3} + \frac{1}{3})^{12}$.

[2] Not such close agreement as occurs in the case of card-drawing and tossing, for dice are never theoretically perfect, and a persistent bias has been observed in them.

experiment is demonstrated and can only be demonstrated by actual experience.

Now this conclusion is so important that it ought

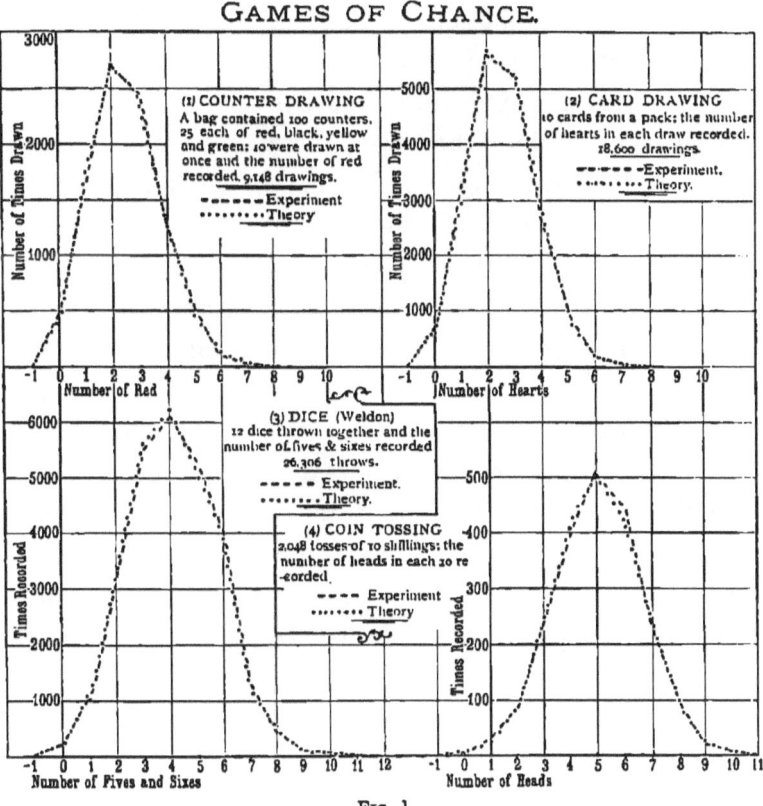

Fig. 1.

to be supported by still further evidence, and I accordingly draw your attention to one or two other results of a like character.

In the first place, we have on the same diagram a figure for the drawing of ten cards together 18,600 times[1]

[1] For these experiments I am indebted to members of my audience at Gresham College, and for the counter experiments to Miss Whiteley.

out of a pack of 52, and then one for the drawing 9148 times of 10 counters out of a bag containing 25 counters each of four different colours. Again, we see a very close approximation between the mathematically possible sets of combinations and the frequencies given by actual experiment. Here, however, there is a fundamental distinction between dice and cards or counter-drawing. In the former case each die gave its own result, uninfluenced by what its fellows might give. But if we draw ten cards in a set from a pack, or ten counters at once from a bag, it is clear that the cards or counters are not each independent; if, for example, we take the ten cards successively out of the pack, the first draw will influence the chances of all that succeed it, the first and second all that follow both, and so on. This is of vital importance for the consideration of mortality curves, the frequency of death at later ages must depend on the incidence of death at earlier ages.

But to return to the results we have already reached, we may sum them up as follows:—

First, the chances of the single event, 2 : 1 in our dice, 3 : 1 in our cards, 1 : 1 in tossing (or 36 : 1 in roulette), may be any whatever.

Secondly, the single events may or may not be independent of each other.

Thirdly, when we take a large number of experiments, we see that, however unable we may be to predict the result of a single trial, the frequencies of many trials distribute themselves round the mode in a perfectly orderly manner, and that the law of distribution is precisely that which we obtain by considering all the combinations which might *possibly* occur.

It is not theory, but actual statistical experience, which forces us to the conclusion that, however little we know of what will happen in the individual instance, yet the frequency of a large number of instances is distributed round the mode in a manner more and more smooth and uniform the greater the number of individual instances. When this distribution round the mode does not take place—as, for example, at Monte Carlo—then we assert that some cause other than chance is at work. Our conception of chance is one of law and order in large numbers; it is not that idea of chaotic incidence which vexed the mediæval mind.

The reader will now, I think, be prepared for the next stage in our argument, the conception of a generalised frequency curve. Taking all the individual results or observations, let us sort them into groups by their deviations from the mode, each group containing all the deviations falling within a certain small range, this small range being the same for each group, and corresponding in many cases to a unit change of deviation. Now, taking a point on a horizontal line to represent the mode, measure the deviations from the mode along this line—deviations in excess to the right, and deviations in defect to the left, of the point. Then place at the centre of each small range or unit a vertical line, proportional in length to the number or frequency of observations having a deviation falling within that range. If the tops of all these verticals be joined we have a polygon which approximates more and more closely to a curve the smaller the range of deviation corresponding to each group be taken. This curve is the so-called *frequency curve*. It gives us by its height at any point, or, to speak more accurately, by its area, the frequency of the corresponding range of deviations from the mode.

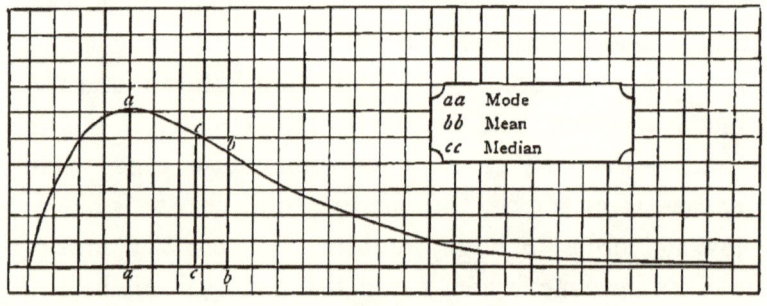

Fig. 2.

We cannot now stay to discuss the mathematical properties of this curve, but attention must be drawn to one or two of its characteristic features.

(1) The mode is not necessarily the same as the mean. For example, suppose we set about counting buttercup petals, then we should find that five petals occur most frequently, but that there are buttercups to be found with ten and even more petals. The mean will be found to lie nearer to six than five petals, and after selection and cultivation may even differ by as many as two petals from the mode. The amount by which the mean differs from the mode gives us a conception of the amount of asymmetry or *skewness* of the frequency curve—the greater length of tail, so to speak, on the mean side of the mode.

(2) Experience soon shows us that very large devia-

tions have little or even no frequency; that the great bulk of the frequency is contained in a comparatively limited range round mode and mean. Now we require some standard by which the degree of concentration of the frequency can be measured. We can realise such a standard in the following manner:—We know that if a body be swinging about an axis, both its energy and momentum will be less the more its mass be concentrated along this axis. Hence we might take the distance from the axis at which all the mass should be concentrated in order to have the same momentum and energy as the actual body, as a good measure of the concentration of its mass. This conception can be applied to our deviations. Suppose a uniform metal disc, or template, to be cut out in the form of the frequency curve, and swung on the vertical through the mean as an axis. Then the distance from this vertical or mean at which the mass of the template must be concentrated, in order to have the same energy and momentum, would not only measure the concentration of mass, but the concentration of frequency (which is proportional to the mass of the template) about the axis or mean. This measure of the concentration of frequency is termed the *standard deviation*. The distance from the axis at which we must concentrate the mass of a swinging body in order to get the same energy or momentum is termed its *swing radius*, and we accordingly see that the standard deviation of a frequency curve is nothing else than its swing radius about the mean. There are various methods used by physicists and statisticians for finding the swing radii or standard deviations of curves,[1] but we must be content for our present purposes with the recognition that a good measure of concentration exists, without entering into details of calculation, which would carry us too far from our present quest. I may, however, remark that whatever be the degree of skewness of the frequency curve, practically the whole of the frequency falls within a range of three times the standard deviation taken on either side of the mean.

Scientifically, we take the ratio of the deviation of the mean from the mode to the standard deviation as the actual skewness. To sum up then, we have these two conceptions with regard to a frequency curve:—

(1) The *skewness*, measuring the amount of asymmetry, or the way in which the mean or average differs from the mode.

For example, in house property the mode is in England a value of about 2s. per week, but the mean is about £15 per year—over 5s. 9d. a week.

(2) The *standard deviation*, measuring the concentration of frequency round the mean.

For example, in tossing twelve coins, and counting the number of heads in each throw, the mean being six heads, the standard deviation is about 1·4 heads, but in throwing twelve dice, and counting the fives and sixes in each set, the standard deviation is about 1·6. There is thus greater concentration in such coin-tossing than in the dice-throwing experiment.

The reader will be curious, however, to learn what

[1] In a whole range of important cases, a piece of uniform card, a pair of scissors, and a fairly delicate balance, *e.g.* a good letter-balance, will suffice.

frequency curves deduced from coin-tossing and dice experiments have to do with mortality? The answer is this: If the laws of frequency we are here dealing with hold very generally for the distribution of artificial frequency in cases where we have no knowledge of how the individual instance will turn out, but only statistics of what happens in the mass, may we not reasonably assume that they are essentially the laws of all large numbers, and that even the frequency of death, its distribution with age, will obey the same laws? Is it not likely that the regularity and order of chance will be manifest even in the apparent chaos[1] which at first impresses us, as it impressed our mediæval ancestors, in the incidence of death?

Let us try and grasp how wide is the field to which results such as these we have deduced from cards and dice apply, and in doing this let us turn to frequencies more directly the product of Nature and less influenced by the hand of man.

In the first place, Mr. Galton has shown by numberless measurements on man, and Professor Weldon by thousands of measurements on crabs and shrimps, that the apparently random sizes of living things have a frequency closely corresponding to our theoretical curves. Personally, I have found skull measurements give good "fits," and I illustrate by a diagram the frequencies of the several cephalic indices for 540 dolichocephalic German skulls found in the Row-Graves of the fifth to the ninth centuries. Theory and observa-

[1] Addison, indeed, considered a bill of mortality "an unanswerable argument for a Providence," since "chance could never hold the balance with so steady a hand."—*Essay on the Bills of Mortality.*

tion here agree with a closeness comparable with that given by counter or card drawing experiments.

The frequency of the various barometric heights is again an instance of the same characteristic type of

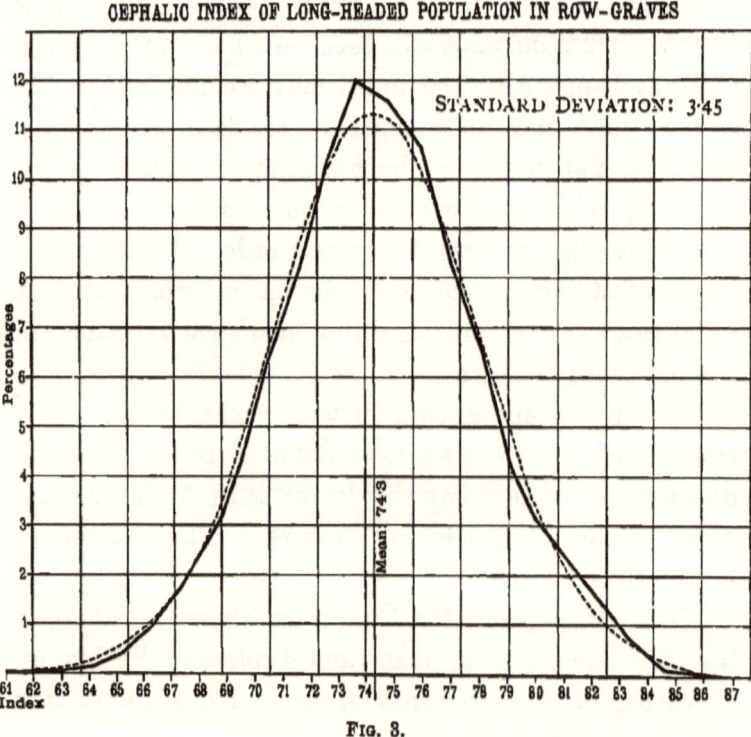

Fig. 3.

curve; the mode differs slightly from the mean, and shows us that extremely low barometer is more frequent than extremely high. Indeed, from paupers to cricket scores, from school-board classes to ox-eyed daisies, from crustacea to birth-rates, we find almost universally the same laws of frequency. I might illustrate my point from the distribution of 8616 Italian marriages in which the bridegroom was in his twenty-fifth year. The mean age of the brides was 22·5 years, but the mode was a bride a year and a half younger. The standard deviation was here 3·945 years, and the statistics show us that the whole frequency of marriage for husbands of twenty-five is practically included in twelve years, or three times the standard deviation on either side of the mean wife. The skewness of the distribution = 1·5 ÷ 3·945 = ·38 about, and the curve starting about the age of thirteen, tails off gradually with a very, very small percentage of wives double their husbands' age. Theory and practice do not, it is true, agree quite as well here as they should do, and I fear this is due to brides understating their ages, especially in cases where they are older than their bridegrooms. The scientific measure of this untruthfulness is a topic, however, which must be postponed for the present.

If birth and marriage fall under the general laws of frequency, we may surely expect that death will do so; and as a step to its consideration, let us examine the distribution of 745 enteric fever cases admitted into the Metropolitan Fever Hospitals during 1891. There are several points of interest to be noted here. The "mode" is 13 years and 8 months, but the mean age for enteric fever is 17 years and 9 months. The two differ by about 4 years. The standard deviation is about 9 years and 8 months, or the skewness is about ·4; thus the distribution is slightly more skew than in the case of matrimony. We may note further that the distribution of 745 deaths for 1891 is very approximately the same as the distribution of 8689 cases for the twenty years 1871-1893.[1] In

[1] The curve for 1871-1893 will be found in the *Phil. Trans.* vol. clxxxvi. Pl. xii.

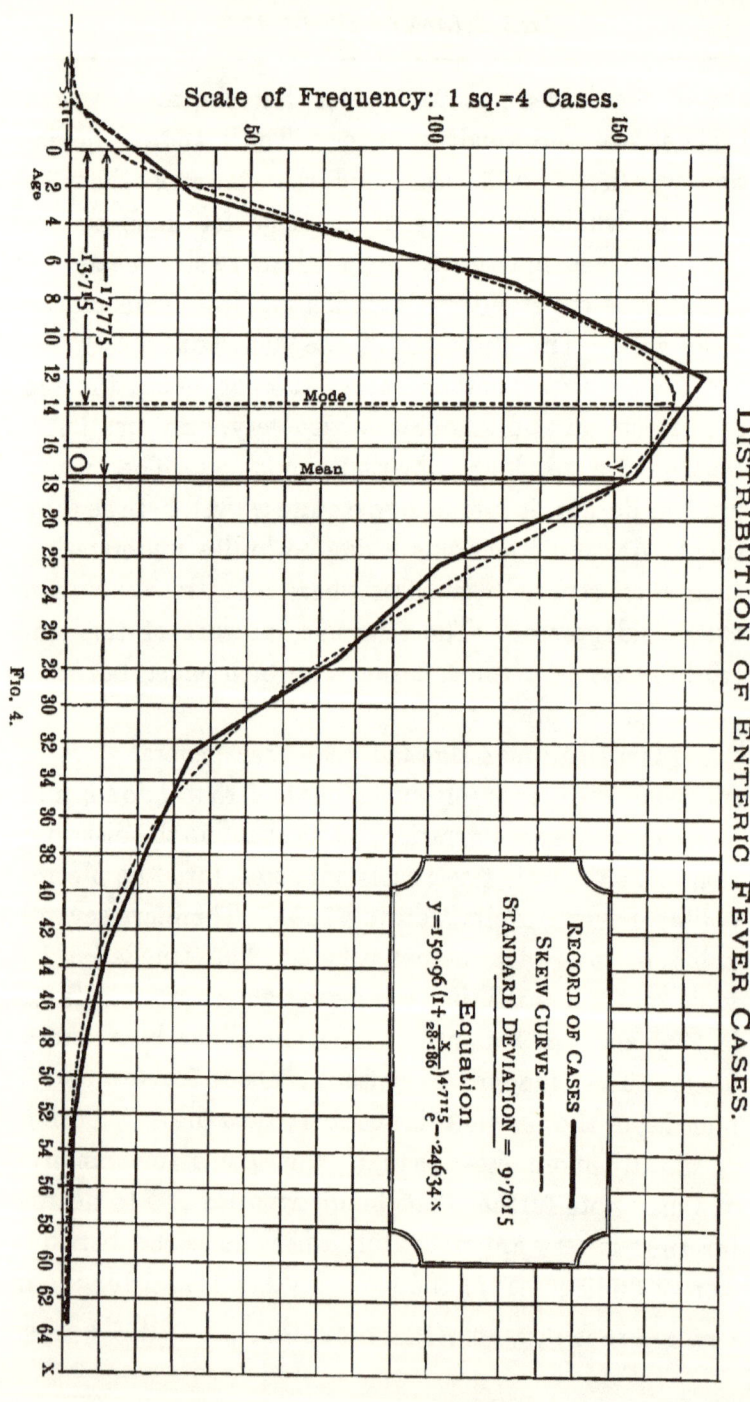

Fig. 4.

other words, the distribution is persistent. Lastly, I would draw attention to this curious feature of theory, namely, that it gives a curve projecting slightly beyond birth, or suggests that there are about three cases per thousand of antenatal enteric fever. To these antenatal cases of illness and of death I shall return later.

The important principle that I want, however, to impress upon the reader by these illustrations is the close-fitting of theory and statistics—the *regularity* in all these chance distributions. I trust that he will now recognise that such distributions are not chaotic, and that the conceptions of skewness and of standard deviation are essential to any just appreciation of variation round the mode.

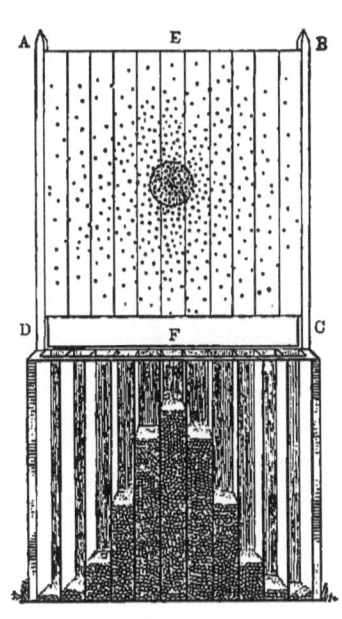

Fig. 5.

Let us turn aside for a brief interval to consider another type of illustration. Suppose a marksman to fire with any weapon at the bull's-eye of a target ABCD, and let a vertical line EF be imagined drawn on this target, passing through the centre of the bull's-eye. Now, it is clear that, however good the marksman and his weapon, all the shots will not strike the bull's-eye, but be concentrated more or less densely round it according to the accuracy of the man and his weapon. Now, we will place under the target a series of columnar receptacles, and suppose each bullet after striking the target to fall without rebound into the receptacle immediately beneath its point of incidence. After several hundreds or thousands of shots these receptacles will be partly filled with bullets, but to different heights. Those at the extreme edge of the target will probably have few or no bullets, those towards the centre will have more, till we reach a maximum under the bull's-eye. The distribution of bullets in our receptacles will form a frequency distribution exactly similar to those we have already discussed. In this case very probably the mean and mode will coincide. The standard deviation which scientifically measures the concentration of frequency is at the same time a measure of the precision of the marksman or of his weapon; the smaller the standard deviation the more closely are the bullets concentrated round the bull's-eye. This example is not wholly imaginary; something like this is actually done in the testing of machine guns passed into the navy; a chance surface instead of a chance curve is constructed, and the measure of the precision of the weapon obtained in a very similar manner. What I would ask the reader to notice, however, is that in any frequency distribution we can look upon the standard deviation as a measure of the precision peculiar to a marksman or to his weapon. Further, we will suppose that, owing to some peculiarity of marksman, weapon, or target—for example, that the bull's-eye is not circular in form, or that, owing to some light effect, the marksman is more liable to miss badly to the right than to the left of the target—the distribution of frequency of hits is not symmetrical but skew. We are thus in a position to conceive any frequency distribution as due to a marksman of a certain skewness of aim using a weapon of a certain degree of precision.

It is by a conception of this kind that I wish to replace the old mediæval notion of the Dance of Death. Our ancestors were correct in supposing the frequency of death to be a chance distribution, but we now know that such a distribution follows regular laws, and this regularity we are able to picture to ourselves by thinking of Death as a marksman with a certain skewness of aim and a certain precision of weapon.

Let us try and follow up this idea. Suppose we imagine a thousand babes to start together along the bridge or causeway of life. The length of that bridge shall represent the maximum duration of life, and our cohort shall march slowly across it, completing the journey in something perhaps over the hundred years. No,—not the cohort completing the journey, the veriest remnant of the thousand who started together! At each step Death, the marksman, takes his aim, and one by one individuals fall out of the ranks—terribly many in early infancy, many in childhood, fewer in youth, more again in middle age, but many more still in old age. At every step forward the target alters; those who fall at twenty cannot be aimed at, at sixty, and the long line of life which serves Death as a target reduces almost to nothing at the extreme end of the Bridge of Life. Such is the picture which I wish my readers to keep before them as they turn with me to the Registrar-General's figures.

Probably they are all familiar with *Whitaker's Almanack*. On p. 357 of the edition for 1894 they will find a table dealing with the number of survivors left year by year out of a company of a million entering life together. If we confine our attention to males, for female mortality differs in some essential points from male, we can deduce from this table the number of males who die in each year of 1000 who start life together. Taking a horizontal line (see plate). I divide it up into equal elements, each of which represents a year,[1] and plot up to each year a like element for each death that occurs in that year among 1000 contemporaries. Thus we see at once from the diagram that of 1000 males born together Death hits 159 in the first year of life, 51 in the second year, 26 in the third, 17 in the fourth year, and so on.

The curve formed by the long series of little crosses on the diagram represents the "mortality curve" thus obtained. The reader will notice at once that it is as a whole unlike any of the frequency curves we have hitherto dealt with. It starts very high in infancy, falls to its least value at thirteen to fourteen years, with only 2·36 deaths. It then slowly increases till it reaches a maximum in the seventy-second year of life, and falls more rapidly than it rose, till scarcely two isolated stragglers of the 1000 reach ninety-one, and hardly one in 10,000 remains for Death to aim at in the hundredth year of life.

---

[1] In the actual diagram, reproduced by kind permission of the Council of the Royal Society from my memoir on "Skew Variation," only two year elements are represented.

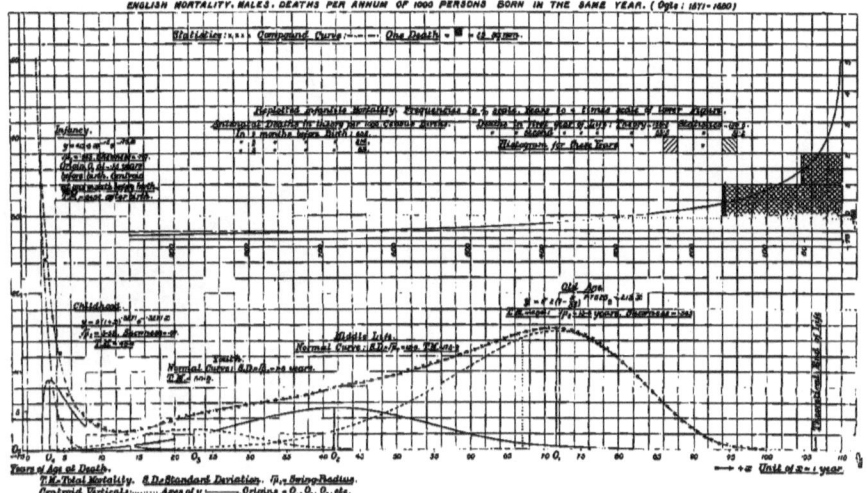

Unlike, however, as the *whole* curve is to a frequency distribution of the type we have been considering, still the old age portion is strikingly like the half of such a distribution, and Professor Lexis some years ago suggested that the old age death is the normal death, and that this would be found to be closely represented by a normal chance distribution.[1] I tried to apply this suggestion of Professor Lexis to French statistics of mortality for both sexes, but only with moderate success. It failed completely on English males. Only when a wide series of experiments on cards and lotteries, and a wider knowledge of variation in the organs of animals and plants had convinced me that there was need of an extension of the ordinary theory of chance, by the introduction of the concept of skewness and its mathematical treatment, did I overcome my difficulty as to old age mortality. I then found that I could represent it with very close accuracy by a skew frequency curve. But it was not only old age that could be thus treated. Once that portion of mortality was removed, I could subtract a second chance distribution covering the next portion of the mortality curve, and so on, till I was left with the mortality of infancy alone to be fitted. This remainder was a frequency distribution of the type I have since found common in economic and botanical statistics; but try as I would, no theoretical frequency curve could be made to fit it, until I had shifted its start some nine months before birth. Thus theory provides us with a certain

[1] See his *Einleitung in die Theorie der Bevölkerungsstatistik*, 1875, where old age mortality is dealt with on this hypothesis.

number of "antenatal" deaths — deaths which also occur in the theoretical distributions which I find otherwise fit fever statistics of all kinds. Now in order that the reader may better realise what has been done, let us return for a moment to the conception of Death as a marksman firing at the living column crossing the Bridge of Life. The mortality curve is not one simple frequency curve, but is made up of several components; in other words, we can only complete our picture by supposing several marksmen aiming with different degrees of precision and with different skewnesses of aims at different portions of the column of life—that is, at different ages. At each step in life we may be hit by more than one marksman, for although they *aim* at one portion of the Bridge of Life they may hit another, for their shots are scattered as those of a rifleman on a target.

Now although I will not assert that my resolution of the mortality curve is final in its values for the chance constants, I am still fairly confident that it is correct in its main features. There are five component chance distributions in the resultant mortality curve—five grim marksmen aiming at the throng of human beings crossing the Bridge of Life. However many are the diseases and accidents from which men die, I cannot doubt that they may be substantially classed into five great groups centring round five distinct ages in life.

Starting, as I was compelled to do in the actual solution of the problem, with the old age end of the mortality curve, I have termed the first chance distribution which may be separated off, *old age mortality*. The point at which this first marksman aims is the seventy-second year, but the mean of his hits is the sixty-seventh year. In other words, the mode of those who die from old age mortality is to die in their seventy-second year, but there is a skewness of aim, and the mean differs from the mode. The period of maximum mortality is very close to the Psalmist's "threescore years and ten." The skewness of this Death's aim is ·345, and his measure of precision, or standard deviation, is 13 years and 5 months. Realise this rather wide range by considering that only slightly more than half the total mortality of old age falls between the fifty-fourth and eightieth years of life. The total number of these old age deaths is 484, or it is within twelve of one-half of the whole number 1000, whom we have considered as entering life together.

There are several facts to be noted about this first component; its skewness is towards youth, and the curve which sweeps right away to infancy on one side is limited at 106·5 years on the other. Thus 106·5 years would form the theoretical limit of life. Not much stress, however, can be laid on this limit, as an almost insensible change in the form of the curve sent up, I found, the theoretical end of life some ten years. What is of significance, however, is that a skew curve of this type does give somewhere a theoretical limit to life. The normal chance distribution suggested by Professor Lexis would make the age of Methuselah (969 years) only extremely improbable, not impossible. In dealing with old age mortality in France, where I tried a normal distribution, there resulted some ten people in the million born who lived beyond their 115th year—a result, I should imagine, hardly in keeping with experience. That there is a superior limit to life seems highly probable, even though we need a very wide range of statistics to establish exactly its theoretical value. On the other side of the Psalmist's "threescore years and ten," we see old age mortality with diminishing intensity running down across middle life, and even with very small frequency across youth into infancy. Death, aiming at the old, sometimes shoots wide of the mark and hits the young. This need not, however, astonish us; what we have termed old age mortality is only that special group of causes most active in old age, that group which in England carries off nearly one-half of human beings. This group corresponds in some sense to the natural end of life, but this natural end may come long before old age. It would probably be the only necessary or essential part of mortality, if the conditions of parentage were perfect, and the freedom from external disease and accident complete. It is death apart from the selection of infancy, the danger of infectious disease in childhood, or of excess or accident in youth or later life. So much, then, as to the last, and the most destructive of the five marksmen whom we have to face as we cross the Bridge of Life.

Having separated old age mortality, the next simple frequency curve was found to centre in the forty-second year, and, further, to have a negligible skewness. This element of mortality I term middle age mortality.

The marksman here is slightly more accurate in his aim than the old age marksman, his standard deviation being 12·8 years. He is far less rapid, however, in his proceedings; he hits only 173, as compared with 484, and his maximum destruction (in the forty-second year of life) is only 5·4 deaths, about $\frac{1}{13}$ that of his old age colleague. His fire is thus slow and scattered, and his curve of destruction a very flat-topped one. His work might be typified by a blunderbus as compared with the rifle-fire of old age death.

In the case of French statistics for both sexes, the total mortality of middle life is 180, its maximum 6 deaths at 45 years, and the standard deviation 12 years. On the whole, considering the greater longevity of women, and the rougher character of my labours on the French statistics, there is a striking closeness in the two results. It is hardly possible to classify the special diseases which are most deadly in the twenty years or so round forty-two. I have not been able to obtain much light on the matter from medical friends. One element, at any rate, might be cancer, the mortality from which is significant from the twenty-fifth year onwards. Accidents also would fall largely into this group. On the whole, it does not appear to me that the causes grouped together in these components—with the possible exception of childhood—refer so much to the special severity of certain diseases, as to the special prevalence during the periods considered of various susceptibilities, relative capacity to resist, or it may be incapacity to resist death,—whatever be the form of its attack — predispositions peculiar, for example, to the periods covered by old age or middle age mortality. However this may be, I feel fairly confident that there can be no great shifting of the mortality components as I am giving them. A little moving of the centre of fire, or its degree of precision may be possible, but that is all, the solution of the problem is practically unique and not arbitrary.

The third component, which I have subtracted from the total mortality curve, is also practically without skewness. It centres in the twenty-third year with a mortality of 2·6. The total number of deaths due to this marksman is only 51, and his accuracy of aim is measured by a standard deviation of 7·8 years. This mortality I have termed the mortality of youth. It centres at a period when new functions and new responsibilities are being exercised. That it is half as large again in the French statistics is, perhaps, largely due to the fact that those statistics embrace both sexes, and this component of mortality covers that critical and sole period of woman's life—eleven to twenty-four years—during which her mortality is known to be greater than man's. The comparatively small mortality of youth, and its not very wide range, might possibly be symbolised artistically by placing in the hands of Death a bow and arrow.

If we now remove from our total death curve the three mortalities of old age, middle life, and youth, we are left with a strange-looking curve generally resembling the frequency distributions found for wealth, flower petals, and cricket scores. To this mortality distribution I tried in vain to fit a theoretical frequency curve. It was only when I returned to the subject, after a further study of fever mortality curves, that I perceived that two points must be borne in mind in any attempted solution. First, there is a mortality of childhood quite distinct from that of infancy; and secondly, the mortality of infancy must, at least in theory, be extended across the antenatal period to a distance which is very approximately nine months.

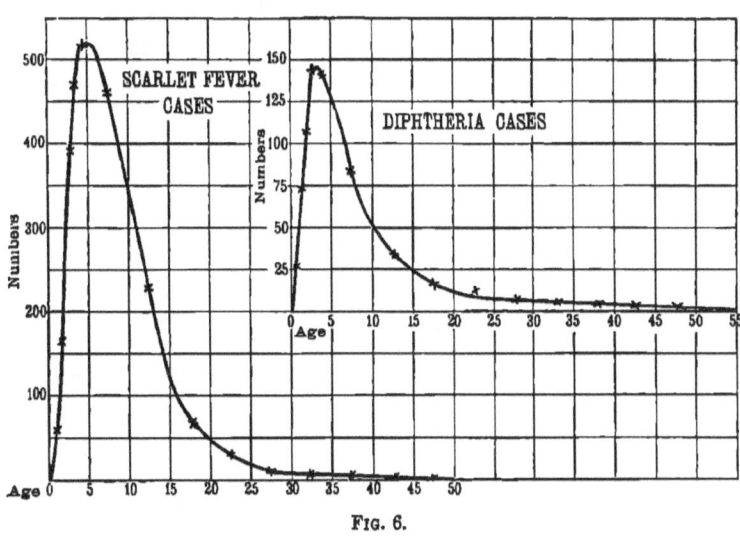

FIG. 6.

The accompanying diagrams show at a glance the distribution, with age, of cases of scarlet fever and diphtheria, and the reader will recognise at once from the manner in which two of the chief foes of child-life arrange their attack, that it is not an attack on the first year of life. The maximum incidence appears in the fourth and fifth years of life. If we pass, however, from the number of cases to the mortality, the maximum deadliness is found in the third year of life—

still well removed from babyhood. The insight obtained from a study of these fever curves enabled me to separate off a mortality of childhood. It contained a total mortality of 46. It rises almost abruptly to a maximum mortality of nine deaths in the third year of life; but while this is the mode, the mean lies at six years. The standard deviation is 3·52 years, and the skewness ·87. It will be seen at once that we have here a far more concentrated fire than anything we have yet come across. The mortality of youth is slightly larger, but the maximum deadliness of the marksman who aims at children is nearly three and a half times as great as that of him who aims at youth. His weapon is more like the Maxim gun than the bow, and it is only the concentrated character of his attack which enables us to pass rapidly through the sphere of his destructive powers without appalling loss. Had we included, as in the French statistics, girls as well as boys, the centre of the mortality of childhood would have been higher up in life, as it is in the third, fourth, and fifth years of life that girl-mortality exceeds boy-mortality.

Lastly, having removed the mortality of childhood, we are left with a remaining mortality in the English statistics of 246 deaths, and in the French of 284 deaths. These form what I term the mortality of infancy. Since the French statistics contain both male and female, and the English only male, and since, in the first two years of life, the excess of male over female deaths is in England very marked—about one-seventh—we ought properly to compare not 284 French deaths, but rather

310 to 320 French deaths with 246 English deaths. If this be done, we see at once that infantile mortality is much greater in France than in England. In England about a quarter, in France nearer a third than one-quarter of all persons born die as infants! A comparatively small reduction in the number of infants who die would be a readier means of checking the decline in the French population than any plan for fostering a higher birth-rate.

Our own infantile mortality—amounting to a quarter of all males born—is quite sufficient, however, to occupy our attention, without turning to our neighbours' shortcomings. This is not the occasion on which to enter into the mathematical difficulties of fitting with a theoretical curve the infantile mortality distribution.[1] Suffice it to say that, though I am far from completely satisfied with my labours, I still think I have reached a curve giving the main features of this mortality component. I consider its constants subject to modification and improvement, when our friends the doctors will provide the sort of statistics we need.

Now as to the nature of the theoretical fit. According to statistics the total postnatal infantile mortality = 246, theoretically our curve gives 245·7. Of this in the first year of life we have theoretically 156·2 and statistically 158·5 deaths, and in the second year of life theoretically 53·5 and statistically 51·2 deaths. After this the mortality of childhood begins to contribute its quota. The divergence, it will be seen, is not significant.

[1] Mathematically the chief difficulty is that, owing to the steepness of the distribution, we can only consider areas, not points, to be given.

The interesting theoretical point of this infantile curve lies in the fact that to get any fit at all, it had to be started very approximately nine months before birth. The bulk of its mortality lies in the first dim stages of life, and the centre of Death's aim is the beginning of the last antenatal month. The precision of Death's aim is measured by $\cdot 943$ years or a little over eleven months—the skewness of his aim, which, as in childhood, is towards age $= \cdot 707$. The total postnatal mortality is 246, the total antenatal mortality 605. Thus we see that this marksman combines intense concentration with extreme deadliness. He is very close to infantile life and unremitting in his destructiveness. The peculiarity of his blows are that they are dealt alike at antenatal and postnatal life. Thus the sources of this mortality must be sought for in causes common to both periods. These causes must be inevitably associated with parentage. Bad parentage is probably largely the source of this great infantile mortality—bad parentage, showing itself not only physically, but mentally in the want of proper care of the young life, is the one possible cause of death continuous from the antenatal to the postnatal period. The marksman Death strikes down the young life with the bones of its ancestry.

As to the antenatal deaths of which theory makes us cognisant, they are distributed as follows:—

(1) Total for the 9 months preceding birth, 605 for every 1000 born alive. Of these, 391 alone fall into the first three months of antenatal life.

(2) Total for the 6 months preceding birth, 214 for the 1000 born

alive. Of these, 131 fall into the period between the third and sixth months.

(3) Total for the last 3 months preceding birth, 83 for every 1000 born at the proper period.

Now it is very difficult to get statistics of these occurrences, and so determine how far our theoretical continuation of infantile mortality into the antenatal period has any meaning for actual facts. The 391 deaths of the first three months would be nowhere recorded, in many cases they would possibly pass unregarded.[1]

The 214 deaths of the remaining six months would be noted as abortions or still-births. The proportion of one such antenatal death to five actual births may seem high. I cannot, however, obtain any sufficiently definite statistics to prove or disprove the point. Dr. Galabin, who has the repute of a very careful and judicious writer, says: "On an average every woman who has borne children, and reached the limit of child-bearing, has had at least one abortion or premature labour." To these, I presume, must be added the not infrequent cases of women who have never borne children, but have had one or more experiences of this kind. Roughly, therefore, taking the average number in a family born alive to be 4 to 5, our proportion of antenatal deaths[2] to actual births at the proper period does not seem exaggerated.

[1] A medical friend writes: "For my own part, I should not think 3 antenatal deaths to 5 actual births would turn out too many, considering the practical impossibility of diagnosing a miscarriage or even a pregnancy of only a few weeks."

[2] The term antenatal death must be supposed to include those born before their proper time and dying before their proper birthday. It might be defined scientifically, despite the paradox, as "the death of a fertilised human ovum within 281 days of conception, whether *in utero* or not."

Lastly, in the three months of the antenatal period which immediately precede birth, we have 83 deaths to every 1000 born at the proper time, or 83 in 1083 = 7·66 per cent. Now this percentage may consist of two factors—still-births, and children born viable, but dying before the date of their proper birth. The latter births would not be recorded, or not recorded in anything like their real proportions in any statistics based on the census returns.

With regard to still-births, I may cite the following returns :—

Dublin Rotunda Hospital :—
1847-54, the ratio of still-births to total births = 6·9 per cent.
1871-75   „   „   „   = 6·1 per cent.

Maternity Charity, St. Pancras (Dr. J. H. Davis) :—
1842-64 (13,916 births) . . 3·86 per cent.

Guy's Hospital Lying-in Charity (Sixth Report) :—
1875-85 (25,777 births) . . 3·84 per cent.

Newsholme's *Vital Statistics* (without any statement of authority or reference) 4 per cent.

We thus reach 4 to 5 per cent as about the percentage of still-births, leaving 2·7 to 3·7 per cent to be accounted for by viable children dying before their normal birthday, or, if dying afterwards, not recorded in the census returns. Still-births are not registered in England, but as all viable children are, it is possible that we might obtain some measure of the second factor in this last period of antenatal deaths, by considering the difference between the census totals and the Registrar-

General's return for births in the twelve months preceding the census.[1]

So much, then, as to these antenatal deaths. Our resolution of the general mortality curve does not depend upon our right to give any interpretation to the portion of the curve preceding birth. But the interest attaching to the infantile mortality component will be much enhanced, if full statistics of antenatal deaths show that it gives intelligible results even for the period preceding birth. Nothing that I have yet been able to ascertain is decisively opposed to the conclusions which may theoretically be drawn from this extension of infantile mortality.

Our investigations on the mortality statistics have thus led us to some very definite conclusions with regard to the chances of death. Instead of seven we have five ages of man, corresponding to the periods of infancy, of childhood, of youth, of maturity or middle age, and of senility or old age. In the case of each of these periods we see a perfectly regular chance distribution, centring at a given age, and tailing off on either side according to a perfectly clear mathematical law, defined by the total mortality of the period, its standard deviation, and its skewness.

Artistically, we no longer think of Death as striking chaotically; we regard his aim as perfectly regular in the mass, if unpredictable in the individual instance. It is no longer the Dance of Death which pictures for us

---

[1] No attempt to do this is possible so long as, in the census returns published, the distribution of population in the first five years of life is obtained by dividing the total "in proportions determined by calculation from the registers of births and deaths"!

Death carrying off indiscriminately the old and young, the rich and the poor, the toiler and the idler, the babe and its grandsire. We see something quite different, the cohort of a thousand tiny mites starting across the Bridge of Life, and growing in stature as they advance, till at the far end of the bridge we see only the graybeard and the "lean and slippered pantaloon." As they pass along the causeway the throng is more and more thinned; five Deaths are posted at different stages of the route longside the bridge, and with different skewness of aim and different weapons of precision they fire at the human target, till none remain to reach the end of the causeway—the limit to life.

It would need a great artist to bring that human procession vividly before the reader. Such alone could fully realise my dream on the Mühlenbrücke at Luzern of twenty years ago. But I ventured to put the roughest of sketch suggestions before two artists. The one, trained in the modern impressionist school, failed, I venture to think, in fully grasping the earnestness of life; the other, reared among the creations of Holbein, Flaxman, and Blake, shows more nearly the spirit of my dream (see frontispiece).

In conclusion, let me point out that the problem here dealt with is one which will have to be solved for other forms of life than man. One of the chief difficulties of the theory of evolution is the want of an exact measure of selection, and, in particular, of selection at different ages. The analysis of the mortality curve enables us at once to reject much that passes for science in the discussion of social evolution. It enables us to localise the time and manner of selection, and until that is done for many forms of life, we shall hardly be able to separate the effects of growth from those of selection, when we come to consider numerical measures of the processes described by Darwin. Unfortunately, with few exceptions, man is the only form of life whose age at death is at any rate approximately known. One of these exceptions is the thoroughbred racehorse, and it has been suggested to me that a study of the *Studbook* would enable me to complete for the horse what the Registrar-General's statistics allow us to do for man. Should the material prove sufficient, and the leisure to deal with it be granted, I should have no doubt to make some changes in the theory dealt with in this essay; but I have little doubt that we should still find distributions following the laws of chance, and that an artist might be induced to render them for us in pictorial symbols.

Man has for man, however, more than the purely scientific interest which he shares with the horse. The great problems of life—its labours and its affections—centre for most of us in the chances of death. It is Death which brings the pathetic and the tragic into our midst, and if the ravages of war and the horrors of the plague are not so continually with us as they were with mediæval man, we still may feel somewhat of the same fascination in our own Bridge of Life, as he did in his weird and ofttimes gruesome Dance of Death.

II

THE SCIENTIFIC ASPECT OF MONTE CARLO ROULETTE[1]

> Many games of skill and hazard
> Have I seen in different nations,
> Have I played in different countries.
> He who plays with old Iagoo
> Must have very nimble fingers.—*Hiawatha*.

THAT it does not pay to gamble has been the oft-repeated theme of the moralist, and has been demonstrated with much brave show of symbols by mathematicians from Lagrange to De Morgan and onwards. While the moralists have boldly asserted that the service of the goddess Chance leads to a complete demoralisation of her worshippers from the high priests downwards, the mathematicians have based their arguments on the fact that the individual with a limited fortune plays against the public with an almost unlimited one, or against a banker with a small but persistent advantage. The mathematicians, however, start from the hypothesis that gambling is a game of chance — chance being defined in their own perfectly clear and definite sense. My object in the present essay is to show that chance

[1] *Fortnightly Review*, February, 1894.

in this sense, chance as it applies to the tossing of an unloaded coin, has no application to Monte Carlo roulette.

It may appear to some of my readers that the goddess Chance is only the personification of ignorance—of *inscientia*—and that accurate reasoning cannot, as it certainly does not, play a part in her worship. But for science chance is identical with knowledge, not with ignorance,—with partial knowledge, it is true, but none the less with knowledge. What the natural philosopher understands by chance is *not* his ignorance of how any individual event—*e.g.* the spin of a teetotum—may result, but it is his knowledge of the percentages of successes and failures which are sure to occur in a considerable number of trials. This knowledge is based, like the physicist's, on past experience, on the widest possible range of statistics as to events of the same or of a similar character which may be available. The scientific conception of chance is that of a measure based on experience; a knowledge of the average results of many events is used to replace ignorance of the result of any individual event. Science has, accordingly, every right to invade such a temple of chance as Monte Carlo itself, and to apply her tests of what is and what is not a worship of the goddess. The judgment which Science gives in this case is decisive; judged by the so-called "permanences," or runs of colour, Monte Carlo roulette is no true worship of the goddess at all—it is a standing miracle, not a game of chance.

Some few years ago I was occupied with the preparation of a course of popular lectures on the laws of chance. Not being able to lead my audience through the mazy and not oversure paths of mathematical theory, I adopted the experimental method of an appeal to statistics, and the deduction by easy arithmetic of the characteristic laws of my subject. The chief difficulty of this method was to make or to discover the necessary material. I required each individual event recorded, and this consumed much time in the case of new experiments. 25,000 tosses of a shilling occupied a good portion of my vacation, and, being conducted frequently in the open air, gave me, I have little doubt, a bad reputation in the neighbourhood where I was staying. A friend and former pupil supplemented the shilling results with 8200 penny trials and the drawing of 9000 tickets from a bag, while another kindly provided me with the details of nearly 23,000 drawings of coloured and numbered counters. In all these cases the results were in close, and indeed strikingly close, agreement with theory, and were of considerable service for purposes of illustration. A machine to show within the brief period of a lecture the result of several millions of tosses of twenty coins at a time, or the like number of throws of dice, only failed owing to the views of the British carpenter on the variability of the British inch.

Looking still further afield for extensive and readily accessible material, I turned, at the suggestion of a friend, to the Monte Carlo roulette-tables. At Monte Carlo is the most sacred shrine of the goddess; in the directors and croupiers of the famous gambling establishment are to be found her high priests. There, if nowhere else on earth, Chance reigns supreme. In my enthusiasm Monte Carlo appeared to me in a new light; it was clearly a scientific laboratory preparing material for the natural philosopher. How to obtain this material in a workable form was the next problem. To spend several months in Monte Carlo recording the spin of the roulettes was personally an impossibility, nor did it seem likely that the Royal Society or the British Association would award a grant to pay the expenses of an agent engaged in such a novel form of scientific investigation. Luckily, however, further inquiry led to the discovery that the records of the tables are published in a special journal entitled *Le Monaco*, and issued weekly in Paris at the price of a franc. The body of this newspaper is devoted to seven columns of the numbers which have occurred on the seven days of the previous week, and in the four weeks of July and August of 1892 upwards of 16,500 throws of the ball are recorded. In another four weeks, which Mr. L. G. de Whalley has kindly tabulated for me, there was about the same number of throws, so that eight weeks' roulette gave a grand total of 33,000 events to illustrate in an endless variety of ways the laws of chance. With such a wealth of material before me, I felt that M. Blanc deserved a niche in the temple of science, and *Le Monaco* a shelf in every mathematician's library.[1]

[1] The authenticity of the returns in *Le Monaco* having been called in question, I think it desirable to publish the enclosed letters, merely remarking that, so far as I am aware, the Directorate of the Casino has not repudiated the numbers given in that journal:—

I

LONDON, *lc* 14 *Février* 1894.

Monsieur—Veuillez avoir l'extrême obligeance de me faire savoir si les listes

In order that my readers may appreciate the manner in which this wealth of material was dealt with, I must briefly describe, for the benefit of those who may be ignorant, the manner in which chance enters into the game of roulette. Let us imagine an ordinary teetotum capable, after spinning, of falling and resting on any one of thirty-seven different sides, these sides being numbered from 0 up to 36 in the manner indicated in the accompanying cut.

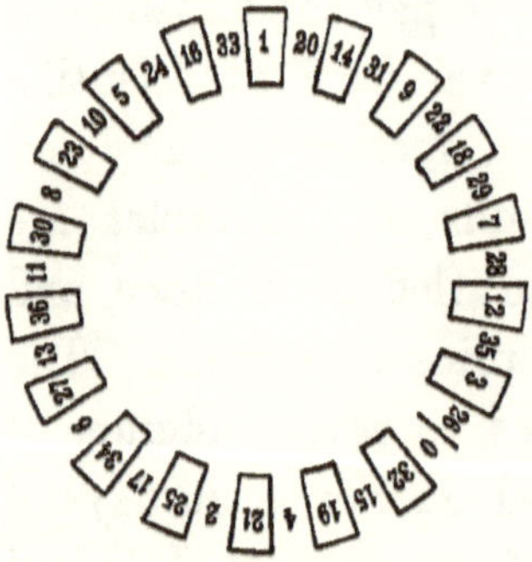

Here the numbers completely surrounded shall be *red* numbers and the remainder *black* numbers, the zero counting as a black number. The whole game of roulette practically consists in betting with the banker on which side such a teetotum will fall after presumably *random* spinning. It may be in betting on the teetotum falling on a

Fig. 7.

des résultats obtenus à la roulette et publiées dans votre journal *Le Monaco* forment un compte-rendu exact et journalier des "coups" qui se font aux différentes tables du Casino de Monte Carlo. Dans l'espoir que vous voudrez bien m'honorer d'une réponse, je vous prie d'accepter avec mes remercîments l'assurance de ma parfaite considération. KARL PEARSON.

Monsieur le Directeur du journal *Le Monaco*.

II

PARIS, le 17 *Février* 1894.

Monsieur Pearson, Londres.

Nous avons l'honneur de répondre à votre estimée du 14. Il nous serait impossible de donner le résultat de toutes les tables, puisque pendant l'hiver "Monte Carlo" fait fonctionner 7 et 8 tables. Nous donnons le résultat d'une seule table, presque toujours la même avec quatre marqueurs, se remplaçant d'heure en heure; généralement la table N° 2, quand il y a de la place. Sinon, à celle qui porte le N° 1 ou le N° 3. Nous vous prions d'agréer, Monsieur, l'expression de nos sentiments les plus distingués. PHILIP.

particular number, or on one of the red numbers, or on a black one, or on an even or an odd one, or on one out of a group of two, three, four, or more numbers, etc., a great variety of bets on such combinations being indicated by the player placing his money on one or another of the many divisions of the roulette-table. The odds, however, against a particular combination are calculated on the basis of thirty-six and not thirty-seven sides to the teetotum, and this forms the "advantage"—the obvious and admitted advantage—of the bank. Clearly, random spinning being assumed, the distribution of chance in the game depends upon the mechanical perfection of the teetotum; it must be equally likely to fall on all its thirty-seven sides, *i.e.* the *frequency* of all the numbers must in the long run be very nearly the same. As a matter of fact, no teetotum is used at Monte Carlo, but the *roulette* is a cylinder containing thirty-seven compartments numbered like our teetotum. This roulette is spun by the croupier, and while it is still rotating a ball is projected in the opposite direction to the rotation on a circular path above the cylinder, and sloping towards its centre; from this path the ball ultimately rolls off into one of the thirty-seven compartments. The whole apparatus is supposed to be made with extreme accuracy, and to be readjusted with the greatest care before the table is used. Admitting the mechanical accuracy of the instrument, and remembering the keen and watchful eyes of the numerous players, it is difficult to conceive a machine better calculated to illustrate the laws of chance than a Monte Carlo roulette. Here, if anywhere, we ought to find excellent material for scientific inquiry. Let us see what we can make of it.

We will start with the easiest conception, that of the chances for and against an event being equal. If we consider the falling of the teetotum on the side marked 0 (or of the ball into the 0 compartment of the roulette) as a blank, we have an equal number of black and red possibilities, or the chances of black and red are equal. Thus in a very great number of throws there ought to be 50 per cent of both. The table below gives the numbers of trials, the percentages of success and failure in the case of roulette as compared with various other cases of equal chances. I premise that "success" means throwing into a red compartment, or drawing a counter or ball of a given colour out of a bag containing equal numbers of two colours, or tossing a tail (a head in Mr. Griffith's case), or drawing any of the first forty-five numbers out of a bag containing ninety tickets numbered from one to ninety.

Method.	Percentages.		Trials.	Experimenter or Calculator.
	Success.	Failure.		
Roulette . . .	50·15	49·85	16,141	Pearson.
,, .	50·27	49·73	16,019	De Whalley.
Bags of balls . .	50·11	49·89	10,000	Westergaard.
,, . . .	50·4	49·6	4,096	Quetelet.
Tossing	51	49	4,040	Buffon.
,, . .	50·05	49·95	4,092	De Morgan's pupil.
,, .	50·04	49·96	8,178	Griffith.
,, . . .	50·16	49·84	12,000	Pearson.
,, . . .	50·05	49·95	24,000	Pearson.
Lottery . .	50·034	49·966	7,275	Westergaard.

In theory the result of an indefinitely great number

of trials ought to be 50 per cent success and 50 per cent failure. In no case, however, are the results exactly reached, but in all the cases of large numbers we have but small deviations from 50 per cent. Thus 16,141 roulette throws give slightly better results than 12,000 and slightly worse results than 24,000 tosses. We notice that Mr. de Whalley's 16,019 roulette throws give nearly the worst percentage, 50·27 instead of 50; and here arises the question which is fundamental to the remainder of our inquiry concerning Monte Carlo roulette: Is such a deviation as ·27 per cent in a case like this a probable or an improbable one? This question may be put in rather more general terms. Let the result of a large but definite number n of trials be known and be represented by s successes; let the result of an indefinitely great number of trials be also known, and let it be represented on the average by S successes for every n trials. How great must the deviation $S-s$ be in order to lead us to assert that we are not dealing with a game of chance? What are the odds against such a deviation? When we say that the odds are 999 to 1 against an event happening in a particular manner, we mean that *on the average* we should expect the event to happen once, and only once, in 1000 trials. Our problem may accordingly be reduced to the following one:—What will be the frequency on the average of the deviation $S-s$, if we repeat an indefinitely great number of times the n trials? To take a concrete example: If we throw 16 coins in the air and count the resulting heads and tails, with what frequency will the result, 4 heads and 12 tails, occur? Here the deviation from the most frequent result of an indefinitely great number of throws, *i.e.* 8 heads and 8 tails, is 4. The question then becomes: What is the frequency with which a deviation of 4 will occur in an experiment of this nature? What are the odds against such a deviation? Now the full answer to this question cannot be given here; the mathematician can provide it by somewhat recondite reasoning, or it may be demonstrated experimentally from well-selected experiments in tossing, ball-drawing, or lotteries—a year ago I should have supposed from the Monte Carlo roulette returns.

It must suffice now to say that for every type of experiment there is a numerical quantity, depending partly on the chance of the single event succeeding, and partly on the total number of the trials of it, which we may term the *standard deviation*.[1] This standard deviation may be calculated, when we know the details of the experiments, either theoretically or from the results themselves; and it gives us a measure of the frequency with which deviations of various sizes will occur. Thus a deviation of more than one half the standard occurs with a frequency of 61·7 per cent of trials, a deviation greater than the standard in 31·7 per cent of trials, of more than twice the standard in only 4·6 per cent of trials, of more than three times the standard in only ·27 per cent of trials; while four times the standard and over is only reached six times on the average in 100,000 trials, or the odds are 99,994 to 6 against it. The standard deviation of our illustration of

---

[1] The standard deviation is a scientific measure of the fluctuation of results round the average or mean. The mean height of 1,350,799 Italian recruits was 162·4 centimetres, their standard deviation 6·67 centimetres.

the 16 coins may be shown to be 2, and a deviation of 4 is just double this; the odds against so large a result being about 954 to 46.

We have now to return to Monte Carlo roulette, and must inquire whether the odds against the deviations exhibited by the returns in *Le Monaco* are so great as to lead any reasonable man to deny that they are the results of chance in the scientific sense—that is, in the only proper sense of the term.

In Mr. de Whalley's numbers we find, out of 16,019 trials, 8053 red numbers, instead of 8009 or 8010. We have a deviation of 43 to 44. The standard deviation is about 63; a deviation as great as or greater than 44 would occur in about half the number of times in which 16,019 returns were examined. It presents, therefore, nothing of the remarkable or improbable. My own results for 16,141 trials confirm this conclusion. We may safely say that so far as the average total numbers of *rouge* and *noir* results go, Monte Carlo roulette obeys the mathematical laws of chance. Indeed, had it not done so, the fact would probably have been discovered by even non-mathematical players at an early date.

These reasonable deviations in red and black were no more than I had expected, and, so far as they went, served to illustrate the laws of chance. The next point to which I turned my attention was the frequency with which the several numbers themselves occurred. Clearly each number, if the roulette were mechanically accurate, should in an indefinitely great number of random throws occur an equal number of times. In the 16,563 throws of my four weeks' play, each number might be expected to have occurred either 447 or 448 times (the mean = 447·65). Recording the frequency of the various numbers, I found that they fitted to a standard deviation of 15·85, while the theoretical standard was 20·87, giving a difference of 5. A new problem thus arises: What is a reasonable amount for the standard deviation of an experiment of this kind to differ from its theoretical value by? The mathematician answers this problem for us by finding the "standard deviation of the standard deviation."[1] It turned out in this case to be 2·43, and it showed me that the odds against a divergence as large or larger than 5 occurring were more than 478 to 23, or something like 21 to 1. In every two years I might expect such a deviation from the most probable results to occur *once*. Now, 37 groups, experiments so to speak, are not very valuable for basing any conclusions upon, and I accordingly increased my groups to 148, by counting the numbers for each week in the month instead of the total month. Here the experimental standard deviation turned out to be 7·2, the theoretical being 10·34, a difference of 3·14, while the standard deviation between experiment and theory was only ·60. The odds against a divergence so great as this are roughly about 2,000,000 to 1.

At this result I felt somewhat taken aback. I did not immediately assume that the laws of chance did not apply to Monte Carlo roulette, but I considered myself very unfortunate to have hit upon a month of roulette

---

[1] If n be the number of trials, and σ the standard deviation, then the standard deviation of the standard deviation $= \sigma \div \sqrt{2n}$.

which was so improbable in its characteristics that it would only occur, on the average, *once* in 167,000 years of continuous roulette-playing. Such were clearly not the most suitable returns for illustrating the laws of chance! Had I then been in possession of the analysis of another 16,000 returns, which Mr. de Whalley has kindly made for me, and which show nothing like the same improbability of distribution *as to the numbers*, I should perhaps have concluded that I was very unlucky in my selection of a month's play, but I should not have been led to a sure conviction that Monte Carlo roulette, as exhibited in *Le Monaco*, is from the scientific standpoint anything but a game of chance.

Not wishing to put aside as useless my very improbable month's returns, I determined to treat them in another manner; namely, to investigate how closely the runs, that is, successions of numbers, of the same *colour* were in accord with theory. To reduce the roulette to the same theory as the coin, I considered the number zero, when it occurred, to be a draw, and simply disregarded it—*i.e.* it was equivalent to a toss in which the coin may be supposed to alight on its edge and balance there. The chance of head or tail is half, the chance of a red or black was thus half. Now, the theory of runs is a very simple one. The chance of a head $=\frac{1}{2}$, of two heads succeeding each other $\frac{1}{2} \times \frac{1}{2} = \frac{1}{4}$, of three heads $\frac{1}{2} \times \frac{1}{2} \times \frac{1}{2} = \frac{1}{8}$, and so on. Calling a "set" the run of tosses or the throws of the roulette ball till a change of face or of colour comes, the chance of a change $=\frac{1}{2}$, of a persistence followed by a change

$\tfrac{1}{2} \times \tfrac{1}{2} = \tfrac{1}{4}$, and so on. Hence, in 2048 "sets" we should expect 1024 sets of 1, 512 of 2, 256 of 3, 128 of 4, 64 of 5, 32 of 6, 16 of 7, 8 of 8, 4 of 9, 2 of 10, 1 of 11, and 1 of some number above 11. Thus one run of 11 heads is on the average to be expected in 2048 sets of coin-tossing. To bring vividly before the reader the divergence between theory and practice,[1] I will place here for comparison my 4274 sets at roulette and 4191 sets of tossing a penny, due to my former pupil, Mr. Griffith:—

Runs.	1	2	3	4	5	6	7	8	9	10	11	12	Over 12
ROULETTE—													
Experiment	2462	045	333	220	135	81	43	30	12	7	5	1	0
Theory	2137	1068	534	267	134	67	33	17	8	4	2	1	0
Standard deviation	33	28	22	16	12	8	6	4	3	2	1·5	1	—
Actual deviation	325	123	201	47	1	14	10	13	4	3	3	0	0
TOSSING—													
Experiment	2163	1056	479	240	120	68	40	15	4	5	0	1	0
Theory	2095	1048	524	262	131	65	33	16	8	4	2	1	0
Standard deviation	32	28	21	16	11	8	6	4	3	2	1·5	1	—
Actual deviation	68	8	45	22	11	3	7	1	4	1	2	0	0

Now let the reader study these numbers, remembering that whenever an actual deviation reaches three to four times the standard deviation, we are approaching the very improbable. In the case of the tossing the actual deviation is slightly over *twice* the standard on two occasions; in the case of the roulette on one occasion the actual deviation is nearly *ten* times the

---

[1] To show how accurately the laws of chance may be verified, even by a Monte Carlo game of chance, I give the following series of 284 sets, forming 590 deals of *trente et quarante*, for the details of which I have to thank Mr. Frank Harris.

Runs.	1	2	3	4	5	6	7	8	9	10	11	12
Theory . .	142	71	36	18	9	4	2	1	One	run	above	eight
Actually .	139	72	36	17	8	4	2	4	1	—	—	1

standard, on another occasion *nine* times the standard, on a third occasion *four* times, and twice it is *three* times it. *The odds are thousand millions to one against such a deviation as nine or ten times the standard.*[1] If Monte Carlo roulette had gone on since the beginning of geological time on this earth, we should not have expected such an occurrence as this fortnight's play to have occurred *once* on the supposition that the game is one of chance. My doubts as to the applicability of theory to predict the averages in Monte Carlo roulette were now fairly aroused, but I determined to get, if possible, independent confirmation of my results. My pupil, Mr. L. Giblin, tabulated for me the runs in a second fortnight's play, with the result that his fortnight was so improbable that it was only to be expected once in 5000 years of continuous roulette. Nothing like as bad a fortnight as mine, but quite inconsistent with a reasonable man applying the laws of chance to Monte Carlo roulette. Finally, Mr. de Whalley investigated 7976 throws of the ball, forming a fortnight's play, at a slightly later date than my returns. There resulted deviations 4·63, 4·62, and 4·44 times the standard deviation, or odds of upwards of 263,000 to 1 against such a result. That *one* such fortnight of runs should have occurred in the year 1892 might be looked upon as a veritable miracle; that *three* should have occurred is absolutely conclusive. Roulette as played at Monte Carlo is not a scientific game of chance. Such results as those published in *Le Monaco*

[1] The odds against a deviation even six times the standard deviation are more than a thousand million to one!

give the deathblow to the mathematician's theory of the random spinning of a mechanically accurate roulette. The man of science may proudly predict the results of tossing halfpence, but the Monte Carlo roulette confounds his theories and mocks at his laws!

It remains, if possible, to localise the exact points in which Monte Carlo roulette rebels against theory. Mr. de Whalley has kindly tabulated for me the runs of odd and even numbers in 4052 throws, with the result that the actual deviation is on *only one occasion* larger, and then only very slightly larger, than the standard. Thus we see that the totals of red and black, the succession of odd and even numbers, are obedient to the laws of chance; the special numbers themselves are in all probability occasionally very chaotic; *the succession of reds and blacks, however, sets the laws of chance at defiance in the most persistent and remarkable manner.* The exact nature of this anomaly will be best brought to the reader's notice by the following table of the runs in 8178 throws of the ball, to which are added for comparison the runs in 8178 tosses of a coin:[1]—

Runs.	1	2	3	4	5	6	7	8	9	10	11	12	Over 12
Theory ..	2044	1022	511	256	128	64	32	16	8	4	2	1	0
Roulette .	2462	945	333	220	135	81	43	30	12	7	5	1	0
Tossing ..	2163	1056	479	240	120	68	40	15	4	5	0	1	0

The abnormal character of these results may be clearly summed up in the words, "superabundance of intermittences and deficiency of small permanences."

[1] As before, a run means a permanence of colour for two, three, or more throws of the roulette ball, or permanence of face for two, three, or more tosses.

Short runs are deficient, and the colour changes much more frequently than the laws of chance prescribe. There is too great a tendency to give red, black, red, black, red, ad infinitum. It is not my object to inquire how this redundancy of intermittences must upset the calculations of those players, if there be any, who follow scientific theory;[1] it suffices to note that its existence demonstrates that roulette at Monte Carlo is not a game of chance, and that no scheme, were there indeed such possible, based on the laws of chance, would suffice to "break the bank." It was, perhaps, some suspicion of the lawless character of his roulette which led M. Blanc to say that he would give a million to any one who would prove that money could be won with certainty at roulette.[2]

[1] During a course of popular lectures on Chance at Gresham College, I was invited to consider more than one scheme for "steadily earning money" at Monte Carlo. As might, perhaps, be imagined, I was in most cases requested to give pecuniary support, others were to provide the "theory." From the little I was allowed to see of these bank-breaking schemes, they were entirely based on the distribution of runs of colour, of permanences and intermittences.

[2] Since the above essay was written I have investigated the runs at various places and times with the following results:—

(1) *Saxon-les-Bains.*—Rouge et Noir, 18,355 coups. These returns were twenty to thirty years old. The distribution of runs was perfectly normal.

(2) *Monte Carlo.*—Roulette, published in *Le Marqueur.* Several thousand coups for, I think, the year 1885. I had only the loan of this publication for a very short time, and could not therefore make as elaborate calculations as in other cases. The runs, however, were slightly improbable, but not sufficiently so for me to assert a definite discord between theory and experiment.

(3) *Monte Carlo.*—Roulette returns published in *Le Pointeur* 31,074 coups from October to November 1887. These returns are of special value, because *Le Pointeur* appears to have been a semi-official publication. They give the following results:—

Black, 15,292.   Red, 15,283.   Zero, 499.

Intermittences	. . .	7917	Set of 6 . .		.	243
Set of 2 .	. . . .	3779	,, 7 .	.		122
,, 3 .	. . . .	1892	,, 8 .		.	48
,, 4 .	. . .	942	,, 9	.	.	35
,, 5 .	. .	459	10 and over 10		.	32

In conclusion, I may remark that there is no way of testing from the Monte Carlo returns, other than by long and somewhat elaborate calculations, whether the game played is one of chance in the scientific sense. As a typical example of fallacy in this matter, I cite the following extract from an evening paper of the year 1893:—

> Some time since, at Monte Carlo, a student of the game of roulette sat for 48 days at one particular table noting the spin of the ball. During the time the spins amounted in all to 31,374, or nearly 700 a day.[1] He found that the black[2] had come up on 15,292 occasions, and the red on 15,283. One colour was thus 9 in advance of the other. The daily average of difference was only 16, and the greatest difference on any one day 57. The inference is that, if a man played steadily at the colours for two months, he would leave off very much where he began. Doubtless this would be equally the case if, furthermore, he backed the even-money chances, the *pair* and *impair*, *passe* and *manque*. The equality of the chances all round is made more striking when the result of the various numbers is given. Each of the thirty-seven numbers, or, to be accurate, of the thirty-six and zero, which makes a thirty-seventh, should have come, as nearly as can be calculated, 847 times, and, as a matter of fact, the 17 did so appear. Ten other numbers were so close to the total that they ranged from 5

Now the proper number of intermittences for 30,576 red and black throws is 7644, or there was a deviation in excess of intermittences of 273, and this equals 3·6 times the standard deviation (75·71). The odds are therefore 5000 to 1 against such an *excess* of intermittences. We may conclude, therefore, that the Monte Carlo returns were beginning to be mathematically improbable in 1887, although they were not then so miraculous as in 1892.

(4) The Rev. T. C. Simmons kindly favoured me with the results of an experiment made by him on 8192 runs of odd and even numbers. The experimental result was in close accord with theory, there being, for example, 4172 intermittences, or a deviation of 76. The odds against this deviation are only about 10 to 1.

This confirms the view expressed in the above essay that, in well-conducted experiments on runs, there is a close accord between actual results and mathematical theory.

[1] Query, 653? [2] Presumably the black zero is omitted.

below it to 5 above—that is to say, they came up from 842 to 852 times, whilst fifteen other numbers appeared from 834 to 858 times. One number was 79 from the average, but this was the exception. All this strengthens the notion one naturally has that, if a number has not come up for a very long time, the chances of its appearance increase with every turn which does not give it, though, theoretically, the fact is unquestionable that every time the wheel is spun the odds against each number are precisely the same, for the ball is just as likely to fall into any one stall as into any other. . . .

Now this paragraph gives us, it is true, very little reliable data to go upon, but what data there are appear to me to strengthen, not to allay, the doubts of the philosophical student of chance.

The general equality of red and black numbers we have already seen to hold, but the "student" tells us that the daily average of difference was 16. The total number of throws of red and black being 30,575 (there appear to have been 799 zeros), the daily number of throws without zero would be about 637, the standard deviation of which number of even chances is 12·6, corresponding to an average difference[1] of about 10 instead of 16. An average difference of 16 would connote a standard deviation of 20. Here theory gives 12·6 and experiment 20, while the standard deviation of theory from experiment equals about 1·29 for the number 48 of the experiments. Thus experiment differs from theory by about 5·7 times the standard deviation. The odds are accordingly more than 50,000,000 to 1 against such a large deviation. We are next given a system of ranges by which the frequency of the numbers differs from the mean, which may be tabulated thus :—

[1] The average difference, or "mean error" of some British mathematicians, = ·8 × standard deviation, nearly.

Range.	Groups of Nos.	Percentages.	
		Experiment.	Theory.
1	1	2·7	1·4
11	11	30	15
27	26	70	36

While theory gives a standard deviation of 28·7, the data, so far as they go, point to a standard deviation of about 14, which would give for percentages of the three ranges about 2·8, 31, and 66.

The standard deviation between theory and experiment is here about 3·39, while the actual deviation is more than 4·3 times this; such a deviation would on the average occur less than three times in 200,000 trials, or the odds are very nearly 200,000 to 3 against it. These are, perhaps, not such gigantic odds as we have come across before; but, so far as these data can be trusted, we see the same tendency as in the 16,563 throws analysed by the present writer—namely, the deviations from the average in the distribution of the individual numbers are *less* than we should expect. There is a tendency to come nearer the average than the laws of chance would allow of; the totals, to be paradoxical, are too near the most probable result to be themselves scientifically probable. We agree with the naïve statement of the paragraph writer that "the equality of chances all round is most striking." The reader cannot be too often reminded that what is popularly termed "chance" may be chaos or it may be design, but it cannot be scientifically chance unless the improbable happens in its due proportions. The absence of the improbable, the redundancy of the probable, is just as much conclusive evidence against conformity with scientific law as the too frequent occurrence of the improbable itself. Hence while in the matter of runs Monte Carlo roulette defies theory by improbabilities repeating themselves in two or three months' play, against which the combined odds are many hundred thousands to one, yet such paragraphs as we have cited, without being themselves of any conclusive weight, are, if interpreted by an accurate theory, by no means calculated to reinstate Monte Carlo roulette as a scientific game of chance. No statements of mere *averages* like those we have just seen emphasised are of the least avail against our statistics. *Fluctuations from the averages* are the sole reliable test, and to this test any defender of Monte Carlo must appeal should he wish for a hearing before the tribunal of science.

To sum up, then: Monte Carlo roulette, if judged by returns which are published without apparently being repudiated by the *Société*, is, if the laws of chance rule, from the standpoint of exact science the most prodigious miracle of the nineteenth century. Yet even the supernatural would be discredited by fortnightly recurrences; we are forced to accept as an alternative that the random spinning of a roulette manufactured and daily readjusted with extraordinary care is not obedient to the laws of chance, but is chaotic in its manifestations. It is no exaggeration to say that such a conclusion is of the very highest moment for science. The theory of chance has been developed by some of the most acute and learned of natural philosophers, and is being almost daily applied in various forms of recondite investigation of the highest importance. We appeal to the French Académie des Sciences, to obtain from its secretary, M. Bertrand, one of the most distinguished students of probability of the present day, a report on the colour runs of the Monte Carlo roulette-tables for the summer and autumn months of 1892. Should he confirm the conclusion of the present writer that these runs do not obey the scientific theory of chance, then science must reconstruct its theories to suit these inconvenient facts. Or shall men of science, confident in their theories, shut their eyes to the facts, and, to save their doctrines from discredit, join the chorus of moralists who demand that the French Government shall remove this gambling establishment from its frontier? Clearly, since the Casino does not serve the valuable end of a huge laboratory for the preparation of probability statistics, it has no scientific *raison d'être*. Men of science cannot have their most refined theories disregarded in this shameless manner! The French Government must be urged by the hierarchy of science to close the gaming-saloons; it would be, of course, a graceful act to hand over the remaining resources of the Casino to the Académie des Sciences for the endowment of a laboratory of orthodox probability; in particular, of the new branch of that study, the application of the theory of chance to the biological problem of evolution, which is likely to occupy so much of men's thoughts in the near future.

III

REPRODUCTIVE SELECTION

The Method of investigating truth commonly pursued at this time, therefore, is to be held as erroneous and almost foolish.—WILLIAM HARVEY.

Introductory.—It is so much the fashion for writers on social subjects to apply in a loose and unscientific manner such terms as natural selection, heredity, and panmixia, which are drawn from scientific terminology, to phases of social evolution, that it is of importance at the present time to insist upon one or two precepts being observed when any argument is based on the use of such terms.

In the first place, the cause (or group of causes) referred to by any term ought to be so clearly and concisely defined that a quantitative measure thereof can at once be formed. For example, the true measure of natural selection is a selective death-rate; the true measure of heredity is the numerical correlation between some characteristic or organ as it occurs respectively in parent and offspring; and the true measure of panmixia is a rate of regression; but we search in vain for these numerical measures in the writers alluded to.

In the next place, even if a sufficient definition has been given, it will still be necessary to demonstrate—and this can only be done from a careful statistical investigation—that the factor thus defined is a *vera causa* of progressive change.

Lastly, when these two stages are satisfactorily surmounted, the comparative weight of the various factors of evolution must be ascertained, and ascertained *numerically*, before any safe conclusions can be drawn with regard to social evolution.

It is needless to say that popular writers on sociological subjects almost invariably avoid definition and number when they apply biological conceptions to civilised man. Could they but realise how nearly insurmountable are the difficulties in the way of demonstrating the existence of natural selection in a population of, say, many thousand crabs, they would surely hesitate to base far-reaching moral theories on biological principles applied to man without a single numerical argument. Yet I have no hesitation in saying that it is just for civilised man that we shall first be able to use safely such terms as selection, regression, and heredity. The reason for my statement lies in this: that statistics of mortality, disease, organic growth, fertility, and parentage either are available or can be collected in the case of civilised man with an abundance which, however much it falls short of the theoretically desirable, could only be equalled in the case of lower forms of life by experiments of duration and magnitude such as no biologist has yet ventured to contemplate.[1] For the

---

[1] Take the case of determining the selective death-rate of a population with regard to any organ. We require (1) the law of growth of the population for this organ, and (2) the mortality table. It may be safely said that the only case in which these are even approximately known is that of man.

very reason that partial statistics are available for man, and are not yet available for other animals, plants, or insects, the reader may safely disregard any writer who, adopting current biological terms in dealing with social problems, still neglects the precepts I have stated above.

The present essay is intended to indicate how it is possible to approach one side of the problem of selection in man, and to give a due weight to some of the various factors influencing his social evolution. The importance of the relative fertility of individuals and of classes, —the restraint on population—the fecundity, thriftlessness, and high death-rate of the labouring classes, are often insisted upon; it may not be without value to measure their real or numerical relations.

(1) If there be any sensible correlation between fertility and the size of any organ or intensity of any characteristic in male or female—that is, if deviations in excess (or defect) from the mean of this organ correspond to a greater fertility than deviations in defect (or excess)—then under the action of heredity we have a *vera causa* of progressive evolution in this organ, for an increasing number of individuals will be born with the organ in excess (or defect), and consequently the mean, and most probably the variation about the mean, of the general population will be progressively modified. The result is somewhat similar to that due to artificial selection in the case of domestic animals, where without extermination greater fertility is given to selected parents by pairing them only, or by pairing them more frequently than others. In a memoir on *Regression*,

Heredity, and Panmixia, recently published,[1] I have ventured to term this possible factor of progressive evolution *Reproductive Selection*. It would perhaps be more logical to term it reproductive evolution, were it not that the word selection has been conveniently appropriated to the special factors of organic evolution. Until we have careful statistical measures of the correlation between fertility and organic variation, it seems impossible to determine whether reproductive selection is an actual as well as a potential factor of evolution. It may, indeed, be a source of progressive change controlled, if not completely masked, by natural selection. For example, if tall mothers be sensibly more fertile than short mothers,[2] a progressive change in human stature results, if stature itself be not subjected to a stringent natural selection. In other cases, reproductive selection may assist natural selection by providing for its action a larger quantity of the suitable variation. For example, this may occur in cases wherein strong physique is correlated to fertility.[3]

---

[1] As "Contributions to the Mathematical Theory of Evolution," part iii., in the *Philosophical Transactions*, vol. clxxxvii. A, p. 253.

[2] In a paper recently presented to the Royal Society, I have stated that there does appear to be evidence of correlation between fertility and stature in women, and that the corresponding reproductive selection, if unchecked by other factors of evolution, would lead to an alteration in the mean stature of women of between 3 and 4 inches in a thousand years. In the face of such a progressive factor as this, the indefinite regression which supporters of the theory of panmixia assert would follow the suspension of natural selection, must be looked upon as a very questionable quantity. See *Proc. Royal Society*, vol. lix. p. 301.

[3] Several biologists have asserted the existence of "innate tendencies" to vary in definite directions in certain species. If such tendencies have any real existence, it is conceivable that certain of them may find a natural explanation in an unobserved correlation between fertility and organic variation. The skewness of variation during the period of growth deserves consideration from this standpoint.

As it would appear that reproductive selection has not hitherto been fully discussed by biologists,[1] and as its discussion must open up several interesting fields of observation and experiment, some remarks on fertility in man may be of service.

(2) I pointed out in the memoir above referred to that in man the fertility of mated pairs gives a markedly asymmetrical or skew distribution. I had not at the time my memoir was written, however, sufficient data to determine with any approach to accuracy what may be termed the curve of fertility. For man, I shall define this curve to be one in which the area between the ordinates corresponding to the abscissae x_1 and x_2 measures the frequency of families containing between x_1 and x_2 children, each family being due to a single-mated pair.

Many difficulties arise when we attempt to obtain a curve of what may be termed "natural" fertility in man. Three of these are deserving of special notice.

(i.) The variation constants for fertility vary markedly from race to race or nation to nation.

(ii.) The variation constants for fertility vary markedly from class to class in the same race or nation.

(iii.) There are clear traces in the statistics of some special action influencing fertility in families with between three and seven children.

If we draw a curve of fertility, it will be found that it runs with exceptional smoothness between 7 and 22

---

[1] The late Mr. Romanes used the idea of differential fertility in his *Physiological Selection*, but that application of it to account for—not the progression of one species, but its bifurcation—seems essentially distinct from the present.

children, which latter number approximates to the extreme fertility. On the side of 7, corresponding to small families, we as a rule observe almost a dip between 3 and 7. The first conclusion to be drawn might easily be that the fertility curve is a compound. If so, its components are not class components, for the same feature occurs in fertility curves confined to special classes of the community. It is noteworthy also that this characteristic is less marked in statistics drawn from pedigrees than in more recent natal statistics. I cannot, therefore, avoid the conclusion that the dip between 3 and 7 is not due to compoundedness, that its origin is comparatively recent, and that it is an artificial break in the natural smoothness of the curve of fertility. I believe it to be entirely due to a Malthusian restraint on population. Families which reach 7 and over appear to be those in which no check is placed on the "natural" growth. Below 7 there is a tendency to restraint which is marked by a transference of frequency from families which should lie between 4 and 7 to those lying between 0 and 4. If this view be a correct one, it is only needful to draw a curve of frequency corresponding to the tail distribution of fertility in order to obtain a fairly good measure of the amount of restraint in reproduction at present exercised by any race or class. But even if a frequency curve be found which fits the statistics of fertility from 1 up to 22 with considerable exactness, a great divergence will be found between theory and observation in the matter of barren marriages. While the theoretical curve will be found to give only 6 to 8 per cent of marriages without issue, we find in modern statistics 11 to 18 per cent of marriages with no issue. In other words, the absolute infertility of modern marriages appears to exceed its natural value by about 5 to 10 per cent of all marriages, and this even in countries like England and Denmark, where restraint is not usually supposed to be so prevalent as in France.[1]

(3) For some time I was not clear how to find statistics of a fairly homogeneous character on which to base a curve of fertility natural to man. The Danish statistics are too irregular between families of 3 and 7, and some data of my own for five or six hundred English families presented a similar difficulty. Luckily Mr. F. Howard Collins most kindly gave me statistics which he had been collecting for another purpose, and

---

[1] Rubin and Westergaard (*Statistik der Ehen*, Jena, 1890) give most valuable statistics for Copenhagen. They divide their material into five social groups corresponding to—(1) Professional men, manufacturers, merchants, bankers, etc.; (2) tradesmen, etc.; (3) schoolmasters, musicians, clerks, commercial travellers, etc.; (4) messengers, waiters, servants, etc.; (5) artisans, factory hands, day labourers, etc. They give for marriages without issue in these classes respectively — (1) 12·9 per cent, (2) 13·2 per cent, (3) 15 per cent, (4) 13·5 per cent, (5) 11·5 per cent, taking only those marriages which have lasted fifteen years or upwards. This gives for the total community 12·6 per cent of barren marriages.

If we consider a marriage which has lasted ten or more years without issue as a barren marriage, we find also that the following are the percentages of such marriages for—

10-14 years.	15-24 years.	25 and more years.
15·9	13·5	11·5

Some of the difference here may be due to cases of issue after ten or more years, but the increasing percentage in the more modern marriages seems to mark, on the whole, an increasing restraint on reproduction. This can hardly be due to an increasing age at marriage, for while class (1) marries in Copenhagen at an average age of 32·2 years for men and 26·5 for women, it has a less percentage of absolute infertility than class (3), which marries at an average age of 29·7 for men and 26·5 for the women. It would accordingly appear that if this absolute infertility be much greater than its natural value, it is not peculiar to a special class, and that it has a secular increase.

which contain data of the size of 4390 families. These data seem in several respects suited to our present purpose. They were extracted from (1) the *Whitney Family of Connecticut* (New York, 1878), 2279 families; (2) *Burke's Peerage* and the *Almanac de Gotha*, 841 families; and (3) Forms filled up by friends of Mr. Collins, 1270. The Whitney family is an old Quaker family, and it will be seen that we are—excepting the comparatively few families extracted from the *Almanac de Gotha*—dealing with fairly homogeneous material of Anglo-Saxon race of the middle and upper classes. The statistics themselves give a remarkably smooth curve and exhibit less evidence of a shift towards infertility than any I have yet come across. Unfortunately they comprise no record of barren families. They run as follows:—

Size of family	1	2	3	4	5	6	7	8
Frequency	546	656	682	628	496	383	336	282
Size of family	9	10	11	12	13	14	15	16	17
Frequency	172	118	63	47	22	8	2	1	2

Reduced to percentages they are plotted in the accompanying figure. With some possible but probably very slight errors of record they represent *gross* fertility, *i.e.* total children born without deduction for those dying in infancy or childhood. I shall term *net* fertility the offspring surviving after fifteen years of married life. This limit is purely arbitrary, but

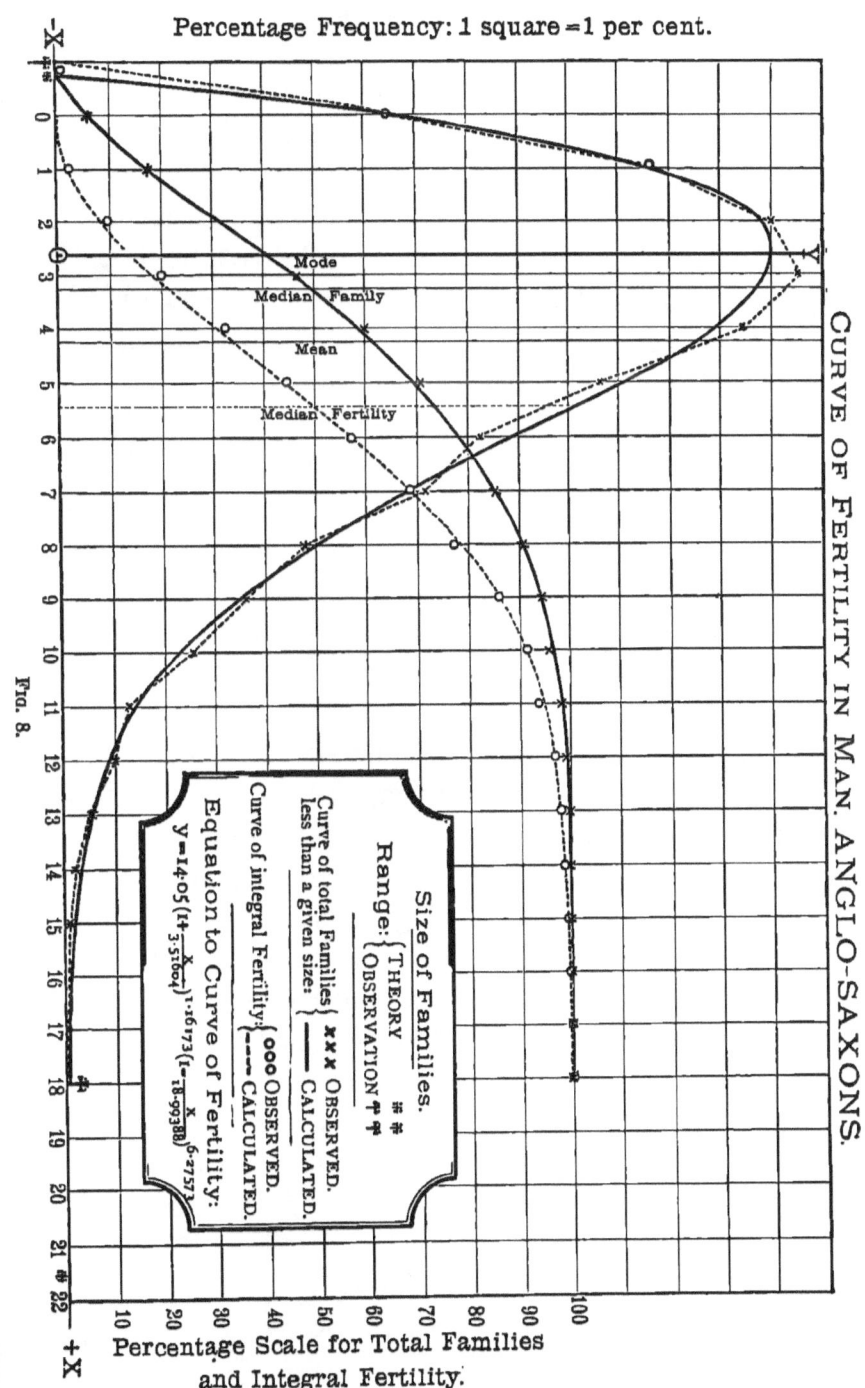

it fits conveniently the recorded Danish statistics. A better distinction would be the number of children in families of different sizes surviving to fifteen years of age, but statistics on this point are wanting. If we take the marriages which have lasted fifteen and more years, and distinguish between the number of children born and the number which have survived, we shall not, it is true, have by any means a perfect measure of net fertility, but we shall probably have a sufficiently exact measure to appreciate how far mortality is correlated to gross fertility, *i.e.* how far natural selection is countcracting reproductive selection. It will be seen from the plate given at p. 26 of this volume that the two components—mortality of infancy and mortality of childhood—are of little influence by the age of fifteen, which is indeed not very far removed from the age of minimum mortality. These components of mortality, however, are those to which must be due the largest amount of periodic selection in man, *i.e.* selective mortality during growth. In taking the surviving offspring in marriages of fifteen years and upwards, we shall undoubtedly be neglecting a certain proportion of child mortality, but at the same time we shall be including a considerable amount of adult mortality. Accordingly, the net fertility thus measured will be a closer approximation than we might at first assume to be the case. The correlation, however, between size of family and mortality will be to some extent marked by increased mortality —adult and possibly non-selective mortality—in the families of much longer than fifteen years' standing, and excessively large families will of necessity fall into this class.

Bearing in mind the need of checking our results for gross fertility by allowing later for its difference from net fertility, we may now return to Mr. Collins's statistics. We assume that they may be represented by a skew frequency curve—an assumption made on the *à priori* ground of our experience of vital statistics, and justified *à posteriori* by excellency of fit. The first difficulty arises from the absence of any record of barren marriages. A guess had to be made at their probable number as a first approximation. This was done from the plotted statistics. The polygon for frequency of families had to vanish at a unit before zero offspring, and rise at unit after to 546. I took 350 as a plausible value. The moments of the whole system were then calculated, and the skew curve fitted. The result was a skew curve (see *Phil. Trans.* vol. clxxxvi. A, p. 367), with a range of families approximately from 0 to 24 children. It gave 328 barren families. Clearly my first approximation to the number of barren marriages was too large. I accordingly made a second approximation, assuming the number of barren marriages to be 300. The skew probability curve was again found. It was of the same type as before, and gave 312 barren marriages. It was accordingly clear that my second approximation was slightly too small. But the ordinates of the two theoretical curves found differ so little from each other, and the labour of approximation is so considerable, that I think we may rest content with the second curve as a very close approximation to the distribution of fertility in human marriage—substantially in the Anglo-Saxon race. The mean would give about 320 naturally sterile marriages to 4390 more or less fertile marriages, or about 6·7 per cent of all marriages.[1]

Reduced to percentages, we have the following results:—

Size of Family.	Frequency per cent.		Difference.
	Observed.	Calculated.	
0	(6·397)*	6·660	+ ·263
1	11·642	11·569	− ·073
2	13·966	13·754	− ·212
3	14·542	13·926	− ·616
4	13·390	12·809	− ·581
5	10·576	10·994	+ ·418
6	8·166	8·918	+ ·752
7	7·164	6·879	− ·285
8	4·861	5·057	+ ·196
9	3·667	3·450	− ·217
10	2·516	2·353	− ·163
11	1·343	1·478	+ ·135
12	1·002	·871	− ·131
13	·469	·475	+ ·006
14	·171	·237	+ ·066
15	·043	·083	+ ·040
16	·021	·040	+ ·019
17	·043	·012	− ·031
18	0	·003	+ ·003
19	0	·0004	+ ·000
20	0	·000019	+ ·000
21	0	·00000004	+ ·000
22	0	·00000000	+ ·000

* On the basis of the second approximation, that 300 barren marriages occur with 4390 fertile ones.

---

[1] The constants of this curve of fertility are as follows, the notation being that of my second memoir on evolution:—

It will be seen that the agreement here is a very close one for such statistical results, and this will be still better realised by a glance at the theoretical curve and the observation polygon given in the figure above.

The observations having been calculated by the method of trapezia, the observation polygon starts at -1 before zero family and the curve starts at $-\cdot 9273$. The range being $22\cdot 50992$ just crosses $21\cdot 5$, and therefore gives a possibility of a family of 22 children from one pair of parents. This may seem a somewhat limited range, especially when it is noted that the corresponding theoretical maximum in Denmark is 26 children. At the same time it must be noted—(1) that the Scandinavian races are, on the whole, much more fertile than the Anglo-Saxon, from which the bulk of our present statistics are drawn; (2) that we are dealing principally with middle and upper class families; (3) that the observed limit of the present statistics is 17 (in two cases, yet one is that of an artisan family), and in the Danish statistics it was 22 (one case in 34,000 marriages). 18 was in Copenhagen, however, the limit

$\mu_2 = 8\cdot 57276$　　$\beta_1 = \cdot 5306915$
$\mu_3 = 18\cdot 28528$　　$\beta_2 = 3\cdot 249620$
$\mu_4 = 238\cdot 82180$　　$\nu = 9\cdot 437454$
　　　　　　　　　$\epsilon = 15\cdot 72813$
Mean family $= 4\cdot 22835$　　$m_1 = 1\cdot 161726$
Modal family $= 2\cdot 58830$　　$m_2 = 6\cdot 275728$
Median family $= 3\cdot 28503$　　$a_1 = 3\cdot 516036$
Range $= 22\cdot 50992$　　$a_2 = 18\cdot 99388$
　　　　　　　　　$y_0 = 658\cdot 952$

The number of decimal places retained is, of course, of no significance, and only served for purposes of calculation.

Equation to curve of fertility—

$$y = 658\cdot 952\left(1 + \frac{x}{3\cdot 516036}\right)^{1\cdot 161726}\left(1 - \frac{x}{18\cdot 99388}\right)^{6\cdot 275728}$$

for the professional classes. Bearing in mind, therefore, that our limit of 22 is for a particular race and substantially for a particular class,—not a limit for human fertility in general[1]—the theory of the skew curve seems to give a very satisfactory result, even for the range of fertility.[2]

Turning to the mean, and excluding the barren marriages, we find 4·52 children for the mean of the fertile marriages. In 204 marriages noted by Mr. Galton, the mean was 4·65, and in 378 fertile marriages collected by myself, I found 4·70 children as the mean.[3] Taking into account the sterile marriages, we have 4·23 for the mean number of children in Mr. Collins's statistics. Taking this as our standard, Mr. Galton's fertile marriages ought to have been accompanied by 10 per cent of barren marriages, and my 378 marriages by 11 per cent of barren marriages. In the former case there are no data to go upon, but I actually took at random 434 marriages and found 56 of these (378 = 434 − 56)

---

[1] Exceeding the limit of 22, we have cases of 24 reported from Finmark, of 24 from Trinidad, of 26 from Cuba, of 27 from Nicaragua, and of 34 from Colombia. In the cases from Central America twins must have been frequent, and the evidence for the children being the product of a single pair is not perhaps absolutely conclusive (see Ploss, *Das Weib.* Bd. i. S. 315 *et seq.*).

[2] It is worth while, however, to calculate the probable error of the range found. A memoir on the probable errors of the constants of skew variation, which I hope shortly to publish, shows that the probable error of the range

$$= \cdot 6745 \frac{b}{\sqrt{n}} \sqrt{\frac{(\nu-2)(\epsilon-2\nu+4)}{(\nu-1)(2\epsilon-3\nu+4)}},$$

where n = total number of observations, b is the range, and ν and ϵ are the constants given numerically on p. 75.

Substituting the values of the constants, we find ·072 for the probable error of the range, or it seems extremely improbable that for the race and class we are dealing with, the limiting family could be raised even one unit above 22.

[3] For Danish marriages of the professional classes, the mean of fertile marriages which have lasted twenty-five and more years is above 5·5, and is 4·8 including sterile marriages.

without issue—that is, about 13 per cent of English middle class marriages. This is somewhat less than the percentage of the more recent Danish marriages. Now the curve of fertility only gives 7 per cent[1] of sterile marriages, or only a little more than one-half of the marriages without issue can be ascribed to the same series of causes as determine the general distribution of fertility. We may then conclude with a considerable degree of probability that: *In the middle and upper classes only about 6 per cent of the marriages without issue are naturally sterile, and between 6 and 7 per cent of all marriages are without issue, owing to causes other than those which naturally determine the distribution of fertility in man.*

If it be objected that any limitation of the family would not render itself sensible solely in childless marriages, the answer must be that the curve of fertility does give marked evidence of such limitation. Although our statistics are taken from material where limitation is not likely to have played a very large part, they yet show a distinct tendency to decreased frequency of families of 5 and 6, and corresponding increased frequency for families of 2, 3, and 4. An examination of the figure on p. 71 shows that a portion of the curve is cut away between 4 and 7, and piled up between 1 and 4. The influence of this appears in both the Anglo-Saxon and Danish theoretical curves as a tendency to throw the start of the range too much to the left of zero.

Beyond 6 children the theoretical and observational

---

[1] Actually 7·1. The ordinate at 0 is 6·66, but the area from start to 0·5 = 7·1 about.

curves of fertility cross and recross each other without exhibiting the same tendency as between 4 and 7. We may, therefore, I think, conclude that limitation of offspring is rarely practised after families number 7 or more children. We shall find these conclusions are practically confirmed by the Danish results.

(4) If it be objected that somewhat far-reaching conclusions are here based on the fit of a certain curve of frequency, it must be borne in mind that this fit is markedly better than that of the majority of cases in which statisticians, and even physicists, are satisfied with the correspondence between theory and observation. In order to illustrate this better, and also with a view to the problem of reproductive selection, two further curves are drawn on the diagram. The first is the integral curve of the curve of fertility. The ordinate of this curve measures the percentage of families of and less than the corresponding abscissa. For example, taking families of 4 the corresponding ordinate is 59·94, or we conclude that about 60 per cent of families have 4 or fewer children. The second is the curve of integral fertility, or the ordinate measures the percentage of children due to families of and less than the corresponding abscissa. Thus, for example, 32·34 per cent of all children are born in families of 4 or less than 4. We see then that 60 per cent of the married population only produces about 32 per cent of the children, or about 40 per cent of the married population produce nearly 70 per cent of the children. These curves illustrate concisely the whole problem of reproductive selection.

In order that the reader may appreciate how closely

theory and observation accord, the observed values are placed on the diagram by means of crosses and dots in the two cases. The subjoined table illustrates the same accordance :—

Families of and less than	Percentage of Families.		Percentage of Children.	
	Theory.	Observation.	Theory.	Observation.
0	7·100	(6·397)	0	0
1	18·669	18·039	2·728	2·753
2	32·423	32·005	9·235	9·359
3	46·349	46·547	19·108	19·677
4	59·158	59·937	31·216	32·344
5	70·152	70·513	44·207	44·850
6	79·070	78·679	56·853	56·437
7	85·949	85·843	68·233	68·297
8	91·006	90·704	77·793	77·494
9	94·456	94·371	85·368	85·299
10	96·809	96·887	90·930	91·249
11	98·288	98·230	94·773	94·743
12	99·159	99·232	97·243	97·587
13	99·634	99·701	98·703	99·029
14	99·871	99·872	99·487	99·595
15	99·944	99·915	99·785	99·748
16	99·984	99·936	99·937	99·827
17	99·996	99·979	99·986	100·000
Median	3·285	3·288	5·4588	5·4445

The maximum differences here between theory and observation are ·8 and 1 per cent, occurring of course just where the presumed limitation of families is most effective. In other words theory and observation are in accord in a degree rarely met with in statistics.

This table would enable us at once to appreciate the influence of reproductive selection when the degree of correlation between fertility and any characteristic in either parent has been established. We see that, whereas the median family is theoretically 3·285 (actually 3·258), only half the integral fertility is reached theoretically with a family of 5·4588 (actually of 5·4445). Thus theoretically 25·819 (actually 25·857) per cent of the parents produce one-half of the next generation. That is to say, if we divide into more and less fertile groups by the median fertility, the latter of these groups will be about three times as numerous as the former, and yet, since it produces only the same number of children, its mean fertility will only be about $\frac{1}{3}$ as great. Thus the *subfertile* and *superfertile* groups have numbers originally in the ratio of 3 to 1, but fertilities in the ratio of 1 to 3. To illustrate the effect of reproductive selection, let us take a simplified problem and suppose fertility to depend in the main on one parent, say the mother. Suppose M to be the mean and R the coefficient of regression of any organ correlated with fertility, and let D be the mean deviation from the mean of the mothers of the superfertile group. Then $-\frac{1}{3}D$ will be the mean deviation from the mean of the mothers of the subfertile group, since the two groups are numerically in the ratio of 3 to 1. The mean deviations from the mean of the offspring in the two cases will be approximately expressed by RD and $-\frac{1}{3}RD$, or, since there are 50 per cent of both, the mean of the second generation will be $M + \frac{1}{3}RD$. If the focus of regression were stationary, then the mean deviations from the mean of the original stock in the superfertile and subfertile groups of the second generation would be respectively $D + \frac{1}{3}RD$ and $-\frac{1}{3}D + \frac{1}{3}RD$, giving

$M + \tfrac{1}{3}RD + \tfrac{1}{3}R^2D$ for the mean of the third generation. After n generations the mean would be $M + \tfrac{1}{3}RD\dfrac{1-R^n}{1-R}$. If, on the other hand, the focus progresses in the manner indicated in my memoir on *Regression and Panmixia*, the mean after n generations would be simply $M + \tfrac{1}{3}nRD$. The truth must lie between these two hypotheses, and, as I have indicated in that memoir, there are good reasons for thinking it nearer the second than the first.[1] Hence it would seem that any characteristic or organ—such, for instance, as stature or size of pelvis in the mother—correlated with fertility would be progressively changed, and on the latter hypothesis without limit, owing to reproductive selection.[2]

(5) A very difficult problem arises, however, with regard to the inheritance of fertility. If there be any correlation between fertility in mother and daughter, the superfertile group will rapidly become the dominant

[1] Actual measures of the influence of reproductive selection in terms of the correlation coefficients of fertility and heredity are given in a paper recently presented to the Royal Society, *Proceedings*, vol. lix. p. 301.

[2] I regret the absence of sufficiently ample and reliable statistics to test satisfactorily the influence of reproductive selection in man, but the following data may suggest the unstable condition produced by the wide differences in human fertility. Out of 206 families I found 133 fell into the group 1 to 5 children, and 73 into the group 6 and upwards, there being no corresponding record of barren marriages. The mean height of the 133 fathers was 5'9"·571, and of the 73 fathers 5'9"·103, the difference here 0"·468 appears significant. In other words, the more fertile fathers are sensibly shorter than the less fertile, but the smaller group of more fertile fathers produced 561 children, while the larger and less fertile group produced only 394 children. Thus, while the two groups of fathers formed 64·5 and 35·5 per cent of the father-population, their offspring formed 41·2 and 58·8 per cent respectively of the second generation. Thus the correlation between fertility and height in fathers would seem to mark a tendency to lesser height in man. In the corresponding data for mothers fertility and height were correlated in the *opposite* sense. The data are far too few to allow of very definite numerical conclusions, but they indicate how very delicate must be the balance, supposing a population to be stable and yet no natural selection holding reproductive selection in check.

element of the population. It must also be remembered that assuming a correlation between any measurable organ (such as stature or size of pelvis) which is inherited and fertility is really assuming a correlation between the fertility of parent and of offspring. Hence reproductive selection, if it exists at all, would seem to mark a tendency to increasing fertility in man. To realise the strength of this tendency, we note that the median fertility of the subfertile group is about 3·5, and of the superfertile group about 7·6, or more than double, while the mean fertilities are 2·82 and 8·46 respectively. Now, let us neglect the influence of the male parent, and suppose very complete correlation between fertility in mother and daughter, we should have the following percentages of the superfertile and subfertile groups in successive generations :—

	Superfertile.	Subfertile.
Originally	25 per cent	75 per cent
1st generation	50 per cent	50 per cent
2nd generation	75 per cent	25 per cent
3rd generation	90 per cent	10 per cent
4th generation	96·4 per cent	3·6 per cent
5th generation	98·8 per cent	1·2 per cent

Thus in five generations the mean fertility of the population would be essentially 8·46, *i.e.* that of the superfertile group. Even if we allow for a comparatively small correlation between mother and daughter, and also for a certain amount of panmixia arising from biparental inheritance, we cannot doubt that reproductive selection would tend to steadily alter the mean fertility in man, unless it were somehow held stringently in check. It is a point which seems to me of the utmost significance that, allowing for the proportion of unmarried in the population, about $\tfrac{1}{5}$ to $\tfrac{1}{6}$ only of the adults produce quite one-half of the next generation, and any correlation between inheritable (physical or social) characteristics and fertility must thus sensibly influence that next generation.[1]

If we seek the causes by which reproductive selection may possibly be checked we are at once led to the following:—

(i.) A stringent natural selection. This, I think, would be the first suggestion made by a biologist. He would consider that the fertility of any species was best fitted to its surroundings, and that high fertilities were checked by a selective death-rate. We shall find later that there is such a selective death-rate in man. Larger percentages of larger families die young than of smaller, but the difference does not appear by any means sufficient to check reproductive selection.

(ii.) The random character of fertility. It may be asserted that fertility is not an inheritable characteristic or correlated with inheritable characteristics. There is a potential fertility in man, and variations in this are not due to organic variation in man, but to place, circumstance, and opportunity. Besides, the admittedly slight evidence I have given

[1] I hope shortly to have further determinations of correlation in the matter of fertility. At present the only coefficient known to me is ·18 for stature and fertility in woman. Mr. Francis Galton tells me that he was recently informed by credible medical authorities in Paris that the French population is becoming Breton, owing to the fact that this element of the population does not limit its fertility to anything like the same extent as other elements. Nearly all large families are found to be of Breton extraction.

for a correlation between fertility and height, and the markedly fertile character of a few pedigree families I have examined, it would seem that to assert the random character of fertility is to cut at the very root of the theory of evolution by natural selection under the influence of heredity, and no wise man will readily attempt that to-day. Such an important feature as the degree of fertility in races and individuals could, on the assumption of its random character, receive no explanation by means of the theory of natural selection.

(iii.) Fertility is inherited, but there is a selective marriage-rate, depending upon some unobserved social or physical conditions. In other words, a greater percentage of members of small than of members of large families marry. This is a point on which statistics ought to be forthcoming, but I doubt whether any such selective marriage-rate can be demonstrated.[1]

(iv.) In civilised communities, where natural selection does not sternly hold reproductive selection in check, the fertility is actually increasing, and the increase would be still more conspicuous were it not more or less completely disguised by an increasing limitation of the family. To this it must be replied that, so far as can be judged from the curve of fertility, the limitation of family seems either non-selective in its action, or to be manifest especially in the subfertile group. At the

---

[1] Of 196 marriages taken out of a pedigree, 131 were in the case of *one* parent from families of 6 and over, and 65 from families of 5 and under—excluding children who died before reaching an adult age. Taking the families from which the parent sprung, I found 59 per cent of the superfertile group married and only 53 per cent of the subfertile group. This evidence—of course of no great weight—points in the opposite direction to that required if a selective marriage rate is to check reproductive selection.

same time, the mean family (France excluded) averages in civilised European communities 4·2 to 5·2 children; while from such statistics and reports as are available we find 3-4 rather a high fertility for Hottentots, Bedouins, Ostiaks, Samoiedes, Lapps, Japanese, Aleutians, Alaskans, North and South American Indians, Abyssinians, Loango Negroes, Australians, Papuans, Polynesians, etc.; the fertility of Lapps, Polynesians, and Negroes being, however, to some extent a disputed quantity (see Ploss, *Das Weib*. Bd. i. Kap. vii.) Bearing this possibility in mind, it would seem that a comparison of the gross fertility exhibited in ancient pedigrees with the gross fertility of modern marriages would be of considerable interest. Whichever way we turn, however, the problem of the inheritance of fertility seems beset with difficulties. These difficulties might to some extent be experimentally solved in the case of lower types of life; in the case of man we shall need far more extensive statistics than are yet available (or than the efforts perhaps of a single individual can suffice to procure), if we are to accurately gauge the influence of reproductive selection, or of the variation in fertility, on human evolution.

(6) Before passing to the subject of net fertility as distinguished from gross fertility, it is worth while to illustrate the method of determining a curve of fertility from a second series of statistics—those for Copenhagen published by Rubin and Westergaard. I select from their work marriages of Class I., which have lasted 15 or more years.[1] This class corresponds fairly well to

[1] It has been objected that this limitation of the range of families to 15 and more years neglects a great number of small families, the product of marriages

our professional and middle class, containing officials, lawyers, doctors, and other professional men, manufacturers, merchants, bankers, etc. The total of 1842 marriages is distributed as follows :—

Size of family	0	1	2	3	4	5	6	7	8
Frequency	237	133	181	243	201	203	171	121	118
Size of family	9	10	11	12	13	14	15	16	17	18
Frequency	82*	61	34	31	12	9	2	1	0	2

Reduced to percentages, these results are plotted on not lasting as long as 15 years, and that if the children of these marriages were included, the percentage of children from small families would be much increased. The objectors have overlooked the fact that the total number of families is also much increased, and therefore the percentage of superfertile families which produce half the next generation still further *decreased*. Hence the range I have adopted tends to minimise, not to emphasise, the action of reproductive selection. Thus, taking 34,075 Copenhagen marriages, both parents of which were alive, and which had lasted one or more years, I find that 50 per cent of all the children are due to 17·1 per cent of the mated couples, instead of the 25 per cent reached in the text for couples whose fertility is practically exhausted. The same result of 17 per cent was obtained from marriages taken at random out of Debrett, while 25 per cent was obtained if only marriages which have lasted 15 or more years were included. This result shows the close resemblance of the general features of fertility in two different races of man.

A further objection, that the inclusion only of families in which both parents are alive must upset the conclusions drawn, can be met by the remark that there is no evidence whatever to show that parental mortality is inversely proportional to fertility, and that statistics actually show a much greater number of women widowed in late than in early life. Out of 1603 women who became widows in Elsass in 1872, 1092, or more than two-thirds, were over 45 years of age, or practically had passed the child-bearing age; of 1594 widowers, 1076, or again more than two-thirds, lost their wives when they were over 45 years of age. It will thus be obvious that the great bulk of families without one or other parent corresponds to marriages which have lasted 15 or more years. The remainder, which would not fall into this category, and the natural fertility of which may be considered incomplete, would clearly only tend to reduce the 25 per cent referred to above towards the 17 per cent which arises when *all* marriages are taken into account. The total effect of including orphans would thus only be to emphasise reproductive selection.

Lastly, objections that no account has been taken of miscarriages, and again of deaths at first childbed, only show how little their raisers have entered into the relative statistics of such occurrences.

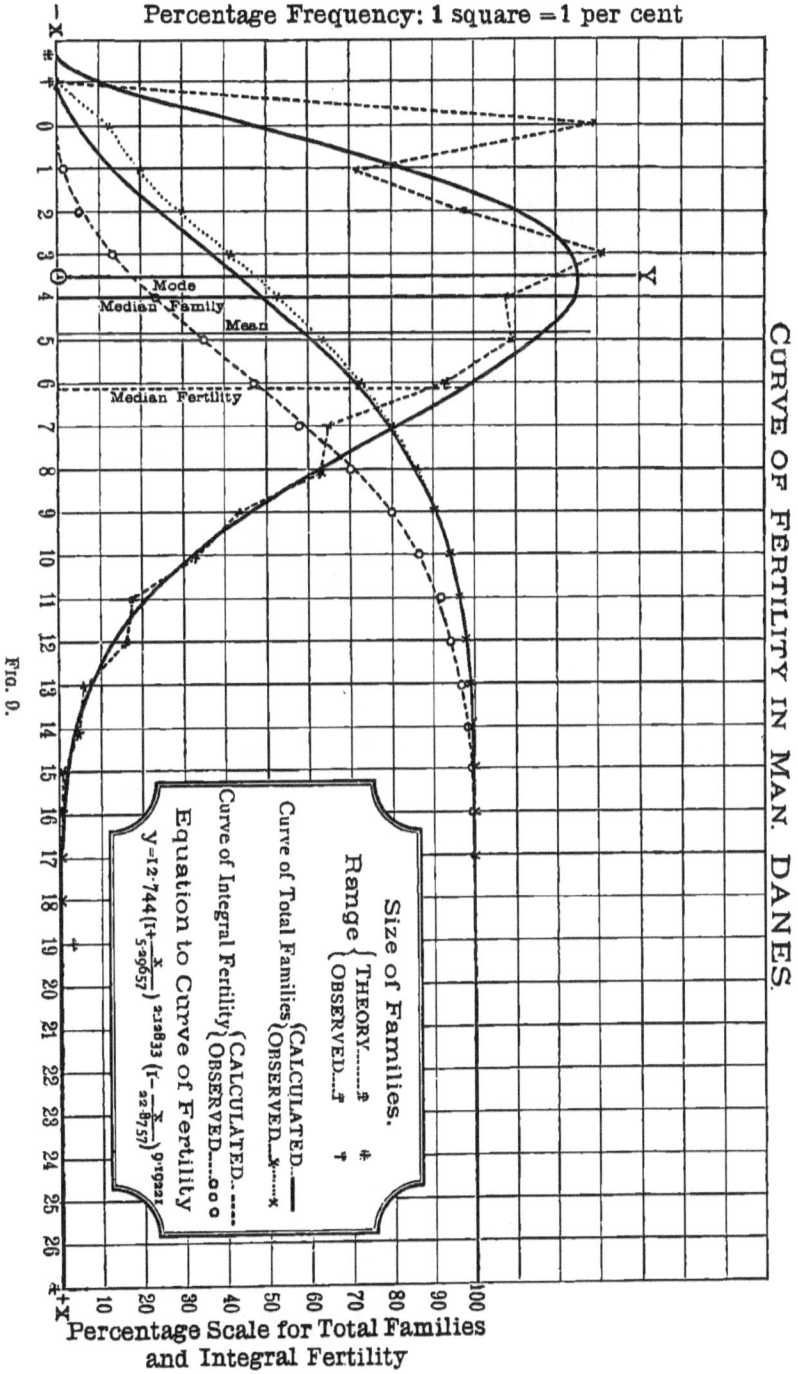

Fig. 0.

the accompanying figure, and they will be seen, as I have mentioned before (p. 69), to be far more irregular than Mr. Collins's data. This irregularity appears, however, to be an exaggeration of the displacement we have found in the latter data, and which I have attributed to a limitation of families peculiar to the subfertile group. Taking the statistics just as they stand, I find the mean family to be 4·5135, the modal family 3·0666, and the curve of fertility to be a skew curve with a range from about − 2 to 23. The large number of families without issue had thrown the curve too far to the left, and yet the curve cut off almost one-half of the barren marriages, showing, as in the previous statistics, that nearly 50 per cent at least of the marriages without issue were not due to the same causes as determined the general distribution of fertility. Accordingly, I re-started the calculations on the assumption that only 6·7, instead of 12·9, per cent of marriages were without issue, owing to the general causes which mainly determine the remaining degrees of fertility. The curve of fertility was again a skew curve of the same type.[1]

---

[1] The following values were found for the constants :—

$\mu_2 =$ 9·959165 . . . $\beta_1 =$ ·381943
$\mu_3 =$ 19·42330 . . . $\beta_2 =$ 3·170176
$\mu_4 =$ 314·43380 . . . $\nu =$ 13·32055
Mean family = 4·83762 . . . $\epsilon =$ 31·88464
Modal family = 3·51791 . . . $m_1 =$ 2·12833
Median family = 3·95405 . . . $m_2 =$ 9·19221
Range = 28·1723 . . . $a_1 =$ 5·29657
$y_0 =$ 12·744 . . . $a_2 =$ 22·87573

Thus the equation to the curve of fertility is —

$$y = 12\cdot 744 \left(1 + \frac{x}{5\cdot 29657}\right)^{2\cdot 12833} \left(1 - \frac{x}{22\cdot 87573}\right)^{9\cdot 19221}$$

The range of this curve starts somewhat (·779 of a unit) before it should do. This is due to the displacement caused by restraint, which is exceedingly emphasised, rather than to our still having the number of barren marriages somewhat in excess of those given by natural sterility. I have not re-calculated the curve, as it seemed sufficiently accurate for the given data, but simply considered all the area to the left of 0·5 to represent sterile marriages. This area is 5·717 per cent, or we conclude that 7·153 per cent of Copenhagen marriages are without issue, owing to other causes than those which determine the general distribution of fertility. These results appear well in accord with the Anglo-Saxon statistics, which gave (p. 77) about 7 per cent of naturally sterile marriages, and about 6 per cent of additional sterility. For, in the first place, the constants of the Danish curve show that we are dealing with a markedly more fertile group than the Anglo-Saxon,—compare the mean, modal, and median families in each — and therefore that the absolute sterility ought to be less; and, in the second place, an examination of the diagrams on pp. 71 and 87 shows a displacement—presumably due to limitation—far greater in the Danish than in the Anglo-Saxon subfertile group, and hence we should expect this greater limitation to manifest itself in the marriages entirely without issue.

The theoretical maximum family is 26, which is again in keeping with the increased Scandinavian fertility. While just as in the previous group there appeared no selective limitation in families of 7 and upwards, so here for families of 8 and upwards we find a close accord between the curve of fertility and the observations. The degree of accordance is illustrated by the following table :—

Size of Family.	Percentage Frequency.		Difference.
	Calculated.	Observed.	
0	5·717	(12·87)	(− 7·15)
1	8·431	7·22	+ 1·21
2	11·212	9·83	+ 1·38
3	12·577	13·19	− ·61
4	12·644	10·91	+ 1·73
5	11·640	11·02	+ ·62
6	10·047	9·30	+ ·75
7	8·187	6·58	+ 1·61
8	6·331	6·41	− ·08
9	4·659	4·46	+ ·20
10	3·265	3·32	− ·065
11	2·178	1·85	+ ·33
12	1·379	1·69	− ·31
13	·825	·65	+ ·175
14	·465	·49	− ·025
15	·244	·11	+ ·13
16	·118	·054	+ ·064
17	·053	0	+ ·053
18	·021	·11	− ·09
19	·007	0	+ ·007

It will be noticed that with 8 onwards the differences become small and fairly alternate in sign. The displacement observable between 1 and 7 is very approximately made up by the superabundance of marriages without issue. On the whole, while it might not have been justifiable to base our discussion of fertility on a distribution of such comparative irregularity, we see that having once fairly established the curve of fertility from smoother statistics, a great deal may be learnt by comparing it with such results as the present.

On the diagram p. 87, the curve of total families and the curve of integral fertility are drawn. The first appears to diverge very considerably from the theoretical curve, but the divergence is more apparent than real, and is due to the large surplus of additional marriages without issue. Had the barren marriages been reduced to their natural value and the percentages recalculated, the crosses marking observations would have been found almost superposed on the theoretical curve. This is obvious when we turn to the curve of integral fertility, in which, of course, the barren marriages do not appear. Here theory appears almost in as close accord with experience as it was in the previous series of marriages.

The following table will illustrate this:—

PERCENTAGE OF CHILDREN DUE TO FAMILIES OF OR LESS THAN

	0	1	2	3	4	5	6	7	8	9
Theory	0	1·74	6·36	14·14	24·57	36·58	49·01	60·83	71·27	79·92
Experience	0	1·60	5·95	14·71	24·38	36·58	48·88	59·08	70·48	79·38

	10	11	12	13	14	15	16	17	18	19
Theory	86·65	91·59	95·01	97·22	98·56	99·32	99·71	99·89	99·97	99·98
Experience	86·68	91·18	95·65	97·53	99·04	99·60	99·59	99·59	100	100

It will be found that half the number of children born fall below and half above the 6·1 family. Hence this is the Danish division between the subfertile and superfertile groups. Examining the diagram on p. 87 we see at once that this division of fertility separates the parents into groups of 25 per cent and 75 per cent on the basis of observation, and into groups of 26 per cent and 74 per cent on the basis of theory. We therefore find the Danish statistics absolutely and fully confirm the conclusion drawn from the previous series—namely, that one-quarter of the married population produce one-half of the next generation.[1] We may take it, therefore, that this rule is a general one, since it holds for two populations differing very sensibly in the constants of their fertility distribution. It is a rule which concisely expresses the whole foundation for reproductive selection. We shall now see that it is not substantially modified when we replace gross by net fertility.

(7) Taking out of Westergaard and Rubin's tables the distribution of children in marriages which have lasted 15 or more years, subtracting the deaths from the totals and reducing to percentages, we have the following tables for gross and net fertility :—

---

[1] Statistics of 1919 bachelor-spinster marriages in which both parents survived the child-bearing age of the mother are given by Charles Anstell in his : *On the Rate of Mortality, etc., and other Statistics of Families*, London, 1874. These statistics, for the upper and professional classes, are for gross fertility including still-births. Anstell had families in his records of 19, 20, 23, and 25, which, "for various reasons," he did not include in his table. His mean family was 5·28 (5·17 without still-births), his modal family 4·51, surprisingly high results even for gross fertility. The number of childless families is only 7·8 per cent instead of the 13 per cent I have elsewhere found ; I suspect their full proportion was not recorded. 26·8 per cent of the families produced 50 per cent of the children. The coefficient of variation in fertility was ·657, it being ·692 for Mr. Collins's statistics, and ·652 for the Copenhagen returns.

Size of Family.	Percentages of			
	Children born of Families of this size or less. Duration of Marriages being—		Children surviving out of Families of this size or less. Duration of Marriages being—	
	15 and more Years.	25 and more Years.	15 and more Years.	25 and more Years.
1	1·60	1·18	1·82	1·35
2	5·95	4·76	6·59	5·44
3	14·71	13·31	15·81	14·43
4	24·38	21·85	26·31	23·49
5	36·58	33·10	38·71	34·73
6	48·88	46·18	51·01	48·04
7	59·08	54·95	61·01	56·61
8	70·48	65·71	72·36	67·38
9	79·38	76·36	80·96	78·12
10	86·68	83·09	88·29	85·04
11	91·18	88·70	92·60	90·77
12	95·65	93·71	96·58	95·22
13	97·53	95·82	97·94	96·67
14	99·04	98·10	99·44	98·85
15	99·40	98·79	99·64	99·24
16	99·59	99·16	99·77	99·51
17	99·59	99·16	99·77	99·51
18	100	100	100	100

The meaning of this table is as follows :—Taking marriages which have lasted 15 and more years, the percentage of children born to families of, say, 7 and under, is 59·08; but if we take only the surviving children, then 61·01 in every hundred were the product of families of 7 and under. If we take marriages which have lasted at least 25 years, then 54·95 of the children born are due to families of 7 and under, but 56·61 of the surviving children are due to such families. If we compare the first and third and the second and fourth columns, we see in every case that the first column of the pair has the lesser number. In other words, there is a selective death-rate increasing with increased fertility. This will be still more clearly shown by the following table :—

PERCENTAGE DEATH-RATE OF FAMILIES OF DIFFERENT SIZES

Size of Families.	Marriages of 15-24 Years.	Marriages of 25 and over.
1 to 3	19·08	23·69
4 — 6	21·15	28·02
7 — 9	25·33	29·82
10 — 12	29·15	30·61
13 — 15	31·18	44·29 [1]
16 — 18	...	55·77 [2]

[1] Depends upon 14 families only and so not very reliable.
[2] Depends upon 3 families only and so very doubtful.

This increase of the death-rate with increased size of family has been pointed out very thoroughly—although in a different manner—by Rubin and Westergaard. Its importance for our present purpose is this. It shows us that: *Natural selection is clearly at work in man tending to check the effect of reproductive selection.*

A death-rate which rises from about 20 to 30, if not higher, with increasing fertility might at first sight be thought sufficient to bring about the survival of lower degrees of fertility with a lower death-rate. But this is very far indeed from being the case. We have seen (p. 91) that half the gross fertility falls to families of more than 6·1 children. The sole effect of natural selection is to shift about 2 per cent of the children from the superfertile to the subfertile group — about 52 per cent of surviving children being in marriages of 15 years and upwards due to families of 6·1 children and under. In fact, the family of 5·92 now represents the median fertility. Turning to our diagram (p. 87), we see that this corresponds to about 27 per cent (actually to 26·6 for the observations) of parents, and no longer to 25 per cent. In other words, 27 to 28 per cent of the married population still produce half the next generation. If we work the corresponding result out for the net fertility of marriages of 25 and more years, we find 26·4 per cent of the married population produce half the children — an almost identical result. Comparing columns 3 and 4 of the table on p. 93, we see that the percentages of children due to small families are considerably larger for the group embracing the shorter marriage term, *i.e.* the more modern marriages. As I have noted before, this appears to be due to an increasing limitation of the family. The difference at the maximum amounts to even 3 per cent. We may therefore conclude that while natural selection is perfectly evident in its action on fertility, it is not more evident than restraint, and that both alike appear to have at the present time no really significant influence on reproductive selection, *i.e. if fertility be inheritable or correlated to inheritable characteristics, then in the case of civilised man natural selection at present would appear to be quite secondary to reproductive selection as a factor of progressive evolution.*

(8) The reader must be reminded that the results we have been considering are not substantially affected by the biparental nature of inheritance in the case of man, or even by a total absence of assortative mating in relation to fertility. Granted that there is no corre-

lation between fertility and infertility in pairing, that a fertile mate does not select an infertile one, but that man mates so far as fertility is concerned "at random," then uniparental inheritance would be quite sufficient to give reproductive selection a substantial influence. Of course the extent and rapidity of its action would be much increased, if we could show that any particularly fertile group largely mated within its own limits. Speaking broadly, most social classes are groups which mate within their own limits. Hence it would follow that if it could be shown that one social class is more fertile than another, then reproductive selection will ultimately tend to give this class greater numerical prominence. We have, in fact, here a means of answering a somewhat important question: Does society ultimately recruit itself from above or below? Really trustworthy and sufficient data for answering this question are hardly at present available, but one or two points with regard to it may be noted.

(a) The fertility of one class must be shown to be sensibly greater than that of another class. Now the curves of fertility for two classes in the same community differ comparatively slightly. Hence the small but sensible effect of natural selection must be carefully estimated and allowed for, $i.e.$ we must deal with net fertilities.

(b) But the net fertility of one class may still be greater than that of a second, and yet the second increase at a greater rate. We have to determine how far the greater fertility is merely potential. We must ascertain what proportions of the two classes remain unmated. Here the difficulty of forming an estimate is extremely great, and so far as any statistics are forthcoming, they are rendered very obscure by their having been collected with other ends in view; the exact details required are generally wanting. I will refer in the sequel to some difficulties of this kind.

(c) Not only may the net fertility be greater—*i.e.* the number of children per family who survive infancy, say, live to 15 years, be greater—but also the percentage of mating may be greater in one class than another, and yet the first class may have no reproductive advantage. We ought further to take into account the *adult* death-rates in the two classes. Natural selection may not only be effective in modifying the gross fertility into a net fertility, but also as an adult death-rate.

It might at first sight appear that the census returns would enable us to surmount most of these difficulties, but, at any rate with regard to the English census, this is not the fact. It is not possible, for instance, to extract returns for even a professional class corresponding to Class I. of the Danish statistics; we find at once that the term 'professional' covers a variety of employments and offices, the followers and occupants of which are essentially drawn from the artisan classes.

Without, therefore, proposing to insist on any very definite conclusions, I will still illustrate these various points from the only available material—Rubin and Westergaard's Copenhagen statistics. I take out of their tables the series for marriages of 15 to 24 years' duration, and for 25 and more years' duration for the Classes I., II., and V., which correspond approximately to our (1) professional and mercantile, (2) shopkeeping and smaller commercial, and (3) artisan classes respectively. I find the following for the mean size of family :—

		No. of Cases.	I. Duration of Marriages being 15-24 Years.	No. of Cases.	II. Duration of Marriages being 25 and more Years.	Both together.
Professional Class	gross fertility	944	4·24	898	4·80	4·52
	net fertility		3·25 (·77)		3·38 (·70)	3·31
Commercial Class	gross fertility	2009	4·32	1622	4·91	4·58
	net fertility		2·91 (·67)		3·13 (·64)	3·01
Artisan Class	gross fertility	2934	4·79	1457	5·26	4·95
	net fertility		3·12 (·65)		3·17 (·60)	3·14

Now a number of important results seem to be suggested by this table.

(i.) Artisan Class, Commercial Class, Professional Class is the order of gross fertility. But this order is entirely altered by Natural Selection, the commercial class falls to the bottom, and the professional class rises to the top. This result has been already stated by Rubin and Westergaard (*loc. cit.* S. 122), except that in the order of gross fertility they place the professional class above the commercial. I am not able to see any error in my figures or method, which differs from theirs. Thus we have a clear instance of natural selection mastering reproductive selection.

(ii.) If we compare columns I. and II. of the table, we see in every case a reduction of both gross and net fertility with the transition from marriages of more to marriages of less than 25 years' duration. Now, undoubtedly children are frequently born after marriages have lasted 15 years, but I am very doubtful whether the full amount of this difference can be attributed to births occurring between the fifteenth and twenty-fifth years of marriage. I believe it is largely due to the increased amount of restraint in the more recent marriages. If this be so, we see that the restraint exercised is greatest in the commercial, slightly less in the professional, and least in the working classes. In the professional and commercial classes the decrease in the gross fertility has not been accompanied by anything like the same decrease in the net fertility, while in the working classes the net fertility has remained sensibly constant. The ratio of net to gross fertility is given in brackets, and shows a sensible increase in all classes in the modern marriages, although the fertility in all is decreasing. A large proportion, however, of this may be apparent rather than real, since in marriages of 25 and more years there will be a considerable effect produced by the adult death-rate. While, therefore, it is possible to assert that both net and gross fertility are decreasing in all classes, we cannot be quite certain whether one is really decreasing at a greater or less rate than the other.

(iii.) If we might judge simply from net fertility, we should conclude that reproductive selection would ultimately cause society to be recruited from the professional classes; for not only have they a greater net fertility, but admittedly a smaller adult death-rate. The net fertilities of the three classes differ, however, so inconsiderably that just as natural selection upsets the conclusion drawn from the gross fertility of the three classes, so a selective marriage-rate may easily again place the artisan class, or even the commercial class, in the dominant reproductive position.

Now the statistics given by Rubin and Westergaard (*loc. cit.* pp. 74-79) present many difficulties, especially with regard to the transition from the artisan proper to the servant class. I doubt, indeed, whether any very definite measure of marriage-rate in the different classes can be drawn from them. Rubin and Westergaard themselves consider that the marriage frequency in the professional classes is only two-thirds the average (p. 78). If we assume this to be true, and apply it to the problem of reproductive selection, we see that the net fertility, $3\cdot31$ of the professional classes, must be replaced by a class-reproductivity of two-thirds, $3\cdot31 = 2\cdot21$ about. Since the artisan class have a frequency, apparently only very slightly differing from the average, we conclude that their class reproductivity $= 3\cdot14$ about. Hence we see that the selective marriage-rate replaces the artisan classes in the dominant position, from which natural selection appeared to have ejected them. Thus, so far as the Danish data go, we must conclude that society after all "recruits itself from below." An immense adult death-rate of a selective character, which would restore the balance of the classes, *i.e.* reduce $3\cdot14$ to something below $2\cdot21$, is, we may take it, impossible, for it would connote that the population was essentially stationary.

(9) The object of this paper, which is one rather of suggestion than of conclusion, is now fulfilled. It has been shown that if fertility be inheritable, or that if it

be correlated with any inheritable organ or characteristic, reproductive selection, as man is now circumstanced, is a factor of evolution which is not held in check by natural selection; that the death-rate—within a particular social class—is really correlated with fertility, but that as against reproductive selection it is non-effective. Further, that a selective death-rate between class and class appears to be far more than counterbalanced by a selective marriage-rate—the class in which marriages are most frequent being able in this way to much more than recover the ground lost by a lower net fertility. Whatever may be the conditions which hold among lower types of life, or among races of uncivilised man, where the struggle for existence is more severe, it would seem that the survival of the most fertile, rather than the survival of the fittest, is very possibly now the keynote to evolution in civilised man. The social importance of such a conception as this, even if it be treated merely as a possibility, seems to demand the collection of a wider range of statistics and their most careful examination. It has been usual to associate—and perhaps too readily—certain undeniably anti-social characteristics, such as recklessness and want of thrift, with extreme fertility in man. The limitation of the family seems to be less conspicuous in the superfertile than in the subfertile group of any class, and more marked in the less fertile than the more fertile classes. It has been more than once suggested that natural selection would undoubtedly hold in check any anti-social characteristics correlated with fertility. There has been, I think, sufficient evidence given in this paper to call such a view into question, and to suggest that reproductive selection—emphasised, as it apparently is, by limitation of the family in certain classes—is with some probability the most potent factor of evolution in the case of civilised man. Whether such an evolution may not ultimately produce a state of affairs in which natural selection will again become dominant is another question. At any rate, the relative degrees of fertility in the various classes of a community, and the correlation of various social or anti-social characteristics with fertility seem to deserve the attention of statesmen even more than statisticians. The prudential restraint on marriage and parentage in the more educated members of the community, which we are apt to regard as a social virtue, may after all have its dark side, and the confidence sometimes expressed that natural selection under the form of a selective death-rate will rectify matters, seems to require more justification than can be found in the statistics at present available. Natural selection is sensibly at work, but its influence *within any class* seems to be of an entirely different order to that of reproductive selection. In civilised man the survival of the fittest appears to be replaced by the survival of the most fertile, and the identification of the most fertile with the socially fittest has not yet been asserted by any statist. To bring this identification about may indeed form the hardest problem which the present evolution of civilised man is setting the statesmen of the future.

IV

SOCIALISM AND NATURAL SELECTION[1]

> What a foolish idea seems to prevail . . . on the connection between Socialism and Evolution through Natural Selection.—CHARLES DARWIN.

EVOLUTION is the most striking feature of modern scientific thought, hence all that terms itself evolution must be scientific. Such seems to be the logic of the average reviewer, and, we regret to say it, of some men of science who ought to know better. The fact is, that the word evolution has been so terribly abused, first by biologists, then by pseudo-scientists, and lastly by the public, that it has become a cant term to cover any muddle-headed reasoning, which would utterly fail to justify itself had it condescended to apply the rule of three. A variety of ill-described and ill-appreciated factors of change have all been classed together and entitled the "theory" of evolution; they have been hailed as the expressions of great biological truths, and by taking a little of one factor and neglecting a great deal of another, any result might be deduced from the theory which pleased the taste of the user. Thus the door was opened for that loose, merely descriptive, and semi-metaphysical reasoning, which places a good deal

[1] *Fortnightly Review*, July 1894.

of the biological writing of the past ten years on the footing of the mediæval writers on physics. The progression in the downward course from hard facts to complete metaphysics is well marked in the writings of August Weismann, starting with his fairly sane essay on the *Duration of Life*, and ending in the arithmetico-metaphysical muddle of his theory of amphimixis. Unfortunately a certain section of English biologists have followed him, and "panmixia" and "germ-plasm," ill-defined even in their writings, have now reached the social platform, and are being used as absolutely unassailable arguments against the socialistic movement.

The reader may well ask what right a socialist has to express any judgment whatever on delicate biological problems. The answer is simply this, the questions to be answered are in reality *mathematical* problems, and a slight acquaintance with the rule of three and the theory of statistics is sufficient to dispel all the metaphysics of amphimixis and much of the puzzle-headedness of panmixia. We are not speaking without evidence; a moderate acquaintance with Colenso would have prevented many of the letters from distinguished biologists on the subject of panmixia which have appeared in the pages of *Nature* from ever being indited. The reaction has not come too soon; the movement started by Mr. Francis Galton, and ably developed by Professor Weldon and others, must end in the theory of evolution becoming a branch of quantitative science; the loose qualitative or descriptive reasoning of the older biologists must give way to an accurate mathematico-statistical logic. The trained biologist may discover and tabulate facts, much as the physicist does to-day, but it will need the trained mathematician to reason upon them. The great biologist of the future will be like the great physicist of to-day, a mathematician trained and bred. Here, then, is the justification for a mathematician, however limited his range, interfering when he observes biological principles, first stated without any quantitative theory or statistical basis, and then adopted as valid arguments in dealing with the great social problems of our time.

While at the sources of knowledge vague descriptive reasoning is being succeeded by a more just quantitative theory of evolution, the innumerable conduit pipes represented by popular writers and the press are still providing the public with a fluid so contaminated with the germs of muddle-headedness that it is little wonder if whole classes of the community are poisoned. I venture accordingly to make the following definite statement:—That until the quantitative importance and numerical relationship of the various factors, vaguely grouped together as the theory of evolution, are accurately ascertained, no valid argument can be based on the theory of evolution with regard to the growth of civilised human societies. We must remain agnostic as to these problems until the theory of evolution has been readjusted on its new basis. Any theory of social evolution which professedly grounds itself on merely descriptive biological truths is built on a quagmire, and might be safely disregarded, did not the perversion of the popular taste by our long consumption of the above-mentioned contaminated fluids lead us too often to declare that a most perturbed liquid is a crystal draught of truth. In particular, a recent work on social evolution,[1] which teems with paralogisms and paradoxes, has been hailed as a work likely to have "wide political as well as social effects," and which competent judges will pronounce "to be one of the greatest books we have had since Darwin's *Origin of Species*." It is further "one of the most suggestive and inspiring books which have ever dealt with the problems of the imminent future"; it is "novel in conception," "fertile in suggestion"; the author, challenging attention by his wide "range of illustration," and "lucid and forcible" manner, "supports every proposition with a mass of evidence," and his book "marks a turning-point in the social controversy which is raging all around us."

It may be said that this is only the opinion of ephemeral newspaper reviews, and that although the newspapers, from *Times* to *Daily Chronicle*, are unanimous in praise, this is not the opinion of science with regard to Mr. Kidd's theories. Now this is precisely the point at which real danger arises. Because Mr. Kidd uses the current jargon of evolution, he is hailed as an exponent of scientific truth, even by the *doyen* of evolutionary science. If Mr. Alfred Russel Wallace, in a journal which professes to be the organ of scientific thought in England, can describe Mr. Kidd's work as "thoroughly scientific in its methods,

[1] *Social Evolution.* By Benjamin Kidd. Macmillan. "If you ask me to describe 'Social Evolution' in a word, I should say that it is an endeavour to give a biological basis to our social science." Mr. Kidd to a *Daily Chronicle* interviewer, 20th June 1894.

inasmuch as it is based on the theory of evolution," what wonder is it that the literary journals describe *Social Evolution* as an application of " the most recent doctrines of science to modern society and life," and as " only an application of the laws of evolution enounced in the *Origin of Species* "? Let us be quite clear about the point. If Mr. Kidd's theory be a correct one, then the modern socialistic movement is completely futile; it is opposed to fundamental biological truths, and we had better at once confess the error of our ways and allow the biologists a predominant voice in social legislation. That socialism is opposed to the cosmic order is not, however, an original discovery of Mr. Kidd's, we shall find it proclaimed years ago by biologists and philosophers, but no one has yet put socialism and natural selection in such glaring opposition as he has done, and from this standpoint at least his work is of value. It enables us to put our finger the more easily on the fallacies which underlie the biological arguments against socialism.

In the first place, let us give Mr. Kidd all the support we can from authority. Professor Haeckel, in his well-known *Freie Wissenschaft und freie Lehre*, writes as follows:—

> The theory of descent proclaims more clearly than any other scientific theory that that equality of individuals which socialism strives after is an impossibility, that it stands, in fact, in irreconcilable contradiction to the inevitable inequality of individuals which actually subsists.

And again:—

> Darwinism is anything but socialistic. If a definite political

tendency be attributed to this English theory—which is, indeed, possible—this tendency can only be aristocratic, certainly not democratic, least of all socialistic. The theory of selection teaches us that in human life, exactly as in animal and plant life, at each place and time only a small privileged minority can continue to exist and flourish; the great mass must starve, and more or less prematurely perish in misery. Innumerable are the germs of every form of animal and plant life and the young individuals which spring from these germs. The number of fortunate individuals, on the other hand, who develop to their full age, and actually attain their goal in life, is out of all proportion small. The cruel and relentless struggle for existence which rages throughout all living Nature, and in accordance with Nature must rage, this ceaseless and pitiless competition of all living things, is an undeniable fact; only the select minority of the privileged fit is in a position to successfully survive this competition, the great majority of competitors must meanwhile of necessity perish miserably! We may deeply mourn this tragic fact, but we cannot deny or alter it. "Many are called but few are chosen!" This selection, this picking out of the chosen, is necessarily combined with the languishing and perishing of the remaining majority. Another English investigator even denotes the kernel of Darwinism as "the survival of the fittest," "the triumph of the best." Obviously the principle of selection is anything but democratic; it is aristocratic in the precise sense of the word.

Professor Haeckel here states the biological dogma even more strongly and crudely than Mr. Kidd. If his words are to mean anything, they must indicate that the pitiless competition between individuals crushes out several human beings for every one that survives. It is needless to say that he appeals to no statistics, although the mortality tables were at hand to confirm or refute his views, had he taken the trouble to examine them.

Yet another German biologist, Professor Oscar Schmidt of Strasburg, writes:—

If the socialists would think clearly they would feel that they must do all they can to choke the doctrine of descent, for it declares with express distinctness that socialistic ideas are impracticable.

Coming nearer home, we may remark that the basis of Mr. Herbert Spencer's essay on *The Sins of Legislators* is the assumption that no society can progress in which the ill-endowed do not get killed off in competition with the well-endowed; the "beneficent working of the survival of the fittest" has been so impressed upon modern people that they might be expected to hesitate before neutralising its action.

A society will be unable to hold its own in the struggle with other societies if it disadvantage its superior units that it may advantage its inferior units.

Mr. Spencer is clearly referring to the struggle for existence between individuals of the same community, otherwise his remarks lose all their point. He gives no statistics, and does not explain how A, B, C, and D will be in a better condition to survive in the struggle with an adjacent group E, F, G, and H, if A and B, being the well-endowed, have first killed off C and D, or reduced them according to their lesser merits to a state of "abject misery." " Placed in competition with members of its own species, and in antagonism with members of other species, the adult dwindles and gets killed off, or thrives and propagates, according as it is ill-endowed or well-endowed. Manifestly an opposite *régime*, could it be maintained, would, in course of time, be fatal to the species."

This is Mr. Herbert Spencer's receipt for an efficient society—the struggle for existence between individuals, the "cosmic process" of Professor Huxley, maintained in order to clear off the ill-endowed, and the less-endowed as well, be it noted.[1]

Professor Huxley, in his *Evolution and Ethics*, refers, if I understand him rightly, especially to the struggle of individual with individual by his "cosmic process." He sets it against the ethical process, and indicates that the process of civilised as distinct from savage man has largely depended on the suspension of the individual struggle. Why the effect of the struggle of social group against social group, which has led to more and more organisation—suppression of anarchic competition—within the group, should be contrasted as an ethical process against the *cosmic* process I fail to understand. The development of social instinct and the intensification of the altruistic spirit in the higher types of gregarious animals would appear to be just as much a product of the cosmic process as the evolution of the maternal instinct in the tigress. Indeed, Professor Huxley himself seems to think so, but *only* in a note appended to his lecture. Yet the note is hardly consistent with such phrases as—

> The history of civilisation details the steps by which men have succeeded in building up an artificial world within the cosmos. . . . Social progress means a checking of the cosmic process at every step, and the substitution for it of another, which may be called the ethical process.

---

[1] Pushed to the extreme—and Mr. Spencer's arguments deserve it—a Newton, a Kepler, and a Copernicus should compete to the effacement of two of them, that the world might be populated by the progeny of the best of the three.

Professor Huxley, with far greater insight, indeed, than Haeckel or Spencer, does recognise that social progress has depended on an organisation of society checking very largely the individual struggle for existence within the group. He does not, like the writers to whom we have referred, suggest that the checking of this intra-group struggle must lead to social degeneration, but he does speak of it exactly in the same way as something opposed to the process of cosmic evolution, to the "natural order."

> On the contrary, the natural order tends to the maintenance, in one shape or another, of the war of each against all, the result of which is not the survival of the morally or even physically highest, but of that form of humanity, the mortality of which is least under the conditions. The pressure of a constant increase of population upon the means of support must keep up the struggle for existence, whatever form of social organisation may be adopted (*Essays*, vol. i. p. 427).

If it were not for the use of the words "the war of each against all," there would be nothing in this passage to which a socialist could take exception; the struggle for existence might mean the struggle against physical nature, against disease, of group with group, or of superior with inferior race. No thoughtful socialist, so far as I am aware, would object to cultivate Uganda *at the expense of its present occupiers* if Lancashire were starving. Only he would have this done directly and consciously, and not by way of missionaries and exploiting companies. To a socialist the checking of the intra-group competition is not an ideal of the future; he believes it to be identical with the history of social growth, and that what intra-group struggle goes on now is scarcely for existence, but for varying degrees of comfort and luxury. He no more believes the limitation of that struggle opposed to the "natural order" than the development of the earliest forms of social instinct among gregarious animals, or indeed of the maternal instinct itself.

But Professor Huxley, if recognising what Haeckel and Spencer have not, namely, that social progress was in the past, quite as much as it is in the present, inconsistent with the struggle between individuals in the group, still supposes that the socialists of to-day have set themselves an impossible task :—

> The only true contradictory of Individualism is that more common kind of Socialism which proposes to use the power of the State in order, as the phrase goes, to "organise" society or some part of it. That is to say, this "regimental" Socialism proposes to interfere with the freedom of the individual to whatever extent the sovereign may dictate, for the purpose of more or less completely neutralising the effects of the innate inequalities of men. It is militarism in a new shape, requiring the implicit obedience of the individual to a governmental commander-in-chief, whose business it is to wage war against natural inequality, and to set artificial equality in its place (*Essays*, vol. i. p. 393).

To "wage war against natural inequality" is clearly a *reductio ad absurdum* of the socialistic doctrine. So far as I understand the views of the more active socialists of to-day, they fully recognise that the better posts, the more lucrative and comfortable berths, must always go to the more efficient and more productive workers, and that it is for the welfare of society that it should be so. Socialists, however, propose to limit within healthy bounds the rewards of natural superiority and the advantages of *artificial* inequality. The victory of the more capable, or the more fortunate, must not involve such a defeat of the less capable, or the less fortunate, that social stability is endangered by the misery produced. At the present time a failure of the harvest in Russia and America simultaneously, or a war with a first-class European power, would probably break up our social system altogether. We should be crushed in the extra-group struggle for existence, because we have given too much play to intra-group competition, because we have proceeded on the assumption that it is better to have a few prize cattle among innumerable lean kine than a decently-bred and properly-fed herd with no expectations at Smithfield.

All the above authorities—and very weighty authorities they are—seem to me to look upon socialism as either opposed to the law of natural selection, or as at best setting up an artificial equality in place of a "natural order." Their parable has been taken up and completed by Mr. Kidd with a definiteness and vigour which leaves nothing to be desired from the standpoint of controversy.

Even at the cost of reiteration, let us endeavour to see the magnitude of the problem we are discussing. We have an apparent contradiction between the conclusions of science and the present socialistic trend of both legislation and ethical teaching. The contradiction can be removed only by asserting that there is no socialistic trend, as Mr. Kidd does; or by admitting that our society is decadent and the British race degenerating, which seems to be the opinion of Mr. Spencer; or, finally, by proving that the "biological truths" on which the contradiction is founded are no truths at all, merely misapplications of ill-defined terms; this is the firm conviction of the present writer. The two sides of the contradiction may be summed up as follows :—

On the one hand, socialist writers have time after time insisted that one of the main objects of socialism —by which we are to understand the State ownership of land and capital, and the State control of labour— is to lessen the intensity of intra-group competition; they propose in this manner to reduce the waste of competitive production, and so render the productive basis of society more efficient. In addition, the further lessening of intra-group competition will, in the opinion of socialists, tend to strengthen society against extra-group stress by knitting society more firmly together and spreading the staying powers of the community, as measured by its capital and intellectual traditions, more uniformly over the whole body.

On the other hand, biologists of more or less authority assert that the progress of any group depends on the highest state of rivalry between individuals of the group. This struggle of individual with individual has been spoken of as a natural law ruling all life, and by aid of a mysterious and novel principle termed *panmixia*, added by Weismann to the Darwinian theory, it is said to follow, not only that progress is impossible without natural selection, but that without natural selection degeneration must set in as certainly as death follows life. Either, then, recent social evolution has been misinterpreted, it does not tend to that limitation of the effects of individual competition, which for Karl Marx and for most socialists is the essence of socialism, or else we are rapidly degenerating, and the worst fears of the old school of economists and of the *laissez faire* politicians will inevitably be realised.

It is the first alternative which Mr. Kidd propounds in his *Social Evolution*. His book, by its frank acceptance of apparently proven scientific conclusions, by its clever disguise of paralogisms, by its general tone of indisputable certainty, and last, but not least, by the weapons it puts into the hands of controversial theology, is likely to have an influence far wider than it really merits. It is above all important that it should be met and refuted from the socialistic standpoint.

Mr. Kidd's position, briefly stated, appears to be the following:—He frankly accepts, without the least qualification or the least criticism, as an acknowledged biological truth, that the intra-group struggle for existence is the *sine quâ non* of social progress. All progress from the beginning of life has been the result of the most strenuous and imperative conditions of rivalry and selection (p. 193); without this struggle positive degeneration must set in by the principle of panmixia. The inherent tendency of modern social evolution is not towards socialism, but towards an equality of social opportunity, which, following on an equality of political rights—the product of the older Liberalism,—will bring all the people into the rivalry of life on a footing of equality (p. 314). This is the last and greatest phase of social development; the rivalry and competition of life are not to be suspended, but are to be raised to the highest degree of efficiency they have ever reached; their scope is to be extended, they are to be made still more strenuous, the stress severer, the pace quicker (pp. 53-55). The higher the form of civilisation, the sterner will be the conflict.

Now, as Mr. Kidd fully accepts as an inevitable natural law the struggle for existence between individuals, it follows that this increased rivalry and competition which is to follow from increased equality of opportunity, must result either in the absolute destruction of the defeated or in the greater power of the victorious to reproduce themselves. So far as statistics go there appears to be no marked correlation between reproductivity and success in life. Hence assuming "equality of social opportunity" to connote equal freedom[1] for all men to marry and reproduce themselves, it would seem that Mr. Kidd trusts to starvation to weaken, defeat to maim, or death to absolutely remove the unsuccessful in the still severer individualistic competition which, according to him, is to be the chief factor of the more efficient society of the future. If progress arises from promulgation by inheritance combined with selection and rejection due to the ceaseless struggle between individuals (p. 38), it must connote the extinction of less efficient forms. Now you cannot drive a man out of existence nor check his keen instinct of reproduction without inflicting in the process great pain and misery. This price we suppose Mr. Kidd, like Mr. Spencer, is quite prepared to pay for the great social

---

[1] *i.e.* no State-regulation of marriage of a *socialistic* kind, no legislation against the parentage of the unfit.

boon of progress,¹ the "beneficent working of the struggle for existence." Mr. Kidd asserts, however, that if all men were rationalists they would not pay this price. Regardless of the increasing fitness of the innumerable generations to come, they would sacrifice the future to the present. Hence for Mr. Kidd, reason is an extremely anti-social and anti-evolutionary force. To check the anti-progressive character of the reason, the anti-social tendency of the intellect, Mr. Kidd believes that religion, which essentially involves an ultra-rational sanction for moral conduct, has been evolved.² Thus religion has appeared to prevent man stopping the pain and misery which is assumed to be a necessary accompaniment of the "beneficent working of the struggle for existence"!

Self-assertiveness of the individual must be absolutely subordinated to the maintenance of a process³ in which the individual himself has not the slightest interest, but to the furtherance of which his personal welfare must be often sacrificed. Hence the central feature of human history, namely, the dominance of that progressively developing class of phenomena included under the head of religions, whereby this subordination has been effected (p. 194).

Now so much of this view of religions as is contained in the statement that they have been developed,

[1] It is needless to say that we should be prepared to pay it also, if social progress did not seem to us identical with the reduction and not the increase of intra-group struggle.
[2] It does not seem to have struck Mr. Kidd that under extra-group competition the social instinct may ultimately have become so developed that the discomfort produced by disregarding it is rational ground for obeying it. A tigress of a thoughtful turn of mind would hardly need an ultra-rational sanction for her maternal instincts; she might be capable of balancing physiological discomfort, maternal gratification, and the pangs of conscience against the pleasures of one hearty meal.
[3] The "cosmic process" and intensification of the rivalry of life.

like other tribal superstitions and folk-beliefs, as a means of strengthening the social feeling at the expense of the individualistic, is undoubtedly sound, and has been long held by many scientific investigators of comparative religion. The tribe that believed in a Walhalla for the heroes killed in battle was clearly likely to be stronger in the fight than one which had not evolved a belief in the hereafter; the inspiring idea of the god fighting for his tribe and the conviction that certain forms of animal life are sacred: that the killing of a cow, for example, was not to be undertaken without tribal sanction of the most solemn kind, can be easily recognised as of social utility.[1] Accordingly, that religion has been evolved, not on account of its reasonableness, but as a sanction for social conduct on the part of the unreasoning, upon whom the fear of future punishments and the hope of future rewards could have an effect, is an opinion in which historical science can for once agree with Mr. Kidd. Whether the theologian will be equally willing to see things from this standpoint is another question.

Now admitting that religions have been evolved on account of their social utility, we may follow our author a stage further and recognise that

all classes of society have become sensitive in a high degree to the sight of suffering or wrong of any kind (p. 300).

Indeed, so sensitive are they, that whole classes of

---

[1] Had Mr. Kidd studied such a work as Robertson Smith's *Religion of the Semites*, or Mannhardt's *Wald- und Feldkulte*, he would hardly have made the statements he has done with regard to the superficial treatment of religion by scientific investigators.

the community become occasionally hysterical on reading the account of sufferings of which they have not taken the trouble, in the first place, to investigate the truth, nor in the second, if they be true, the possible justice.[1] But if we admit the existence of this fund of altruistic feeling in society at the present, surely it must be tending to lessen that stress of individual competition and that presumed extermination of the unsuccessful upon the existence of which Mr. Kidd's theory of social progress is based? By no means, according to our author. This

> great fund of altruistic feeling which, gradually saturating our entire social life, has slowly undermined the position of the power-holding classes, and so rendered possible the movement which is tending to ultimately bring all the people into the rivalry of life on conditions of equality (p. 239)

can only, on Mr. Kidd's hypothesis, intensify the suffering by making the struggle more widespread, more strenuous, and more deadly.

If rivalry of life does not bring with it the extinction of the less fit, or check their reproduction, then it is perfectly idle to associate it with the biologists' struggle for existence. If Mr. Kidd uses the term "rivalry of life," and he apparently does, to denote the biological conception of the struggle for existence, then clearly altruistic feeling as developed by religion is supposed by him to have relation only to the struggle of class against class, and not of individual against individual. How far this is in keeping with

---

[1] By justice we understand solely the social utility of a corrective and exemplary punishment for directly or indirectly anti-social conduct.

the wonderfully moving and impressive altruistic ideals which we have in the simple story of the life and acts of the Founder of Christianity (p. 298)

is a question which does not appear to have troubled Mr. Kidd. With him religion seems to be a means of checkmating the reason and altruism to be a dodge for weakening the resistance of the power-holding classes.

Now it hardly needs much width of observation to see that the "great fund of altruistic feeling which is gradually saturating our entire social life" is quite as much opposed to the unlimited triumph of the individually strong in body or mind over the individually weaker, as to the unlimited triumph of one class at the expense of another. While such characteristic features of our age as the trade-union movement, the eight hours' movement, and the movement for the emancipation of women, appear directly to limit the anti-social effects of the triumph of class over class, as well as to lessen the intensity of the struggle of individual with individual, yet the bullying of the weaker by the stronger man, whether it takes a physical or intellectual form, draws just as much on the "fund of altruistic feeling," and calls forth just as stern a public censure nowadays as any oppression of "the power-owning classes."

We are no doubt growing more fully conscious of the social value of power and ability, from whatever class it comes; we are endeavouring to throw the net which shall draw talent into useful social activity over the widest possible area; but, at the same time, we are restricting the power of special ability to crush out the less competent. We recognise that the advantage of rightly-placed ability may be obtained at a less expense than the abject misery of the less capable, and the consequent instability of the social organisation. No dispassionate observer, we are convinced, can study modern legislation and modern social feeling without seeing, like Mr. Spencer, that they are actually tending to lessen the extreme results of intra-group competition; that is, they are tending in the direction indicated by the socialistic thinkers. The future will be socialistic, the intra-group struggle will be weakened rather than intensified. Mr. Kidd's reading of modern social evolution is utterly wide of the mark. But does it follow that the "biological truths" on which he bases his theory are erroneous? May we not be proceeding towards stages of less social efficiency?—shortly, are we not a decadent race?

The exactly opposite proposition appears to me true, namely, that a limitation of competition within the group is likely to lead to increased social efficiency. Further, it is quite unproven in the case of gregarious animals of any kind, including civilised man, that the rivalry to death of individuals of the same group plays any important part in natural selection.

In the first place, it is open to question whether Mr. Kidd has ever studied his Darwin; in the second place, he can hardly have analysed the mortality tables of any civilised human community; and, in the third place, he has made absolutely no attempt to measure the relative importance of the various factors of natural selection in the evolution of civilised man. Now it must be remembered that Mr. Spencer and Mr. Kidd are referring to one special factor of natural selection—the competition between individuals of the same group, which leads to the weaker being destroyed or prevented from breeding. It is this intra-group struggle for existence which is the sole basis of their arguments against Socialism. There is no special power in Socialism which can prevent the action of "physical" selection—the struggle of the group against its physical environment, against disease and climate and physical wear and tear. Nor is the struggle of superior with inferior races, especially of civilised with uncivilised man, likely to cease with the socialistic advent; at least, if past history be any guide to the future, we may safely assert that extra-group struggle for the means of subsistence will invariably precede any severe form of the intra-group struggle for life. A nation, whether socialistic or individualistic, if its population reaches the limits of its food supply, will sooner break its bounds and consume its neighbour's, especially if an obviously inferior neighbour is to be found, than gnaw its own vitals. Here, then, are three factors of natural selection—intra-group struggle, physical selection, and extra-group struggle—of which one alone is likely to be effected by socialistic changes. When, therefore, we are told that socialism is impossible because it checks the "cosmic process"—the fundamental condition for progressive evolution—surely it is necessary for the upholders of such a statement to give us some numerical measure of natural selection in civilised man, and, above all, some numerical statement as to the relative importance of the above three factors?

Almost the whole strength of Darwin's arguments as to the struggle for existence in plant and animal life, is drawn from the conception that we are dealing with a *practically stationary population.* The population has reached the limits of its food supply—"more individuals are born than can possibly survive"; "a grain in the balance will determine which individual shall live and which shall die." And again: "As the individuals of the same species come in all respects into the closest competition with each other, the struggle will generally be most severe between them." "Of the many individuals of any species which are periodically born, but a small number can survive. I have called this principle by which each slight variation, if useful, is preserved, by the term Natural Selection." "A struggle for existence inevitably follows from the high rate at which all organic beings tend to increase," *i.e.* the increase in geometrical ratio. "Hence, as more individuals are produced than can possibly survive, there must in every case be a struggle for existence, either one individual with another of the same species, or with individuals of distinct species, or with the physical conditions of life."[1] It is statements such as these which have been applied without the least reservation to the very different problem of the social evolution of civilised man. Professor Haeckel speaks of the "great mass" of mankind "starving and prematurely perishing in misery," as an inevitable cosmic process reducing all socialistic schemes to absurdity. This is obviously Darwin's "small number" of the many indi-

[1] *Origin of Species,* pp. 71-78, 552-577, etc.

viduals born who can survive. It is clearly on the basis of such teaching that Mr. Kidd, without any statistics and without any demonstration, asserts, as a great biological truth, that only where rivalry goes on will selection and progress remain unchecked. But have these statements of Darwin any relation to civilised man? *Did he himself intend that they should have?*

Do the great majority of civilised men starve or perish miserably before they have reproduced their kind? To answer this question we have only to turn to vital statistics. Let us take the mortality table for English males,[1] where, if anywhere, the intra-group struggle should exhibit itself. If we form a curve in which we represent the deaths in each successive year of age of 1000 males born in the same year, this curve may be analysed by mathematical processes (which cannot be discussed here) into five "chance" distributions of death.[2] They are the following:—

Mortality of old age centring about	67,	484 deaths.
Mortality of middle life	41,	173 ,,
Mortality of youth	22,	51 ,,
Mortality of childhood	6,	46 ,,
Mortality of infancy	—[3]	246 ,,

Within fairly narrow limits such a distribution of mortality is not peculiar to our own country, nor is it peculiar to the last decade. It is typical of civilised man.

[1] The French mortality statistics for both sexes give nearly identical results.
[2] See the first paper on *The Chances of Death*.
[3] Almost entirely in the first two years of life; but carrying the curve backward I find an additional "antenatal mortality" of 200 (per 1000 born) in the last three months of pregnancy.

Now this result teaches us many things. If more than 480 male deaths in the 1000 fall into the *old age* chance distribution, it is idle to speak of the very small number out of those born who are able to survive. Further, it may safely be assumed that a very large proportion of those who fall under the mortality of middle life, centring about 41, have already reproduced themselves. There is no *large majority* which "dies prematurely" unable to reproduce itself, at most a minority, perhaps 40 in the 100 males, die before reaching an age at which they could many times have reproduced themselves. But how many of these deaths are due to natural selection? In the first place, we can cut off for our present purposes old age mortality, nearly 50 per cent, and at least half the mortality of middle life —which must be selected, if at all, too late to largely affect reproduction. How many of the remainder die from non-selective forms of death? Such, for example, as accident, or fevers, which chance to strike the strong man and miss the weak, or kill both, if not both in the same proportions.[1] Let us say 40 per cent die before practically being able to complete their reproductive activity. We are erring greatly in the opponent's favour if we give 30 per cent of this to a *selective* death-rate. And of that 30 per cent what proportions shall we attribute to intra-group competition? Clearly but a vanishingly small proportion. The great bulk of deaths which are due to natural selection occur in infancy and childhood. Here it is that physical selec-

[1] Typhoid may kill more weak than strong individuals, but it is only the *difference* in the number of weak and strong killed which is a differential or selective death-rate.

tion is chiefly at work. About 300 in the 1000, or 30 per cent, are killed off before reaching the age at which the intra-group struggle between individuals may be supposed to commence. The weaklings of all types, and, with some exceptions, of all classes, are thus weeded out by physical selection long before intra-group competition—"the bitter rivalry of individuals"—has commenced, or has had any chance of producing substantial effects.

If it be argued that this rivalry of individuals—the cosmic process which socialism seeks to upset—acts indirectly, not by destroying individuals, nor hindering them from reproducing their kind, but by killing the offspring of the defeated in much larger proportions, then again statistics can be appealed to to settle the matter. The birth-rate of the well-to-do, professional, mercantile, and superior artisan classes, has been for a long time considerably less than the average birth-rate of the community at large. The causes which produce this—late marriages, limitation of the family, or the frequency of promiscuity unaccompanied by parentage—are largely typical of individualistic stages of society. There appears to be no direct relation between success in the rivalry of life and the extent of reproductivity in civilised man. The lower we go in the social scale the greater is the reproductivity. The infant death-rate is indeed much higher, but does not compensate for the great superiority of the birth-rate and of the marriage-rate.[1] The well-to-do classes, those who are presumably successful in the rivalry of life, are perpetually recruited

[1] See the third essay on *Reproductive Selection*.

from the lower ranks, and if we started a rigid caste system in this country from the present date, the proportion of the "classes" to the "masses" would dwindle more and more with each decade.

Success in the rivalry for life in an *individualistic* community means largely the artificial protection against physical selection of weakly offspring. It is difficult to grasp how socialism will, in this respect, decrease the selective death-rate, be it what it may. It is for those, indeed, who assert that the intra-group struggle is essential for human progress, to point out what percentage of the differential mortality of youth and of early middle life is due to intra-group struggle, and *not to physical selection, i.e.* is due to the struggle for food, where only a "small number" out of the many born can survive. Where in any civilised community is the "great mass of mankind starving and prematurely perishing in misery"? Such expressions can only apply to a stationary population, and Darwin's phrases as to a "grain in the balance will determine which individual shall live," and as to a severe struggle between individuals, have no application to a population increasing by several millions at each decade. Nor did Darwin ever intend that they should be applied; it is only the thoughtless who have caught up these phrases and, in order to push some idle theory of social evolution, use them as bogies for the socialists. Here is what Darwin himself says :—

> With highly civilised nations, continued progress depends in a subordinate degree on natural selection; for such nations do not surplant and exterminate each other as do savage tribes.

And again—

> Important as the struggle for existence has been, and still is, yet, as far as the highest part of man's nature is concerned, there are other agencies more important. For the moral qualities are advanced, either directly or indirectly, much more through the effects of habit, the reasoning powers, instruction, religion, etc., than through natural selection; though to this latter agency may be safely attributed the social instincts which afforded the base for the development of the moral sense.[1]

It is true that in a few other passages Darwin speaks more doubtfully, but in nearly every case he is speaking generally, without any reference to particular statistics, and his remarks apply with greater force to physical or extra-group selection than to intra-group selection. Thus he emphasises the rate at which man tends to increase (*Origin of Species*, p. 74, *Descent of Man*, p. 142), and asserts that natural selection must follow from the resulting struggle, but he does not assert that it is an intra-group struggle. In one passage he does write:—

> Nevertheless, the more intelligent members within the same community will succeed better in the long run than the inferior, and leave a more numerous progeny, and this is a form of natural selection (*Descent of Man*, p. 143).

This conclusion seems to me directly opposed to the birth statistics of any individualistic state. But how little weight Darwin himself really put on any *automatic* action of this kind in a civilised community—for which action he nowhere cites any evidence—is shown by the following paragraph, where he has passed at once from the automatic to the utilitarian conception,

---

[1] *Descent of Man*, pp. 143, 618. The definitions of "highest part" and "moral quality" fail.

from a law of nature to a desirable principle of social custom and legislation :—

> The advancement of the welfare of mankind is a most intricate problem; all ought to refrain from marriage who cannot avoid abject poverty for their children; for poverty is not only a great evil, but tends to its own increase by recklessness in marriage. On the other hand, as Mr. Galton has remarked, if the prudent avoid marriage, whilst the reckless marry, the inferior members tend to surplant the better members of society.
>
> There should be open competition for all men; and the most able should not be prevented by laws or customs from succeeding best and rearing the largest number of offspring (*Descent of Man*, p. 618).

It is, however, one thing to insist on the desirability of breeding from the better members of the community, and another to assert that there is actually an automatic principle at work, which causes social progress to depend principally on an intra-group struggle for existence.

Are we then to conclude that natural selection and the population question have no meaning for the socialist? The very contrary is the truth. He asserts that among gregarious animals, in particular civilised man, there is little, if any, evidence of the intra-group struggle for existence playing an important part. He believes that the progress of man has depended in the main on the minimising of this particular factor of natural selection, in order to emphasise the action of another factor—extra-group selection. He admits to the full the continuous action of physical selection at the present day, and does not see how the influence of this factor will be diminished by increased socialisation of the State; in fact, he conceives that its effects will be more uniform and widespread than ever before. Less artificial protection for the weaklings will be possible, less chance of their surviving and reproducing their kind if they are called upon to take part in the work of life, and earn by their own, rather than by their ancestors' hands, provision for their offspring and themselves. While the socialist denies that intra-group struggle in civilised communities is ever to the death, he is quite ready to admit that intra-group competition may be of great social value, as putting the right man into the right place, and as a means of obtaining a maximum of efficient social work. On the other hand, he holds that this competition can be carried on at too great a price; it may render the group unstable by the overwhelming advantages it gives to individuals; it becomes disastrous the moment it approaches a struggle, not for comparative degrees of comfort within a limited range, but for absolute existence. The socialist feels that in proposing to regulate this competition, he is not flying in the face of biological laws and cosmic processes, but taking part in the further stages of that evolution by which civilised man has been hitherto developed; this is just as much "biological" and "cosmic" as the evolutionary history of ants or bees.

The limitation of intra-group competition is not, therefore, a question for biological specialists, but for practical politicians; it is a utilitarian problem: How far by still further lessening intra-group competition can a community be made more stable, better able to resist extra-group selection?

This extra-group selection is nowadays much disguised, and to some extent spasmodic. Societies prepare for years, perhaps for centuries, for the extra-group struggle, which eventually changes the predominant races of continents. In a lesser form the struggle is ever going on. One after another inferior races are subjected to the white man; it is an extra-group struggle for markets and trade routes and spheres of influence, and only indirectly, but none the less really, for food-supply for the teeming multitudes at home. Meanwhile the stability and power of any group depends on the preservation and increase of its traditions, on its technical education, on its stores of knowledge, on its material resources, and on its limit of endurance, far more than on the perpetuation of any struggle for existence within the group itself. When the extra-group struggle with inferior races abroad has run to its end, then, if not sooner, the population question will force on a severer struggle for existence between civilised communities at home. Whether this struggle takes the form of actual warfare, or of still keener competition for trade and food-supply, that group in which unchecked internal competition has produced a vast proletariat with no limit of endurance, or with—to use a cant phrase—no "stake in the State," will be the first to collapse. It is extra-group competition which will more and more force the nations of Europe in the direction of socialism, just as on a much smaller scale the semi-socialistic organisations of the German mediæval towns were largely the product of the almost perpetual state of warfare of the time.

If we accept the standpoint of the socialist, that the

evolution of civilised man depends on other factors of natural selection than intra-group[1] struggle for existence, Mr. Kidd's theory of social evolution falls to the ground like a pack of cards; it finds no bottom on great "biological truths," and the supposed incompatibility of socialism with the laws of natural selection is only a bogie set up by individualist thinkers to scare the socialist, and if possible to check social changes for which they personally have no liking.

We have endeavoured to show that the particular factor of natural selection—intra-group struggle—plays little, if any, part among civilised man. At any rate, the onus of proof lies on those who assert that it does. The proof to be of any value must be a statistico-mathematical one, not a mere descriptive account of what effects supposed causes *might* bring about without a real numerical demonstration of their actual relative importance. Here we might leave Mr. Kidd and the biologists, but we cannot refrain from one further example of the manner in which bogies are manu-

[1] A characteristic example of the manner in which changes are attributed by descriptive biologists to intra-group struggle occurs in a recently published work by O. Ammon on *Die natürliche Auslese beim Menschen*. It is therein asserted that the inhabitants of Southern Germany were dolichocephalic—long-headed—in the fourth and sixth centuries, and that by intra-group selection they have now become brachycephalic—round-headed. The inference being that the latter are more intellectual, and have survived in the struggle within the group. Herr Ammon compares the mean index of 675 Row-Grave skulls with that of 6748 Baden recruits. Allowing for the difference between head and skull indices, I find on mathematical investigation of the frequency curve for Row-Grave skulls that it breaks up into normal components, one of which is identical with the Baden recruits both as to mean and distribution about the mean, while the other closely fits in mean and distribution about the mean the modern Low German skull curves. In other words, we have in the Row-Graves a *mixture* of races, and it would appear that extra-group and not intra-group struggle has led to the replacement of a dolichocephalic by a brachycephalic population. I believe most cases of supposed intra-group selection in man would disappear if they were examined by an adequate statistical theory.

factured to enforce the good behaviour of socialists. The last and biggest bogie is panmixia.

The paralogistic stages in the manufacture of this bogie are peculiarly instructive. In the first place, intra-group selection is widened out into natural selection, which embraces several other factors. Socialism is then asserted to contemplate the checking of the whole action of natural selection.[1] But it is not enough to saddle the socialists with a desire to check the "cosmic process," and so stop progress. It is demonstrable that their action would lead to the steady degeneration of the human race. This depends upon panmixia, which is introduced by Mr. Kidd as a recent development of biology, "the almost illimitable significance of which science is beginning to appreciate." He speaks of panmixia as "a necessarily inherent part of the doctrine of evolution," and asserts that

> the selection of the fittest acquires an immensely widened significance, if we realise it to be an inherent principle of life, that, by the simple process of the individuals of each generation propagating their kind without selection, the higher forms of life would tend to gradually sink back again by a degenerative process through all those stages of development by which they reached their present position.[2]

Push this to its logical result and the effect of socialism would not be to leave man where he is, physically and mentally, but to reduce him again to

[1] "Marx contemplated our Western civilisation culminating in a condition of society which it was difficult, if not impossible, for any one who had realised the essential unity and continuity under all outward forms of the developmental forces at work in human society to imagine; a state in which the laws that had operated continuously from the beginning of life were to be suddenly interrupted and finally suspended" (Kidd, *Social Evolution*, p. 228).

[2] *Social Evolution*, pp. 36, 37.

the simian condition. Now a great "biological truth" of this kind, if it be not self-obvious, and panmixia is certainly not that, should at least be supported by appeal to an ample range of accepted biological authority. Mr. Kidd gives us nothing of the kind, only a vague reference to "the investigations and conclusions of Professor Weismann." Now panmixia is like the majority of Weismann's theories—suggestive, nebulous, and utterly unproven. If any organ of a species be measured, say in one thousand specimens, and the number of organs between certain small ranges grouped together, the statistician can construct from these numbers a curve, which the researches of Professor Weldon on crustacea, and Mr. Galton and others on man, show to be practically continuous.[1] This curve is fully defined, and fully describes the variation of an organ, when we know the mean, the mean deviation from the mean, the total range and the skewness, or preponderance of variation on one or other side of the mean, the two latter qualities having hitherto been somewhat overlooked by the statistical biologist. Now the whole question of Panmixia turns upon a comparison of this frequency curve of variation for an adult population which has been subjected to natural selection since birth, and one for an adult population in which natural selection has played no part. To obtain a population in which natural selection has played no part since birth, would be a difficult if, perhaps, not impossible task. It is a feat which Mr. Spencer and

[1] The curves which I have constructed for several hundred skull measurements for different races and different ages are also sensibly continuous. See the diagrams in Essays I. and X.

Mr. Kidd imagine the socialists wish to attempt. But a fair appreciation of the variation of population with and without natural selection might clearly be obtained by studying the growth of individuals, and then comparing the birth and adult curves of variation. We should then have some definite ground to go upon in judging of panmixia. Will it be believed that although no biologist has yet published any statistics worth a moment's consideration bearing on panmixia—least of all Weismann—Mr. Kidd glibly talks of panmixia as a "necessarily inherent part of the doctrine of evolution"! He tells us, as if there were not a vestige of doubt about it, that

if all individuals of every generation in any species were allowed to equally propagate their kind, the average of each generation would continually tend to fall below the average of the generation which preceded it, and a process of slow but steady degeneration would ensue (p. 37).

The average of *what* of each generation we ask in amazement—the average variation, the mean or the range, or the skewness, of one or all, or of how many organs? There is not a grain of statistical evidence at present extant to say what effect the suspension of natural selection would have on average anything, and the only straightforward course is to suspend judgment till the statistical evidence is forthcoming. At present panmixia is only a name for what would happen if natural selection were suspended, but what would happen, nobody at present is in a position to say.[1] To

[1] The whole argument as to panmixia may be represented symbolically, and in a manner possibly suggestive for other branches of biological inquiry, as

speak of degeneration ensuing from panmixia as an "inevitable law of life among the highest forms" is follows:—Let B be the frequency curve of the variation of an organ at birth; A the corresponding curve actually found for adults when natural selection is at work. Let $A_1, A_2, A_3 \ldots A_n$ be the adult curves after 1, 2, 3 ... n generations in which natural selection is suspended, and $B_1, B_2, B_3 \ldots B_n$ the corresponding birth curves of each corresponding generation of adults. Then P_n, the effect of panmixia after n generations of suspended selection, will be represented by

$$P_n = A - A_n.$$

Now if f be the symbol of operation by which a birth curve gives rise to an adult curve without natural selection, S the operation of selection, and d the operation for converting an adult curve into the next generation birth curve, we have $fB = A_1$, $SfB = A$, $dSfB = dA =$ birth curve for generation following A, and this is sensibly B again, if the population has reached an equilibrium with its environment.

Thus—
$$dSfB = B;$$
or
$$dSf = 1.$$

Further,
$$dfB = dA_1 = B_1,$$
$$SdfB = SB_1,$$
or
$$B = SB_1.$$

Similarly, $B = S^2B_2, = S^3B_3 = \ldots = S^n B_n$, whence we easily deduce $A = S^n A_n$. Thus—

$$P_n = (1 - S^{-n})A,$$

that is, the effect of panmixia is quite unknown until we have ascertained what S, *i.e.* the difference of the curves of adult variation for one generation with and without natural selection may be. There seems no reason whatever for supposing that the operation S^{-n} can possibly be identical with either S^{-1} or d, *i.e.* that panmixia reduces the adult curve *merely* to the birth curve, or to the adult curve flowing from that birth curve without selection, as some have suggested. Still less likely is it—if S_r be the selective operator in the rth generation backwards of those earlier generations preceding A, when selection was actually modifying A—that

$$S^{-n} = S_1^{-1}, S_2^{-1}, S_3^{-1} \ldots S_n^{-1},$$

for each S_r differs from the others and from S in that it is a function of the special biological and physical environment of the species in the rth generation. Thus, while the suspension of natural selection would doubtless modify species which have reached a stable condition, it is not only utterly unproven, but most highly improbable, that such species "would sink back again by a degenerative process through those stages of development by which they reached their present position."

The writer has dealt with this subject more fully in a memoir entitled, *Regression, Heredity, and Panmixia*, published in the *Philosophical Transactions*, vol. clxxxvii. A, as *Contributions to the Mathematical Theory of Evolution*, No. III.

not science; it is pseudo-science rushing to conclusions and manufacturing bogies for its own special ends. When Professor Weismann or Mr. Kidd have measured the influence of panmixia by a study of the birth and adult frequency curves of variation, then it will be time to question whether the limitation of intra-group selection in gregarious animals indicates that the gregarious animal, in particular man, is destined to disappear in the ultimate struggle of species, before the pressure of some thoroughly individualistic and presumably cannibal carnivora.

If such "biological truths" as panmixia, and the necessity of intra-group selection for progress, are idle as far as socialism is concerned, it is not to be inferred that socialists are prepared to disregard such important social problems as those of variation and heredity. While recognising that in the past social evolution in man has been almost entirely the product of extra-group selection and of physical selection acting automatically, they are inclined to believe that increasing sense of social responsibility with regard to parentage, followed, as it is sure to be, at a due distance by regulative legislation, is likely in the future to supplement the automatic action of natural selection by a more rapid process of human selection. They do not understand how the success of theories which inculcate greater social regulation in this respect, places socialism from the biological standpoint at a disadvantage as compared with that individualism which to-day seems directly to encourage the unlimited breeding of the physically and mentally most degenerate classes in the community, and refuses to impose any test as to physique or intellect on the pauper aliens it allows to enter the social group. The pious wish of Darwin that the superior and not the inferior members of the group should be the parents of the future, is far more likely to be realised in a socialistic than in an individualistic state.

In conclusion, then, if biology is very far from being in a position to lay down the dogma that socialism spells degeneration, it is still quite possible that the socialistic movement will react on biological science as it has already done on economic science. No portion of the material for the study of evolution is nearly as plentiful as that dealing with mankind. We have most wide-reaching statistics as to growth and as to mortality; we have most elaborate measurements of a very great variety of organs in many races of men, and even of men separated by considerable intervals of time. The record is, of course, fragmentary in the extreme, but it is probably far better than can ever be attained for any other form of life. Here, then, we may look for some approximate measurement, if it be but a rough one, of the relative numerical importance of the several factors of natural selection. When these investigations have been carried out, it will be time enough to talk about the antagonism of socialistic theory to biological laws. All the evidence, however, that I individually have been able to gather from a naturally limited examination of anthropometric statistics and anthropological facts, distinctly points to the very small part played by intra-group selection in the case of civilised man. If this be so, then the manufacture of biological bogies for socialists is as idle an occupation as that process of planting economic scarecrows round the field of social reform, by which the Manchester School strove for a time to delay their political bankruptcy.

V

POLITICS AND SCIENCE[1]

Throughout Lord Salisbury's address there was the spirit of the student, the spirit of the man of science.—LORD KELVIN.

MEN of science are accustomed to do their own work in their own way without paying much attention to the movement of political or social thought outside the limits of their own little corner of the field of knowledge. The men whose mental powers enable them to accurately survey a wide area of scientific work must in our generation of specialised research be very few, and even if they do exist, they are too often voiceless. Still fewer are those who, like Huxley or Clifford, not only have width of vision and power of speaking to their generation, but can grasp the relation of scientific progress to the social movements of their time. Great as are the advantages of a cloistered life for the scholar and the man of research, we must still remember that the highest types of scientific work are not remunerative, and that in these days of democratic government those who live on the labour of others must justify themselves to the people. The reader must not for a

[1] *Fortnightly Review*, September 1894.

moment suppose that we consider it is either right or necessary to preach that some grossly material profit will ultimately arise from every recondite research. What men of science, above all, have to do is to cultivate a widespread delight in reasoned truth for its own sake, to show that scientific processes are only applications of the ordinary laws of logic—a refined common-sense—and that accordingly they are not beyond the ken of the normally constituted human mind; nay, that they are indeed capable of giving keen pleasure to the average man.

In a word, popularisation of science in its truest and widest significance, while it is a perfectly sufficient, is yet the perfectly necessary justification of science from the social standpoint. Unluckily, men of science, carried away by the excitement of their own particular hunt for truth in the darker recesses of the jungle of ignorance, are too apt to look upon the masses as of necessity ignorant, and the populariser as perforce superficial, if not, indeed, as a complete charlatan. That the charlatan is occasionally to the fore is largely due to the neglect of the real student and scholar to come out into the open and show how much more lasting are his wares than those of the man of the marketplace. Not every man is capable of "going among the people," but it is the grave weakness of science in our day that there is not one of the younger generation who, standing well in the front rank of natural philosophers, is yet understood of the people. There is no one who can act as a mediator between the cohorts of science and the growing democracy. This democracy, be it remembered, is the product of a great industrial crisis, of the widest reaching social upheaval which Europe has witnessed for a century; and its growth is involving and must involve almost revolutionary changes in the relationship of the classes and of the hand-workers and mind-workers of every grade.

It is all very well for the younger generation to shrug their shoulders at the mention of Tyndall, to hint that Huxley has not made any very great or permanent contribution to biological knowledge, or that Clifford would have done more for mathematics had he devoted less time to a popular warfare with superstition. But the younger generation is too apt to forget that these men justified science in the eyes of the people, that their names became household words in very humble ranks of life, and that fifteen years ago, before social questions became as prominent as they are to-day, these men of science were looked upon in the working-men's clubs throughout the country as quite as much the champions of freedom as parliamentary tribunes like Gladstone or Bright. If the latter worked for the political emancipation of the artisan, the former largely contributed to his mental emancipation, and the value of the one was recognised in no lower degree than that of the other.

Men must and will be hero-worshippers, they need a personality to embody their ideal; and if science and men of science were popular among the working-classes at the end of the seventies, it was largely due to the personal force of two or three men, and the subtle charm of their written and spoken words, which fitted

them so essentially for the " going among the people."
Those were days when science and labour could look
back on a near past when they had fought for and won a
common emancipation, and the sympathy of the common
cause was still quick. To-day, when our British democracy is approaching a far graver crisis in the national
life, when it has every need of " common-sense "—
simple clear logic, which is the essence of the scientific
spirit, and is in nowise so easily learnt as by the study
of genuine science—we find science without its popular
champions, very generally apathetic if not anti-pathetic
to the new intellectual problems of labour, and what is
a still more disastrous feature, its soldiers wanting in an
esprit de corps which would enable them to foresee and
meet the real dangers of the near future. Circum-
stances and even parties to-day are much as they were
at the beginning of the sixteenth century in Germany.
We have not, it is true, Catholics and Lutherans,
Humanists and Anabaptists, but we have an old and a
new bigotry, and we have the men of science and the
socialists. In the sixteenth century the new bigotry
displaced the old, and, crushing out the Humanists and
Anabaptists alike, checked in Germany for nearly a
hundred years the progress of learning, and until the
days of the French Revolution all serious social reform.
The new bigotry masquerades to-day in the mantle of
science, even as it did of old in the mantle of Humanism. It professes to use the processes and adopt the
conclusions of science, but having once established itself
among the people, its prophets will turn round, like
their Lutheran prototype, and term reason " the Devil's

chief whore." As in the days of Worms and Augsburg the politician again will rush in and profit by the victory of the new bigotry. The belittling of science cannot but bring grist to *his* mill.

Is it want of insight or want of faith which at such a time of danger could allow the "lower house" of British research to invite Lord Salisbury to "convey the voice of English science"?[1] It is perfectly true that men of science themselves value in exact proportion to the contents the presidential addresses and other products of the long vacation picnic. But to the layman the British Association gathering is the great annual palaver of the scientific tribe, the one occasion in the year when science is brought prominently to his notice, and for him the presidential address does "convey the voice of English science." At a time when everything spells REACTION, when there is a peculiar need for men of science to stand shoulder to shoulder and justify their methods and their work to the people, the "voice of English science" conveys a message of despair and of ignorance which finds not the least justification in the facts, and, albeit unintentionally, gives disastrous support to that new bigotry which is likely to prove such a powerful engine of political warfare in the days to come. Science, like Humanism, puts into the hands of its pseudo-friends weapons for its own destruction. Whether it was a thoughtless bid for the State endowment of physical research by a lavish Tory Government, or an unhealthy

---

[1] Lord Salisbury's own words as to the function of his office, not really modified by his protest that he is "a layman."

craving for political support against the increasing vigour of the anti-vivisectionists,[1] there can be little doubt that the evil results of this year's presidential selection will be felt for many a long day to come.

Some readers may think I overrate the danger of the reaction which is spreading among us; they may hold that Lord Salisbury's address will have but the transient influence which must be ascribed to Virchow's famous *Halt!* or Du Bois Reymond's *Ignorabimus!* If they do so, I believe they have but a very imperfect appreciation of the forces of reaction at present at work, and of how subtle are the methods of the new bigotry; nor can they in the least have grasped the part it is preparing to play in the political warfare of the next few years. Mr. Gladstone's casuistical defence of the Mosaic cosmogony was, however undesignedly, nevertheless a powerful appeal for the political support of the old bigotry. The danger to science, and through science to human progress, was in truth small. The least cultured of the dissenting sects might be a real power at the hustings, but they had no spokesman in the world of letters, and the more powerful organs of the press were already in the hands of men who had felt the influence both of the German textual critics and of the scientific teachers of evolution. Catholic theologians were beginning to find that the doctrine of evolution had been propounded by St. Thomas, Anglican divines taught from university chairs that belief in the authenticity and divine inspiration of the Old Testa-

[1] Note that it is especially in the direction of researches such as those of Pasteur, that Lord Salisbury sees the social value of science; the rest of the scientific progress of the nineteenth century men may possibly overrate.

VOL. I   L

ment was optional; the more educated dissenters had already discarded dogma for a social activity based upon a somewhat nebular theology—upon a religious feeling rather than upon an intelligible creed capable of verbal expression. Shortly, historical, physical, and biological science had thoroughly undermined the foundations of the old bigotry. The prophets of this *Aufklärung*, however, had forgotten the intense emotional feelings—largely intermingled with social instincts developed in the extra-group struggle for existence—which had been satisfied in the old religious beliefs, and their neglect to provide for the social gratification of these feelings opened the door alike to the new bigotry and to the new social reformers. It is history repeating itself—the Humanists preparing the way for Luther and for the Anabaptists. The politicians of the old days threw in their lot with Luther and crushed social reform because the Humanists had no touch with the masses, and neither the will nor the sympathy to guide them. In the struggle learning disappeared, as science will disappear to-morrow, if either the politicians by aid of the new bigotry are effectual in checking social reform, or a triumphant democracy finds men of science apathetic or even hostile to its intellectual needs.

What, then, is this new bigotry of which we speak, and why does Lord Salisbury's address form another link in the chain which is binding it to an important political movement?

If we turn to the leaders of the Liberal Party at the present time, Lord Rosebery, Sir William Harcourt, or

Mr. John Morley, we find, rightly or wrongly, that none of them have a popular reputation for strong piety or keen theological interests. Indeed, at some time or another the "Nonconformist conscience" has been stirred by the real or supposed conduct or opinions of one and all of them. In this respect the loss of Mr. Gladstone is a loss the full extent of which the Liberal Party has not yet realised. It is true that his support of the old bigotry could not have been a lasting factor of strength, but it sufficed to disguise for a time the want of sympathy between the Liberal lieutenants and both conforming and nonconforming wings of the theological party. This party has been steadily reconstituting itself since its complete discomfiture at the hands of the historical and natural sciences. In the first place, it has retreated from the old biblical standpoint as untenable; it professes to accept all the results of modern science, but it takes care to emphasise our ignorance rather than our knowledge, and having learnt something of the critical spirit from its opponents, is able, not without effect, to point out the grave weaknesses in the present foundations of both physics and biology. It passes lightly from the true *Ignoramus!* of science to the *Ignorabimus!* of pseudo-science, and thence by an easy stage, the illogic of which is scarcely noticed by the untrained mind, to the characteristic theological *Credendum est!* " There is grandeur and truth in the evolutionary view of life, but natural selection has not been proved to the hilt, *ergo* benevolent design and an ever-acting creator and ruler are shown us with an irresistible force." There is a *non-sequitur* at every turn, but the religious spirit, rendered uncomfortable by the attack of science on the old bigotry, is impressed by the frank acceptance of scientific truths, and hails this apparent reconciliation of all that it is longing to believe with the little that science has at last forced it to admit.

This apparent reconciliation of religion and science is accompanied by a nebular theology, which is quite unassailable because it disclaims all written creed and bases itself upon no definite passages of any inspired book. The next stage in the process of reaction is, as of old, to claim for religion a monopoly of the moral basis, and hence, by an easy paralogism, a monopoly of morality. No distinction is made in the analysis of conscience between its objectively rational evolution and its subjectively ultra-rational enjoinders;[1] thus it is argued that naturalism can provide no basis for ethics, and that all morality requires an ultra-rational sanction. From this stage a slight verbal jugglery leads us to the reason as an anti-social and anti-progressive force. This is at present the culminating point of the new bigotry. If it be argued that this new bigotry is not becoming a force in the land, I can only reply that it seems already to have carried away the Conservative leaders in both Houses. Mr. Balfour's demonstration that naturalism affords no basis for ethics, and Lord Salisbury's attack on science — his new appeal to the argument from design—will go far, in the absence of any prominent theologically-minded

[1] I hope on another occasion to deal more at length both with the causes which have produced the present Reaction, and also with] the relation of Rationalism to Ethics.

Liberal politician, to bring the new bigotry into line with the Tory party.

That this union will not, in the long run, tend to the profit of those whose sole claim to public support lies in their possession of that "anti-social and anti-progressive force," the reason, can hardly be doubted. If doubt there be, a slight study of the chorus of praise which greeted Lord Salisbury's "well-timed reminder to science of its own fallibility," will suffice to dissipate it. It proceeded from all organs of the press alike. The same Liberal (?) journals which hailed the address were, but a few days previously, attributing to the materialism of science and to "naturalist" ethics the appearance of criminal anarchists of the type of Caserio and Vaillant. This is only another phase of the anti-social character which the new bigotry attributes to all rational processes. But saddest and most significant of all in this reaction (of which so many scientists appear as yet unconscious) is the welcome given to its prophets in the ranks of science itself. Scientific journals not only deign to discuss, but even praise pseudo-scientific works like those of Kidd and Drummond, works which ought to have been sternly repudiated on their first appearance; and now the typical representative of British Science, the man whose position, if any, entitled him "to convey the voice of English Science," hails Lord Salisbury's address as exhibiting "the spirit of the student, the spirit of the man of science"! This is the unkindest cut of all, for no courtesy required the adoption, no usage enforced the choice of this particular form of words. They are words which will be echoed everywhere, where the bigot seeks to belittle the achievements of science, and to raise the ultra-rational to its old supremacy over the spirit of man.

We have studied, and carefully studied, Lord Salisbury's address; but seen apart from a certain glamour of style, we find nothing in it which shows the spirit either of student or of man of science; it teems with fallacious conclusions, and whatever may have been intended by its author, it can only serve as an appeal to that gallery which is occupied by the reconstructed theological party. Let us run through its chief features in brief detail, and the demonstration of this assertion will be convincing.

In the first place, Lord Salisbury discards the old bigotry; but in the same breath that he renounces it, he takes away from science the credit of having rendered it impossible. What is it that has destroyed our belief in the Mosaic cosmogony, which has then naturally deprived the Old Testament of its character as a divinely inspired book, and, in doing so, thrown an entirely new aspect on the Messianic revelations of the New Testament? In this country it has been essentially the work of science in the broadest sense of the word. Nor is this an isolated feature of human intellectual progress; the growth of natural knowledge has, throughout the whole history of man, been modifying and remoulding from century to century his religious belief. What man could believe in one age, a Copernicus or a Darwin have rendered it impossible for him to believe in another, and the microscope and the laboratory have just as much influence over the manner and substance of man's belief to-day as the telescope and the collector's box have had in days gone by. Lord Salisbury admits that even the old learning is no longer "blind to the supreme influence which natural knowledge is exercising in moulding the human mind," and yet he supposes that a great factor like this of man's intellectual development can leave untouched the religious beliefs of the human mind. The history of man and of his religions shows that this view is utterly untenable. The soul of man cannot, indeed, be put under the microscope, but what man thinks of the destinies of his soul, and of his own relations to the cosmos, will be inevitably influenced by what the physicist and biologist tell him of the probable past and the possible future of the universe. Here is what Lord Salisbury says of the old bigotry, here is his skilful advocacy of the new :—

> Few men are now influenced by the strange idea that questions of religious belief depend on the issues of physical research. Few men, whatever their creed, would now seek their geology in the books of their religion, or, on the other hand, would fancy that the laboratory or microscope could help them to penetrate the mysteries which hang over the nature and the destiny of the soul of man.

If *few* men recognise how physical research has moulded and is moulding religious belief, it is simply because few study the history of religious thought. If the theology of to-day escapes the critical influence of microscope and laboratory, it is simply because its doctrines are so nebulous, its nature so perturbed, that no definite theogenetic or cosmogenetic fact is allowed to crystallise out. Thus, in the spirit of the new bigotry, Lord Salisbury accepts the facts, and in part the terminology of science, but disregards its intellectual methods, and belittles its achievements in the field of religious emancipation.

Turning from this prefatory matter to the substance of the address, we find that Lord Salisbury sets himself the perfectly legitimate task of surveying scientific ignorance — the "undiscovered country which still remains to be won." In other words, he starts, as every honest man of science ought to start, from an *Ignoramus!* But in his case it is soon to be converted into an *Ignorabimus!* and will conclude with a *Credendum est!* The three points which he has chosen to enlarge upon are, indeed, the three chief barriers of scientific knowledge to-day: the nature of the atom, the nature of the ether, and the problem of biogenesis. There has not, so far as I am aware, been any attempt to hide our ignorance on these points. More than one recent writer has emphasised that ignorance,[1] and it has been left entirely to an always limited, and now practically discredited school—that of Moleschott and Büchner—to "explain" the whole universe by "matter" and "force." So far as I am aware, no first-class physicist anywhere, and no English biologist of repute, has ever been a member of this school. It must always be impossible for any one who has the least acquaintance with logical processes to deduce an "explanation" of anything by attributing "laws of force" to an inexplicable "matter."

[1] See, for example, the present writer's *Grammar of Science*, where these three points at which our present knowledge halts are strongly insisted upon.

If science be far from unconscious of its ignorance, if some of the best powers of the mathematical physicists have for years past been expended on these problems of the atom and the ether, it was still open to Lord Salisbury, if he thought it profitable, to cry, "in the voice of English science," *Ignoramus!* But it was not "the spirit of the man of science" to emphasise ignorance and speak without hope at a time when we are full of hope. It is not making by any means too great an assertion to say that the discoveries of Maxwell and Hertz, discoveries made in the past twenty years concerning the nature of this very ether, have as much revolutionised our physical knowledge as the Newtonian discovery of the law of gravitation revolutionised natural science in the eighteenth century. We are only now, and shall be for years to come, garnering in the splendid harvest of those achievements, which we are yet too close to, to measure in all their far-reaching importance. In the infancy of the *Principia* was it worth while to cry, "We know nothing of matter"? When the whole of physics is being rewritten as a physics of the ether, is it worth while to cry, "We know nothing of its nature"? To the mind that has once investigated from the philosophical standpoint the origin and development of our physical concepts, the problems indeed are not: what is a material atom? what is an objective ether outside me? They run: What concepts can my mind invent which will describe in brief shorthand the main characteristics of certain physical sensations? The problems are, in the first place, largely those for an inventive intellectual genius, and only in the second place for the laboratory. At present no one can definitely assert that the genius of Lord Kelvin has not given us this mechanical, *i.e.* intellectual concept, not as Lord Salisbury seems to suppose, in Lord Kelvin's "labile" or "foam" ether, but rather in his later gyrostatic medium. We are surely much further here than the President's address would lead the public to imagine. The mystery is not so much in the concept, but in the *Dinge an sich* lying behind the impenetrable veil of sensations which we intellectually mimic and describe by our concepts. It is, in truth, not the ether but sensation which is the mystery of life; and knowledge and ignorance, if they are to be rationally defined at all, can only apply to what lies on this and not on the other side of sensation.

In dealing with the problem of the atom, Lord Salisbury begins his attack on the theory of evolution. So far as I am able to follow him, he limits the possibility of finding any solution of the problem of the elements to the static processes of the chemist, the kinetic considerations of the physicist do not seem to have crossed his field of view. If we assume a "prime atom," by aid of which the atoms of the elements may be conceived as built-up, there is every reason physically to suppose that the dynamical stability of groups of such prime atoms will vary so much in degree that it would be difficult, if not impossible, to form a continuous series of highly stable groups. Under the physical conditions which we may reasonably hold to have ruled in the birth-time of a new planet—conditions extremely hard to reproduce in our laboratories—the prime atoms in their concourse would tend more and more to congregate in the more highly stable groups, and the unstable groups would be eliminated. In this manner we can conceive an evolution of elements, a real physical or natural selection of stable groups. So soon as we treat the elements as *kinetic* groups, there does not appear anything in the so-called "atomic" weights of the chemist inconsistent with the prime atoms of the physicist. Thus it is in the idea of selection itself that we seem to see a glimmer of daylight breaking the night of our ignorance as to the elements. How then does Lord Salisbury treat the problem? Simply with a cynical remark as to the use of the word evolution :—

> Whether you believe that Creation was the work of design or of inconscient law, it is equally difficult to imagine how this random collection of dissimilar materials came together. . . . If they were organic beings all our difficulties would be solved by muttering the comfortable word "evolution," one of those indefinite words from time to time vouchsafed to humanity, which have the gift of alleviating so many perplexities, and masking so many gaps in our knowledge. But the families of elementary atoms do not breed and we cannot ascribe their ordered difference to accidental variations perpetuated by heredity under the influence of natural selection. The rarity of iodine, and the abundance of its sister chlorine, cannot be attributed to the survival of the fittest in the struggle for existence. We cannot account for the minute difference which persistently distinguishes nickel from cobalt by ascribing it to the recent inheritance by one of them of an advantageous variation from the parent stock.

Now this is clever writing, but it hardly shows the "spirit of the man of science." The word evolution has indeed been often abused, but in every field of knowledge it has carried infinite light to our generation, and in this very problem, where our ignorance leads to Lord Salisbury's jest, it is not only conceivable but highly probable that evolution by physical selection of stable forms is the key to the solution.

Let us turn now to the last and the most significant portion of Lord Salisbury's address, the point at which he comes into closest contact with the new bigotry, namely, his treatment of our *Ignoramus!* as to the problem of life.

In order to fully grasp the bearing of Lord Salisbury's attack on natural selection, it is necessary to remind the reader of an old controversy, the details of which he will most readily find, should he be so inclined, in Professor Huxley's *Collected Essays*, vol. viii., and Lord Kelvin's *Popular Lectures and Addresses*, vol. ii. It is more than thirty years ago since Lord Kelvin undertook, on the basis of generally accepted thermal laws, an investigation of the secular cooling of the earth. He concluded that, so far as our knowledge at present reaches, "life on the earth and all geological history showing continuity of life must be limited within some such period of past time as one hundred million years." Lord Kelvin was peculiarly careful to state that his numbers were only *round* numbers, and that his conclusion had only a high degree of probability. There might be other thermal factors of real importance yet to be discovered, or the growth of our knowledge of the thermo-dynamics of slowly solidifying bodies might modify to some extent the estimate given. At any rate Lord Kelvin's estimate has not been seriously attacked from the physical side during the past thirty years, and it still remains, with all necessary reservations, a highly probable conclusion.[1] Professor Huxley, in an address to the Geological Society in 1869, took up, by way of reply, the line that geologists did not really require a longer period than one hundred million years, but if they did require it, Lord Kelvin's calculations by no means amounted to a demonstration that they must limit themselves to this period. In a reply entitled *Geological Dynamics*, Lord Kelvin is, I think, successful in substantiating two points:—

(1) That geologists had, before the publication of his results, demanded far more time than physics with any reasonable degree of probability could allow them.

(2) That there was nothing in Professor Huxley's criticisms which really affected the high degree of probability attaching to the limit set by thermal considerations to geological history "showing continuity of life."

It must not be supposed that Lord Kelvin's limitation of the age of the earth rendered geological history impossible, and an "instant of creation" inevitable. It simply laid weight on a modified "catastrophism" as compared with "uniformitarianism," and Lord Kelvin used his time limit and his theory of an initially far hotter earth to argue in favour of "greater causation" in former epochs. Shortly, there was an age in which temperature and the resulting climate wrought the earth's surface more rapidly than at present. Lord Kelvin, in arguing against an "unlimited bank of

[1] It has, since the publication of this paper, been attacked—and the present writer thinks with much force—by Professor John Perry (see *Nature*, vol. li. pp. 224, 341, and 582).

geological time," was arguing against the perpetual miracle involved in a permanent solar system. We know

that Creative power has created in our minds a wish to investigate and a capacity for investigating; and there is nothing too rash, there is nothing too audacious in questioning human assumptions regarding Creative power. Have we reason to believe Creative power did order the sun to go on and shine, and give out heat for ever? Are we to suppose that the sun is a perpetual miracle? I use the word *miracle* in the sense of a perpetual violation of those laws of action between matter and matter which we are allowed to investigate here at the surface of the earth, in our laboratories and mechanical workshops.[1]

Lord Kelvin, in using these words, clearly indicates that he considers the ordinary laws of matter must be accepted as holding for the universe before we reject the highly probable or before we appeal to the miraculous.[2] He would not assert that we must accept the known laws of physics in preference to supposing a miracle, if the acceptance of those laws in their turn involved the hypothesis of a still greater miracle, *i.e.* the moulding of the earth's surface to its present form within a time which physically was absolutely impossible for its development. This would be merely the physicist thrusting the responsibility of the miracle on to the shoulders of the geologist. According to Lord Kelvin, then — and geologists are by no means now unanimously opposed to his conclusions—100,000,000 years or so has sufficed for the development of all geo-

[1] *Popular Lectures*, vol. ii. p. 45.
[2] Elsewhere in his essay on *Geological Time* (p. 35) he appeals to an antecedent condition of matter obeying the laws of matter as an absolutely irresistible inference, when the alternative is a special act of creation.

logical history showing continuity of life. Professor Huxley has stated that this period is sufficient, and that so far as evolution is concerned, the biologists when, like Darwin, they suggested a longer period for the action of natural selection, were merely taking their time from the geological clock. Thus Professor Huxley writes :—

> The only reason we have for believing in the slow rate of change of living forms is the fact that they persist through a series of deposits which geology informs us have taken a long while to make. If the geological clock is wrong, all the naturalist will have to do is to modify his notions of the rapidity of change accordingly.

Here we might suppose the onus of proof for or against natural selection might have been left to the biologist. But at this point I venture to think that Lord Kelvin made a false step. Hitherto his position had been logically unassailable, but what are we to say when he writes :—

> The limitation of geological periods, imposed by physical science, cannot, of course, disprove the hypothesis of transmutation of species; but it seems sufficient to disprove the doctrine that transmutation has taken place through "descent with modification by natural selection."

Why? we ask in astonishment, when up to the present date NO measurements whatever worthy of the name have been taken of the rate at which natural selection, whether periodic or secular,[1] is proceeding! It is only

---

[1] By *periodic* selection, I understand the selection which repeats itself in each generation and maintains the species in a practically permanent and stable condition. By *secular* selection, I understand the selection which, in long course of time, has brought a species from a less developed to its present form. In either

yesterday, so to speak, that the elaborate measurements of the anthropologists upon modern and ancient man have given us the slightest data to even attempt an answer to the problem of secular selection, or the measurements of Professor Weldon and his pupils on crustacea have led us to even hope for some ray of light on periodic evolution. It is only to-day that biologists are beginning to mimic natural selection in their laboratories, and endeavouring, by repeated applications of an unfavourable physical environment which destroys a large percentage of some low form of life, to ascertain at what rate and to what degree that life can be modified. Surely, when we stand face to face with our ignorance, when we are awaiting the results of experiments and investigations which can alone determine the quantitative rate of natural selection, when, indeed, we have no reason to assert that one hundred million years is or is not sufficient for the evolution of species by natural selection, it is the better, nay, it is the *only* scientific course to suspend our judgment. Surely, because a most distinguished physicist "feels" that the hypothesis of natural selection "does not contain the true theory of evolution, if evolution there has been in biology," we may for the present accept, on faith, his probable estimate of the age of the life-bearing strata, but we are in nowise bound to respect his views, *unless they are supported by actual facts and reasonings on those facts*, when he discusses biological problems, and tells us that he *feels* "profoundly convinced

case the quantitative measurement of selection is a matter for elaborate measurements of a very large number of specimens for a considerable variety of organs, and the treatment of these measurements by a complex statistical theory.

that the argument of design has been greatly too much lost sight of in recent zoological speculations." If the physicist will, if he can help it, have none of the miraculous in the maintenance of the sun's heat, if the geologist in his turn insists on shifting the miracle further and explaining the moulding of the earth's surface by physical causes, then why should the unfortunate biologist alone have his investigations curtailed by being ordered to take into account at every turn a "continually guiding and controlling intelligence," presumably working a perpetual miracle in the way of artificial selection? Does not Lord Kelvin himself tell us that

> science is bound by the everlasting law of honour to face fearlessly every problem which can fairly be presented to it. If a probable solution consistent with the ordinary course of nature can be found, we must not invoke an abnormal act of creative power.

Then why shall the biologist alone depart from such an excellent rule? Why must he alone accept "the solid and irrefragable argument so well put forward in that excellent old book," Paley's *Natural Theology?* As we have seen, the probability or improbability of natural selection has never been determined by exact measurement, and if its improbability had been actually demonstrated, we should only stand face to face with the problem of the transmutation of species. We might legitimately cry, *Ignoramus, laborandum est,* as we do before the problems of the atom and the ether; but it would be to the everlasting dishonour of science to cry, *Ignorabimus, credendum est,* to anything which is material of *sensation.*

We have devoted so much space to this question of the rate of natural selection, and Lord Kelvin's views with regard to it, because his argument is the first objection raised by Lord Salisbury to the Darwinian theory, and, like Lord Kelvin, Lord Salisbury leads us to Paley by exactly the same *non-sequitur*. What he adds to the discussion is not argument, but a smart phrase or two. Speaking of the Darwinians, he says:—

> But it cannot be gainsaid that their theories require all this elbow-room. . . . If we think of that vast distance over which Darwin conducts us, from the jelly-fish lying on the primeval beach to man as we know him now; if we reflect that the prodigious change requisite to transform one into the other is made up of a chain of generations, each advancing by a minute variation from the form of its predecessor; and if we further reflect that these successive changes are so minute that in the course of our historical period—say, three thousand years—this progressive variation has not advanced by a single step perceptible to our eyes, in respect to man or the animals and plants with which man is familiar, we shall admit that for a chain of change so vast, of which the smallest link is larger than our recorded history, the biologists are making no extravagant claim when they demand at least many hundred million years for the accomplishment of the stupendous process. Of course, if the mathematicians are right, the biologists cannot have what they demand.

Now in these sentences there are several assumptions which find no justification in proven fact. If the physicists are right, the further we go back, the more intense was the heat, the more varied the climatic conditions, the more rapid the superficial changes on the earth; in the words of Sir Roderick Murchison, the "grander was the intensity of causation." All this would probably render the action of environment far more influential in the earlier ages of the world's history, and the pace would accordingly be much quicker. Further, the living material would be more plastic, for type by type had not settled down into stable equilibrium with its environment. So soon as that environment became more permanent, so soon as that stability was reached, and this appears largely to have been the case before "the course of our historic period," the function of natural selection would be confined to maintaining the type. Is this periodic selection, by which we might to some extent gauge secular selection itself, really "imperceptible"? Nobody definitely knows; it yet remains to be statistically investigated. Or, are we certain that secular selection is insensible even in the last three thousand years? Would the anthropometric statistics of Americans of the southern states yet of English origin and unmixed blood show no divergence from the like statistics of Englishmen to-day? There appears, at any rate, to be certain distinct differences between the measurements of English school children and American school children of English ancestry. Is it not a process of extra-group selection which has replaced throughout large districts of Europe a preponderant dolichocephalic by a preponderant brachycephalic population? It is mere dogma to assert that the period of recorded history gives us no measurable step in secular evolution. The fact is, that the data on which a judgment could be based are only to-day being properly collected and analysed, and that until this is completed all judgment as to the rate at which natural selection even now[1] works must perforce be suspended.

It would be just as idle, just as anti-scientific to assert on the basis of geological history, that because physicists have limited the time of development, there must have been an instant of creation, as it is idle to assert that because we have not as yet measured the rate at which natural selection can work, we must reject without patient investigation a very probable factor of evolution, and fly to an alternative which shuts the door for ever to scientific research in the field of biology.

Lord Salisbury's second objection to natural selection is at bottom more illogical than the first, but it is for two reasons more dangerous. In the first place, he strengthens his paralogistic jump from natural selection to design as its *sole* alternative by quoting biological authority for the *non-sequitur*; and, in the second place, he uses some smart phrases—indicative rather of a journalistic than of a scientific training—which it is needless to say have been repeated *ad nauseam* by the daily press. As a matter of fact, the smartness of these phrases overreaches its end, for they demonstrate that their maker has gained his views on natural selection, not by a real understanding of its working, but by the same ingrained prejudice which in other directions is characteristic of the new theological school.

English biologists, if they will permit an outsider to

[1] *i.e.* in an age when much leads us to believe that types are highly stable. That the childhood of the world lies in the past is not purely a poet's dream. As the mental and physical growth of the child can hardly be deduced from measurements on the adult, so the plasticity of primitive biological forms very possibly cannot be inferred from types which have been gaining in stability for tens of thousands of years.

say so, have much to be responsible for, in the manner in which they have raised August Weismann to a position of popular authority. Of his actual biological researches it is not for me to express an opinion, but of his reintroduction of metaphysics, of his vague use of physical concepts, both qualitatively and quantitatively, and of his shaky logic, any normally educated man can easily convince himself. If Weismann chooses to assert that design is the only alternative to natural selection, we are not in the least bound to accept his *dictum*. We can only compare it with the assertion of a Newtonian theologian, that if the corpuscular theory of light were not true, then light must reach his eyes from the sun by a perpetual miracle. The fact is, that till an excellent working hypothesis is demonstrated to be false, the minds of scientific men are more profitably occupied with its consideration than with the search for alternatives. The history of science seems to show that a new, wider, and more exact hypothesis is, as a rule, developed by those whose study of the old has convinced them not only of its insufficiency, but also of the *direction* in which modifications are required. It is the paradoxers and circle-squarers who abound in alternatives before the old hypotheses have been fairly tested and found wanting. Now Lord Salisbury tells us of Weismann's *dictum* that "as a politician he knows that argument very well." Surely if he could see through the shakiness of the Weismannian logic, it was —well, rather like a politician—to palm it off again as an argument against natural selection to his British Association audience! The biologists there assembled may have tingled for cremation—but the new bigotry rejoices in what is thus conveyed by "the voice of English science."

We must now pass to the other point made by Lord Salisbury, in the discussion of his second or "gravest objection," namely, his appeal to the doctrine of chance. This contains the sentence which has made his address from the newspaper standpoint. Let me cite the whole paragraph on natural selection :—

No man, so far as we know, has ever seen it at work. An accidental variation may have been perpetuated by inheritance, and in the struggle for existence the bearer of it may have replaced by virtue of the survival of the fittest his less improved competitors; but, as far as we know, no man or succession of men have ever observed the whole process in any single case, and certainly no man has recorded the observation. Variation by *artificial* selection, of course, we know very well, but the intervention of the cattle-breeder and the pigeon-fancier is the essence of artificial selection. It is effected by their action in crossing, by their skill in bringing the right mates together to produce the progeniture they want. But in natural selection, who is to supply the breeder's place? Unless the crossing is properly arranged, the new breed will never come into being. What is to secure that the two individuals of opposite sexes in the primeval forest, who have been both accidentally blessed with the same advantageous variation, shall meet, and transmit by inheritance that variation to their successors? Unless this step is made good the modification will never get a start, and yet there is nothing to ensure that step except pure chance.

There is hardly a sentence in this which can be accepted without extreme reservation. Every man who has lived through a hard winter, every man who has examined a mortality table, every man who has studied the history of nations has probably seen natural selection at work. It is not the existence of natural selection, but its *intensity* and *rapidity* of action in the transmutation of species, which is the problem, and here is the point where we may be called upon to suspend our judgment. That "no men or succession of men have ever observed the whole process in any single case" is a truism arising from the thousands of years over which evolution is spread, and from the probably high degree of stability now possessed by most forms of life, *i.e.* the periodic rather than the secular nature of natural selection at the present day. As the argument stands, however, it applies equally well to the coursing of his satellites round Jupiter. Yet it is an argument which for biology, unlike the case of Jupiter's satellites, can be and may be upset by a well-devised laboratory experiment to-morrow.

We now reach the stage at which Lord Salisbury appeals to the doctrine of *pure chance* to upset the theory of natural selection. To judge from his words he is probably unaware that the theory of evolution is likely to become a branch of the theory of chance, and that very poor comfort is to be obtained from that theory for those who are seeking to establish design as an *immediate* factor of evolution. It is by aid of the theory of chance that a quantitative measure of the rate of natural selection is being sought, but, whether that rate be ultimately found sensible or insensible for the great variety of types of life, what appears to be quite clear, as more and more extensive series of measurements are made on man or the lower types of life, is this: That to a high degree of approximation the distribution of variation in all sorts of organs follows the laws of a chance distribution.[1] This chance distribution is, I think, one which the admirable Paley especially contrasted with and opposed to immediate design. On this distribution of variation we have to fix our attention, for it helps us at once to the solution of Lord Salisbury's difficulty as to the rarity of advantageous individuals of opposite sexes meeting in the primeval forest. The dog-fancier might start with a single pair of fox-terriers, dog and bitch, each standing, say, 10 inches high, and he would find a chance distribution in the litters of this pair, so that when the puppies reached adult age their heights might very possibly vary from 9 to 11 inches, the majority, perhaps, centring round 10 inches. The offspring would not exactly repeat the features of their parents, they would vary with a definite mean deviation about a definite mean. Now the dog-fancier might select the larger dogs and breed solely from them until he obtain a breed, say, 12 inches high. *Or*, he might shoot every dog in each generation of adults under, say, the mean of that generation, and allow the remainder to breed promiscuously. The right mates would thus be brought together without the least problem of direct mating, and a breed also 12 inches high might ultimately be obtained.[2]

The artificial selection may be more humane and direct, but then, as Peer Gynt says of the deity, "economical, that he is not." Now, this law of varia-

[1] Not necessarily the normal curve of errors of the mathematician, but a generalised form of it and this rarely with an average error of more than 4—5 per cent in the frequency.

[2] The example is, of course, purely hypothetical,—yet typical if only explanatory.

tion, that mediocre pairs will produce a majority perhaps of mediocrities, but also a definite percentage of giants and dwarfs, is all that is required by the Darwinians beyond that struggle for existence, of which there is evidence enough. All this is made quite plain and clear by Darwin himself, if it has been left to his successors to get numerical measurements of the degree of variation in populations. It would not be needful to repeat it here had not Lord Salisbury's words shown that he had not in the least grasped it. In the light of this law of variation, what becomes of his statement that there is nothing to set the improved breed going? When we recognise the comparatively wide range of variation which actually occurs in the offspring of each pair, when we grasp the severity of the struggle, when we note the change of climate, the migration, and the scarcity of food which in so many cases intervene between successive breeding seasons, it will hardly be the pretty conceit of that sentence about the advantageously varied bridegroom at one end of the wood and the equally advantageously varied bride at the other which will cause us to smile!

Nay, if the meeting of such a bride and bridegroom would, which is questionable,[1] *very* much accelerate matters, it has not been wanting in primitive man. The irrefragable traditions of brother-sister marriage in the oldest period, and the endogamous habits of innumerable savage peoples, show how the pace of natural selection may have been quickened by the

[1] *i.e.* taking into account parental regression. It is needless, perhaps, to remark that many variations, *e.g.* polydactyly, are as a rule transmitted throu one parent only.

intensification of both good and bad variations in the early history of man.

Thus the last of Lord Salisbury's objections to natural selection is seen to be based on a misunderstanding of the nature of variation; it may remain as a catch-phrase, but it has no validity as an argument. We stand precisely where we did with regard to natural selection, patiently awaiting, if we have a grain of scientific spirit, a quantitative measure of its intensity and of its rapidity of effect. We simply say *Ignoramus*—we have a good theory, and we mean as students to test its validity. This is not, however, the attitude of the President of the British Association, conveying "the voice of English science." He too cries *Ignoramus*, but he follows it up with a paralogistic *Ignorabimus*. He tells us of the great danger scientific research is running at the present time:—

> The acceptance of mere conjecture in the name and place of knowledge, in preference *to making frankly the admission that no certain knowledge can be attained.*

—the italics are ours.

All knowledge is only knowledge of a greater or a lesser degree of probability; but why is science, even if a great hypothesis prove insufficient, to renounce its very function, its birthright to the pursuit of knowledge, to cry *Ignorabimus* before this problem of evolution? Certainly not because of difficulties which as stated by Lord Salisbury are largely the product of the limited attention he has, amid other pursuits, been able to devote to the study of the subject. Nay, if we pass over the inconsequence by which Lord Salisbury reaches the profession of *necessary* ignorance, must we not logically stop there, and let that profession, in his own words, be "our only reasonable answer"? We are under no obligation to go further. Why must we join him in the *credendum est* of Lord Kelvin, and find "overpoweringly strong proofs of intelligent and benevolent design" in the stages of biological evolution, while we have discarded, in the development of the material earth, a perpetual miracle in favour of physical laws? Has it struck Lord Salisbury that the laboratory and the microscope may, after all, at this very moment be establishing the high probability of natural selection, and pushing back from the evolution of species, as they have done from terrestrial evolution, that "influence of a free will" into a dim, unfixed, and indescribable past? May he not ultimately find that the creed of a *benevolent* design, with which he burdens biology, can be overturned by the microscope, and that, notwithstanding his *dictum*, men's religious beliefs are, in fact, largely moulded by knowledge, by that knowledge which to-day is, in the first place, the product of scientific research?

Read them as we will, Lord Salisbury's words do not exhibit the spirit of the student; they do not, we sincerely hope, "convey the voice of English science." They are not the words of a man full of hope in the future, full of just appreciation of the real magnitude of the work which has been done in the immediate past, and is being done to-day. They do not even show an accurate knowledge of where science now stands or what are its immediate prospects. They are the words of that Reaction which is noticeable on every side, and they have been hailed as such by the new bigotry, which, adopting much of the terminology and some of the results of science, neglects its intellectual methods and its instruments of research. That this new bigotry should find what it can thoroughly approve of in the annual dress parade of the scientific world, is an event not without omen for the future of science. It has further a political significance which bodes ill for our modern Humanists.[1]

[1] Two passages in this essay have been criticised by Mr. St. George Mivart (*Fortnightly Review*, September 1895). The author's reply is republished in an appendix to this volume, as notwithstanding its controversial character, it may help to still further illustrate the importance of the points at issue.

VI

REACTION![1]

A CRITICISM OF MR. BALFOUR'S ATTACK ON RATIONALISM

Mr. Balfour has now formulated the views which underlay Lord Salisbury's suggestive address at the last meeting of the British Association. . . . No man can deny that such a work by the most distinguished and most popular of our younger Conservative statesmen is in itself a memorable event in the spiritual life of the British people.—*Times Leader.*

Part I

In criticising Lord Salisbury's Oxford Address a year ago,[2] I ventured to suggest that the full political weight of the "new bigotry" was hardly appreciated by the Liberal Party. I am far from certain that even the Conservative leaders completely realised the influence on the Nonconformist vote of their "fidelity to the traditional beliefs of the race." A study, however, of the reviews and leaders in the religious journals dealing with Lord Salisbury's Address and Mr. Balfour's *Foundations of Belief* might long ago have convinced the electoral prophets that disaster was in store for the Liberal Party. It goes without saying that the majority of these religious journals had not the desire,

[1] Published as a pamphlet, September 1895.
[2] "Politics and Science," *Fortnightly Review*, September 1894.

nor indeed the power, to critically examine Lord Salisbury's pseudo-science or Mr. Balfour's pseudo-philosophy. What was clear to them only was that these statesmen had stepped into the shoes of Mr. Gladstone — presumably too narrow for Mr. John Morley—and stood therein as defenders of Christianity, if not of the verbal interpretation of Genesis. To proclaim in two columns and a half Mr. Balfour's utterances as completely destructive of the detestable rationalism was to satisfy the many who find it easier to dissipate their mental energy in emotion, than to convert it into intellectual products. The sympathy thus aroused was not in the least moderated by a concluding remark that theological concord might be compatible with political dissidence, or by the interjection of a pious wish that Mr. Balfour had adopted theology instead of politics as a profession. How was it possible for the reader to grasp that fine distinction which the writer drew between sound Christianity and bad public policy, especially when enthusiasm for the Derby was demonstrated in the next week's issue to be certainly inconsistent with sound Christianity, and likely to injure a good public policy? The influence of the new bigotry at the recent elections has been, we feel sure, not less decisive than that of either the new labour movement or licensed license. It is, indeed, too subtle to be estimated by electoral arithmetic, and if the Liberal journals recognise generally that the Liberal defeat is due to "Beer and Bible," they associate the latter with Church disestablishment, and not with the direct appeal of Lord Salisbury and Mr. Balfour to the theological instincts and the anti-scientific prejudices of Nonconformist voters.

Even now, in order to reconstruct their party, the Liberal press is striving to find out what the electors want, since it has at last discovered that Home Rule, Local Veto, Abolition of the House of Lords, and Disestablishment do not suffice to procure a majority. Liberalism, if it is to mean anything again, I will venture to assure the Liberal press, must connote certain fixed principles by which modes of thought and action are to be judged, and which are quite independent of what the bulk of the electors for the time being may want or not want. It is an attitude towards social and intellectual progress, which must be reasoned and consistent, and is not an *omnium gatherum* of transient electorial fancies. So little has this need for consistent principle been recognised by the radical newspapers, that we find columns of praise for the new bigotry in juxtaposition with a rationalistic programme of social reform. On the one hand, science is branded as the basest materialism, the reason is proclaimed as an anti-social force, and Christian belief asserted to be the sole basis of ethics; while, on the other hand, the new economics are hailed as the only rational theory of social reform, without the least regard to the fact that their creators and supporters have been almost entirely guided by rational and non-religious views of life.[1]

---

[1] "Contemporary socialism viewed as a whole, unquestionably, rests on a non-religious conception of the Universe, and is plainly inconsistent with any recognition of religious duty in the ordinary acceptation of the term." . . . "Socialism is antagonistic to Christianity, inasmuch as it assumes that man's chief end is merely (*sic!*) a happy social life on earth" (Flint, *Socialism*, pp. 370, 461, and cf. chapter xi. in its entircty).

While a large proportion of the Liberal press has adopted the "logic-tight compartment" mode of thought, welcomed Mr. Balfour's pseudo-philosophy, and treated agnostics and freethinkers to the sort of abuse meted out by their ancestors to our Quaker forefathers, the Tory leaders have been busy with the congenial task of casting out the devil by aid of the devil; in other words, demonstrating the futility of the reason by aid of the reason.[1]

Now that the "memorable event in the spiritual life of the British people" has been followed by a still more memorable event in their political life, Liberals may possibly have the leisure to reconsider the merits of Mr. Balfour's philosophy, and it is partly with this end in view that the following criticisms are published. Intellects sodden in the quagmire of a natural (as distinguished from a revealed) theology are hardly likely to have a crisp and dry political grasp. Should a grave national crisis arise, their want of elasticity and fibre will become suddenly and mayhap dangerously apparent. They will be prating about belief, when they ought to be realising facts; creating an Absolute out of their own relative and vague æsthetic needs, when they ought to be impersonally and with a clear intellect guiding a nation through a period of stress. Shortly, we see once more in power, men who, largely indeed ignorant of the methods of modern science, have yet not hesitated to discredit the sole pathway to

[1] "Looked at from the outside, as one among the complex conditions which produce belief, reason appears relatively insignificant and ineffectual, not only appears so, but *must* be so, if human society is to be made possible" (*Foundations of Belief*, p. 213).

knowledge, men who, placing themselves on the crest of a wave of reaction, are prepared to shout in the market-place with Mr. Kidd that reason is an anti-social force, only endurable so long as its parasitic growth does not kill religious belief.[1] It is not, therefore, without a sense of near danger, that we desire at the present time to criticise the intellectual methods of Mr. Balfour. We are convinced that facility in the use of bad logic in one department of thought cannot be associated with strong intellectual power in a second; that if Mr. Balfour has built his theological house on sand, the foundations of his political belief, and what is still more important, his motives in political action, must be equally irrational and unsound. Such a view may seem exaggerated, but it is the only alternative to the logic-tight compartment theory of Mr. Balfour's mind. The nation has yet to learn—may the lesson be not too bitter!—that an aptitude for defending Genesis or for demonstrating the truth of the Incarnation is not the best test of the intellectual fibre needed in a really great statesman.

But let us turn to Mr. Balfour's work itself. Its main theses appear to be the following:—

(I.) The foundations of Naturalism, Science,

[1] "So it is with those persons who claim to show by their example that naturalism is practically consistent with the maintenance of ethical ideas with which naturalism has no natural affinity. Their spiritual life is parasitic; it is sheltered by convictions which belong not to them, but to the society of which they form a part, it is nourished by processes in which they take no share. And when those convictions decay and those processes come to an end, the alien life which they have maintained can scarce be expected to outlast them" (*Foundations of Belief*, p. 83). The writer apparently imagines that there was no morality B.C. It is the old tale, if your neighbour does not believe as you do, assert that he must be immoral, or would be if your example did not shame him into righteousness.

Rationalism — Mr. Balfour, as we shall show, is not careful to distinguish between the three — are unsound.

(II.) The foundations of Theology may be equally unsound from the rational standpoint, but if practical experience compels man to accept the chief conclusions of science, so the "deepest needs" of man compel him to assert the truth of theological teaching, in particular, of the chief Christian dogmas.

(III.) Apart from religious belief no basis can be found for ethics, and rationalism would lead at once to immorality, were it not for the vitality of the Christian society within which it is bred and on which it preys.

It will be seen at once that this third thesis is only another statement of Mr. Kidd's belief in the anti-social character of the reason. Indeed, there is much similarity between the "psychological climates" and mental equipments of Mr. Balfour and Mr. Kidd. If Mr. Kidd makes, it is true, a braver show of science, Mr. Balfour's philosophic terminology remains to equally impress the uninitiated.

Now we are not in the first place concerned with the truth or falsehood of Mr. Balfour's theses. Did they simply represent Mr. Balfour's belief, we might merely shrug our shoulders, ejaculate, "So many men, so many creeds," and pass on. The national importance of Mr. Balfour's creed lies not in its contents, but in the arguments by which he deduces it. It is Mr. Balfour's logical methods and his intellectual insight which it is of the utmost importance that we as a nation should estimate at their correct value, and these are as easily tested in the theological as in the political sphere.

At the very outset of our inquiry, however, we are met by a formidable difficulty. This lies in the extremely slipshod character of Mr. Balfour's language. It is true that he endeavours to protect himself by stating that his book is for "the general body of readers," and further, by asserting, what is indeed perfectly correct, that words connote ideas and associations which vary from age to age, and from individual to individual. But just because Mr. Balfour is writing for the general reader, it behoves him to be perfectly clear and consistent in his use of terms—such is indeed a fundamental axiom of popular writing or popular lecturing. It was open to Mr. Balfour to use terms in the senses defined for them in standard scientific or philosophical treatises, or to use them in his own peculiar sense, provided he carefully described for us his own range of meaning, his own "psychological climate." I desire no pedantry in the use of words; their number is far more limited than that of the possible permutations of ideas. All I demand is that a writer shall carefully describe—when not writing as a specialist for a technical audience—what is the permutation of ideas he intends his readers to understand by a particular term.

Not a line of this higher type of definition or description occurs throughout Mr. Balfour's book. The same word is used in many different senses, often in nearly contiguous paragraphs; different words are used for the same permutation of ideas, although either their scientific or popular sense, or both senses, connote something very distinct from that of Mr. Balfour's usage.

Subtle distinctions which are none the less vital and real are slurred over at one point, in order to be emphasised at a second after the desired antinomy has been displayed. A parade is made of philosophic terminology, which is neither used in its technical sense, nor in any consistent sense which can be drawn from the context. Now we are accustomed—however much we regret it—to this sort of thing at the hustings, we know it in the exoteric and esoteric renderings of the mediæval theologians, but it is the bane of all exact thinking, and if Mr. Balfour was not writing for the hustings, but exhibiting the actual workings of his own mind, his best capacity for clear thinking, then, alas! for the nation which trusts him as a leader.

Let us take one or two instances. Mr. Balfour is very fond of the word *epistemology*—yet we find not the slightest trace of a definition of knowledge or of a critique of the knowable. The same things are spoken of at one time as "beliefs," at another time as "knowledge." Science and knowledge are used indiscriminately for mere perception of phenomena and for the results obtained by reasoning on concepts ultimately based on those perceptions. As we are given no definition or critique of the knowable, so we are treated to no doctrine—however brief—of cause. Cause is not used consistently in its scientific meaning as an essential antecedent or adjunct to a routine of perception; causes are for Mr. Balfour sometimes causes in the scientific sense, and sometimes "things in themselves," and sometimes the purely geometrical concepts of kinetics, and sometimes things which may be thought of as endowed with a tendency to truth or falsehood. The context very infrequently shows the sense in which the word is to be interpreted, and if the confusion in Mr. Balfour's mind be as great as that which he must leave in his reader's, he is really an object for sincere pity. It is bad enough that two such totally distinct ideas as primary and secondary causes should have received a common name, but it is all the more important that no meretricious argument should be based on so obvious an extension of terms. By a nice little "derangement of epitaphs," belief and perception seem, in Mr. Balfour's opinion, interchangeable in science, while belief, doctrine, and experience are convertible in theology. After such examples as this, it is perhaps of smaller import to add that the terms Naturalism and Science are over and over again spoken of as interchangeable, while Agnosticism, Positivism, Empiricism, and Naturalism are positively asserted to describe one and the same scheme of thought—a thing itself "sufficiently easy to describe."

Mr. Balfour does not only sin in the use of what might perhaps be spoken of as technical terms. He repeatedly asserts that one mode or thing is "higher," "deeper," "lower," "poorer," than another. He will give us the most excellent reasons for accepting the relativity of the moral or of the beautiful, and yet conclude by telling us that "when we are most ourselves," or "when we look back on those too rare moments," or when we realise our "deepest needs," or our "higher selves," we see beyond the ken of discursive reason; then without further demonstration he will point to the ecstatic state thus postulated as an argument against all his previous reasoning. Now if mankind were unanimous as to what is "high" and "low," they might at any rate agree as to what they saw beyond the ken of reason in special moments of their existence. But here, again, the matter of taste is all-important. Krishna Mulvaney found his "deepest needs" satisfied in those "too rare moments" which followed his stepping into the palanquin. If some of us find our "deepest needs" gratified in those "too rare moments," when with reason enthroned we grasp some extension of natural law, who is to arbitrate on "high" and "low" between ourselves and Mr. Balfour, who finds his higher self in those ecstatic moments, when—with reason dethroned—feeling shows him the Universal and the Absolute?

To me the great end of human intellectual strivings *is* "to provide a machinery by which the recurrence of feelings and ideas may be adequately accounted for." Mr. Balfour wonders how any one can "go through so much to get so little." The Agnostic finds in the wealth of his own perceptual and conceptual worlds a field of endless activity. Mr. Balfour finds that if only the "unknowable" exists "outside the circle of impressions and ideas, then is all science turned to foolishness." Who, again, shall arbitrate in such a matter of taste? Surely such terms as "higher," "most worthy," "deepest," etc., only denote in a reasoner a poverty of thought, and weaken a style which current opinion asserts to be brilliant? I fear I can lay no claim to literary instinct, and my idea of style is confined to a clear and consistent use of the right words, an absence of question-begging adjectives and adverbs, which only express individual opinions and not conclusions of universal validity,[1] and lastly, a sparse use of metaphors, even when they are appropriate.[2] Judged from this narrower standpoint, Mr. Balfour's brilliancy only dazzles me, when I strive to grasp what is the actual thought to which he desires to draw attention. Should he really be disappointed, as he states in his preface, if the reader finds both the substance and form of his arguments "unintelligible or even obscure," then we can only hope, in the words of the old *Spectator*, that he may have enough disappointments to save him from ruin.

Having said so much with regard to Mr. Balfour's form, let us turn to his substance, and, in the first place, examine the grounds he adduces for his first thesis:

[1] See *inter alia* the use of "highest," "best," and "most worthy," pp. 248, 249; "most unlovely germ" of instinct or appetite, p. 325; "larger and worthier inheritance," p. 242; "mere" collection of hypostatised sense-perceptions, p. 243; "almost animal" instincts lying at the roots of our judgments about material phenomena, p. 243; "bare" catalogue of utilitarian precepts, p. 77, etc. etc. It is needless, perhaps, to remind the reader that no animal instinct is in itself unlovely, no natural appetite loathsome or disgusting as Mr. Balfour seems to suggest in more than one passage. *Relatively* to man or to social man the unseasonable gratification of appetite or the blind obedience to instinct, may be "unlovely" or "disgusting"—a rather roundabout way of saying that they may be anti-social, but *absolutely* it is worse than childish to stigmatise them by adjectives which only mark how totally unsympathetic one type of the processes of Nature is to Mr. Balfour's individual mind.

[2] Mr. Balfour speaks of a "woven tissue" "proclaiming" to those who can hear and understand (p. 104), of knowledge being caught up and "ordered" in "the meshes of an all-inclusive dialectical network" (p. 105), of forces as sometimes "driving" and sometimes "flowing in channels," and of Nature as "playing tricks," "committing frauds," "attaining her ends," and having "positive objections" and "desires," etc. etc. Indeed, the anthropomorphic imagery of Mr. Balfour extending from tissues to mechanism reminds me of the animism of the primitive African.

The foundations of Naturalism, Science, Rationalism are unsound.

Now a series of questions at once arises. Does Mr. Balfour treat Naturalism, Science, and Rationalism as identical? Is he justified in so doing? Are their foundations really what Mr. Balfour states them to be? And if so, are those foundations sound or unsound?

Mr. Balfour, notwithstanding occasional disclaimers when he finds it convenient, does directly and indirectly identify Naturalism, Science, and Rationalism, and this identification, we believe, if the words be given exact meanings, is perfectly correct. Any logical critique of knowledge can only end by concluding that knowledge (relative to man) is the body of results reached by rational analysis of the contents of the human mind. Science is sometimes popularly supposed to deal with an outside world of phenomena—it can only deal with what is content of the human mind. Sense-impressions have left stored sense-impresses, and these by extension, association, and comparison have become concepts and ideas, before the reason is applied and we reach anything that can be fairly called knowledge. Mere receptivity of sensations, even the collection of sense-impresses is not science. Science only begins with the classification and comparison of concepts. Accurately speaking, theology is here in exactly the same condition; it cannot reason about God *per se*, but only about the concept of God in the human mind. Now Mr. Balfour has stated that the leading doctrine of Naturalism is that we can only know phenomena (p. 7). There seems to be more than one interpretation of the word "know" thus used.

But if he wishes to say that Naturalism teaches us that the most elaborate human concepts and ideas have been *ultimately* deduced by association and suggestion (generally by the method of limits) from stored sense-impresses, and these ultimately from sensations, and that all our knowledge is ultimately based on sensatory experience, then I am inclined to think that Naturalism is absolutely at one with Science. And further, if the Rationalist teaches that knowledge (as distinct from mere sensatory experience) can only be derived by the application of reason to the contents of the mind, then his doctrine also appears to be in perfect harmony with both Naturalism and Science.

Mr. Balfour attempts to introduce confusion by using the words "natural" science, and telling us that the Rationalist holds that nothing deserves "to be called knowledge which does not come within the circle of the natural sciences" (p. 171). Remove the word natural, or interpret it in an accurate sense, and this seems a statement to which every Naturalist, every Scientist, and every Rationalist must assent. It is, indeed, a conclusion to which every logical analysis of the words science and knowledge must lead. If Mr. Balfour means by "natural" science one which does not deal with the "supernatural," then the word is in the right place; if he uses natural science as something apart from exact science on the one hand, or from mental science on the other, then it behoves him to state what Rationalist has refused either to geometry or psychology, say, a place in the field of knowledge. As we shall show when we come to consider the real foundations of science, modern theoretical physics are precisely in the same category as geometry, and neither is more or less of a "natural" science than the other.¹ If, therefore, we are quite prepared to accept Mr. Balfour's identification ² of Naturalism, Rationalism, and Science, we do so with distinct meanings attached to these words, and decline entirely to see them only through the mirage peculiar to Mr. Balfour's "psychological climate."

The next question to be answered is: Are the foundations of Science really what Mr. Balfour states them to be? Now, Mr. Balfour will hardly be able to disguise from any scientific reader that his acquaintance with science is of a very limited character. No man even superficially acquainted with the modern physics of the ether would still speak of ether as a "substance which behaves as if it were an elastic solid"; nor would even a dabbler in biology, after recent publications, slip glibly over from the formation of habits to their inherit-

[1] It is remarkable that Mr. Balfour never cites or refers to exact science in the course of his volume. Had he once tried to realise the relations of mechanics to geometry, he would have found that, so far as these sciences are "knowledge," they are *both* purely conceptual: the *belief* that they will suffice to predict future routines of perception is quite another matter. Yet Mr. Balfour's confusion of knowledge with belief is one of the chief sources of his blunders.

[2] "Naturalism, then, the naturalism whose practical consequences have already occupied us so long, is nothing more than the result of rationalising methods applied with pitiless consistency to the whole circuit of belief; it is the completed product of rationalism" (p. 172). This identifies Naturalism and Rationalism. In his chapter on the "Philosophic Basis of Naturalism," Mr. Balfour makes a series of statements which he considers represent this basis; he then refers to them as "the creed which science requires us to adopt," and in several passages identifies the premises on which scientific theory rests with the same "rationalistic" basis (see pp. 101, 102, 112, 115, 116, 121, etc. etc.) It is true that Mr. Balfour qualifies his sweeping condemnation of modern Science by occasionally asserting that it will survive Naturalism, but the whole object of his work is to show that Theology has as firm a foundation as Science, the foundation of the latter being what Mr. Balfour is pleased to alternately term Naturalism and Empirical Philosophy.

ance without a sign of hesitation. Mr. Balfour, like Lord Salisbury, has spent his life on other things than Science; his profession has not been that of the thinker. There must be many such, and this ignorance of modern scientific views is too often their misfortune rather than their fault. All we ask of them, and surely this is a small and justifiable request, is this, that when they lay down "the creed which science requires us to adopt," they will tell us, not being even 'prentice hands themselves, who are the masters who have taught this creed. The statement will be scarcely credited by those who have not opened Mr. Balfour's pages, yet it is none the less true that, with one exception, not a single modern scientist is referred to by name or work throughout Mr. Balfour's book, either with reference to "the creed which science requires us to adopt," or with regard to any of the extraordinary statements put forward as "truisms of science." The one exception is Professor Huxley. Surely, my reader will remark, he may be allowed to speak for science? Certainly no man was better qualified. Yet Mr. Balfour only mentions him incidentally as one who would certainly have repudiated that independent reality which our author asserts is postulated by Science! It is true that Mr. Balfour cites Locke and Hume, but these philosophers were not scientists, nor were they historically in a position to deal with the philosophic basis of modern science. Science again is not responsible for Mr. Spencer's views, although we fancy that there are but few scientists who would not dub Mr. Balfour's criticism of Mr. Spencer in Part II. as pitiable quibbling.

So far, then, as any evidence to the contrary can be found in Mr. Balfour's volume, "the creed which science requires us to adopt" might be promulgated solely on Mr. Balfour's own authority. He does not tell us that it has been distinctly repudiated for Science by men like Kirchhoff, Clifford, Mach, and others, as well as by Huxley. Now this is rather serious, not to say misleading, especially when Mr. Balfour takes upon himself to tell us that "the view necessarily adopted by the biologist" will "not stand critical examination." We are not only told that we must necessarily adopt what we repudiate, but that, having adopted it, it is absurd. We should have thought that, in the long list of distinguished physicists and biologists, one might have been found who was as sane a thinker as Mr. Balfour, and would have seen that this "necessary" creed of Science would not bear critical examination. Was there no Daniel among the prophets before Mr. Arthur Balfour?

What, then, is the creed which our new prophet thrusts upon us *nolentes volentes?* Briefly, it is the long-exploded materialism of Moleschott and Büchner! So far as we know, it was never adopted by any physicist of repute; and, perhaps, Mr. Balfour will tell us the name of any distinguished biologist who still teaches it.[1]

---

[1] One of the most significant facts, tacitly shuffled out of sight by Mr. Balfour, is this, that those thinkers who have been leaders of the agnostic and rationalistic movements in modern science, and have found it necessary to deal philosophically with the foundations of science, have emphatically repudiated this materialism. What semblance it may have of the scientific, arises from the unconsidered and sometimes slovenly terminology, not the direct teaching of those who are in theological sympathy with Mr. Balfour—men who have pursued science without any attempt to investigate its philosophy, or apply its methods to a general theory of life. They are either engrossed specialists or men with minds constructed on the logic-tight compartment principle.

Its best known exponent in England was the late Mr. Bradlaugh, and Mr. Balfour may possibly have drawn it in with other political humours of the House of Commons atmosphere.

Now it is as well to have clearly before us the crude materialism which Mr. Balfour tells us is the result of the investigations of science; and which, he further adds, "is practically accepted without question by all instructed persons"—a category which may include Mr. Balfour himself, but would undoubtedly exclude a Huxley or a Clifford.

Science, Mr. Balfour tells us, postulates a world of objects "ordered and mutually related in one unlimited space, and one unlimited time; all in their true reality independent of the presence or absence of any observer, all governed in their behaviour by rigid and unvarying laws." This world of objects "consists essentially of innumerable small particles of definite and unchanging mass, endowed with a variety of mechanical, chemical, and other qualities, and forming by their mutual association the various bodies which we can handle and see, and many others which we can neither handle nor see." After stating that these ponderable particles "have their being" in all-penetrating medium or ether, and both are "animated" by a quantity of energy, Mr. Balfour continues: "It only remains to add, as a fact of considerable importance to ourselves, though of little apparent importance to the universe at large, that a few of the material particles above alluded to are arranged into living organisms, and that among these organisms are a small minority which have the remarkable power of extracting from the changes which take place in certain of their tissues psychical phenomena of various kinds;[1] some of which are the reflection, or partial reproduction in perception and in thought, of fragments and aspects of that material world to which they owe their being." Secure in this general view of things, Mr. Balfour tells us, the co-operative work of scientific investigation moves swiftly on. Here this tit-bit of a creed is forced down the throat of Science; on other occasions it is Naturalism which is compelled to swallow it, with a little additional flavouring; as, for example, the doctrine that beliefs, if the result of reasoning at all, are "founded on premises produced in the last resort by the collision of atoms," or the "truism" that molecules, but not degrees of brightness, are part of reality!

Now it may, perhaps, be argued that, although this materialism is hopelessly absurd, and although it is an error on Mr. Balfour's part to assert that it is the philosophical basis of Science, still he has done good service in showing that it is untenable. The reader who takes this view must be reminded that Mr. Balfour's second thesis, the constructive part of his philosophy, is essentially based on the assertion that this materialism *is* the view of Science, and that its insufficiency and incoherency justifies a like insufficiency and incoherency in the foundations of theology.

Mr. Balfour, like "all instructed persons," is ap-

---

[1] This phrase reminds us strongly of that of another person who gave up Rationalism, because "science teaches that brain secretes thought"—a doctrine which naturally did not carry much illumination, although whether Science is to blame for the reason being made a Jonah in this person's case is open to question.

parently prepared to accept what he assumes Science teaches of the phenomenal world; its judgments about the world, he admits, are inevitable and universal, but he argues that they are based on faith and not on reason, that any attempt at a rational deduction only succeeds in showing them to be inconsistent and irrational. He asserts that there is no special characteristic which marks off the central truth of theology, "'There is a God,' from one of the fundamental presuppositions of science .... 'There is an independent material world.'" Whether the latter statement is fundamental to science we shall consider later. What we are at present concerned with is this—that Mr. Balfour does not use the insufficiency of materialism as an argument against its truth, its judgments are "inevitable"[1]—but as an argument in favour of the acceptance of other equally unintelligible beliefs.

"Without any preliminary analysis, nay, without any apparent suspicion that a preliminary analysis was necessary or desirable, they—the advocates of Naturalism—have chosen to assume that scientific beliefs stand not only upon a different, but upon a much more solid platform than any others; that scientific standards supply the sole test of truth, and scientific methods the sole instruments of discovery" (p. 235).

The beliefs of Science are the products of practical

[1] Even his Imaginary Observer who, "quite indifferent to mundane theories," and "in a spirit of detached curiosity," examines the *causes* of our beliefs of perception, finds that when normal they are "invariably due to the action of external objects upon the organism, and more particularly upon the nervous system of the percipient." Mr. Balfour's language shows him over and over again to be more of a materialist than the most naturalistic of scientists we have hitherto come across. For example: "the object as we know (!) it to be—the vibrating molecule and undulating ether" (p. 61).

experience, the beliefs of theology the products of practical needs. Neither has an adequate or consistent philosophy. This seems to sum up Mr. Balfour's position. Indeed, having shown to his own satisfaction that Rationalism is inconsistent with itself, he feels "bound to protest against the assumption that consistency is a necessity of the intellectual life, to be purchased, if need be, at famine prices." This is a maxim which might serve to calm the intellectual scruples of an opportunist politician, but introduced into philosophic thought, it is Nidhöggr gnawing at the root of Yggdrasil, and must ultimately bring the tree of knowledge—which is the tree of life—to the ground. Our opportunist politician may drive the State coach on a known road with the horses' heads towards their stalls, but give him a country new to both team and driver, and he will certainly wreck the coach at the first dip in the road.

We are quite prepared to follow Mr. Balfour, and admit that 'There is a God' and 'There is a material world built up of molecules' are equally unproven statements, but the comparison between Science and Theology ends here, for while Theology is based upon a belief in the former proposition, Science in no way depends upon the truth or falsehood of the latter proposition. The validity of scientific conclusions remains untouched, if behind the veil of sense-impressions, which for the Rationalist limits the field of human knowledge, be postulated *Dinge an sich*, mediate or immediate deities, mind-stuff, the unknowable, permanent possibilities of sensation, or a complex of molecules "endowed with force." Assuming for the moment that the foundation of Science is not the materialism so glibly propounded by Mr. Balfour, but that it must be sought on the perceptional side of the veil of sense-impressions, then it follows at once that theological belief (which treats of things on the other side of the veil) and scientific belief must have foundations of a totally different character; the whole of Mr. Balfour's reasoning based on confused analogies between the two falls to the ground, and his book takes its proper place among that weird collection of paralogistic writings which illustrates the futility of those who would replace or supplement revealed theology by a theology of the reason.[1]

If confirmation were, indeed, needed for the naturalistic, rationalistic, or scientific standpoint, namely, that any sound critique of knowledge must confine its sphere to the perceptional side of sense-impression, it lies in the fact that while innumerable thinkers have given innumerable names to what lies behind sensation, they consciously or unconsciously admit their real ignorance of its nature. It does not matter whether it be Spinoza[2] with his Infinite Substance, or Kant with his *Ding an sich*, or the materialist with his molecule, or the theologian with his personal God—one and all can tell us nothing of the real mode of action of his *idolum specus*. Mr. Balfour makes himself merry at Mr. Spencer's placing solely the Unknowable behind the veil of

[1] The straightforward and proper term would be "natural theology," but Mr. Balfour thinks he has shown that natural theology and rationalist orthodoxy are inadequate, if not paradoxical. None the less, his work is really a contribution to natural theology.

[2] A protest may well be raised by every lover of Spinoza against Mr. Balfour's contemptuous treatment of that great thinker. It would, however, be impossible for Mr. Balfour to appreciate how congruous much of Spinoza's work is with modern science.

sense-impression. Yet when Mr. Balfour comes to his own *idolum specus*, he tells us that we cannot form "I will not say any adequate, but even any tolerable idea of the mode in which God is related to, and acts on, the world of phenomena. . . . How He created it, how He sustains it, is impossible for us to imagine." A thing of whose mode of action we cannot even form any tolerable idea seems very close to the Unknowable, and a much more subtle religious thinker than Mr. Balfour went perilously near to the agnostic position when more than five centuries and a half ago he asserted of his deity that he was a non-form, a non-person, a non-spirit, and a non-god. On the whole, considering the want of unanimity in terminology, if not in vacuity of idea with regard to the source of phenomena among these philosophers, Science, even if it had not a reasonable critique of the knowable, might be justified in crying ἀγνοὲω! if it did not add: A plague upon you both, metaphysicians and theologians, for dissipating the intellectual energy of mankind!

We may stay for a moment to consider whether this agnostic limitation is really depressing. It is true that Mr. Balfour himself tells us that life is not worth living, if we cannot penetrate to the other side of the sensuous. But Mr. Balfour's individual needs cannot be taken as a criterion of what it is possible or impossible for the human intellect to achieve. Personally I was not born nor reared so that Rationalism was to me a "psychological climate";[1] I spent five years of

[1] Mr. Balfour imagines Rationalism, like Toryism, to be inherited. In John Stuart Mill's case perhaps it was, but it would be interesting to know in how many others.

life in struggling with much bitterness out of the mazes of metaphysic and theology, only to find in agnosticism the peace which arises from understanding. To the man who knows the limitation of his powers, life is as a rule better worth living than to the lad, who is yet uncertain whether he means to be prime minister or lord chancellor. Mr. Balfour speaks contemptuously of those who regard the Universe as a "mere collection of hypostatised sense-perceptions packed side by side in space and following each other with blind uniformity in time." He wants "ideas of wider sweep and richer content," and considers that the work of Science would be beneath contempt if it only provided a machinery by which the re-occurrence of feelings and ideas might be adequately accounted for. Most natural philosophers, we venture to think, would consider the work of Science completed and the field of human knowledge exhausted if any such machinery were provided. Those who know how pitiably little of the almost limitless sphere embraced by "feelings and ideas" has yet been surveyed, still less "adequately accounted for," will assuredly smile at Mr. Balfour's pious opinion that all Science is turned into foolishness, if it confines its attention to the region where experience has shown and reason can demonstrate that its labour will be profitably expended.

Mr. Balfour's appeal to his own æsthetic needs for something "higher and richer," sounds like the wail of a child, who considers the astronomer's work contemptible, because although the astronomer can deal with the motion, the phases, the shapes, and even the physical and chemical surface conditions of the heavenly bodies, he still cannot bring the moon into the nursery, cut it open and show its actual contents. Nay, we are by no means sure that any sound theory of æsthetics would justify Mr. Balfour's standpoint. The scientific critic of the drama of life would certainly not have his pleasure increased by seeing the legs of the scene-shifter or by investigating the nature of the stage-props. The true enjoyment of the great landscape of Nature would be rather lessened than heightened by any subsidiary attempt to investigate its canvas backing or the strength of the trestles. It is not a metaphor, but a truism, which I give expression to, when I state that the natural philosopher, like the art critic, deals with the conceptual relations of his subject, and is not concerned with canvas, stage-props, or any other *Dinge an sich*. He may be quite content to think they exist, if it is not intellectually possible nor even æsthetically desirable that he should investigate their nature.

But let us return to Mr. Balfour's opinions as to the basis of Science. It is true that he makes what he considers an even stronger statement in favour of a materialistic creed for Science than the views of the man in the street. He asserts that the whole of Science has been developed in the belief that its conclusions applied to an independent material universe, and that scientific observers of Nature would never have done what they have done if they "had realised from the beginning that all that they were observing was their own feelings and ideas." As usual Mr. Balfour seems to know more about what men of science must necessarily think or feel than they know themselves, or than the history of Science in the least indicates. He has entirely overlooked the fact that large portions of the so-called exact sciences, which for many centuries monopolised the attention of men of science, not only deal with conceptual notions—ideas and not phenomena,—but were at an early period of their development recognised by their devotees to be conceptual, and even appreciated the more highly on that account. Mr. Balfour appears to be equally ignorant that at least a moiety of the scientific work and a moiety of the scientific workers of to-day fall respectively into the categories of admittedly conceptual reasoning and admittedly conceptual reasoners. We have no ground for supposing that Cayley was more lukewarm in his enthusiasm for Science than Newton, although the former must have been fully conscious that his labour was confined to the conceptual field. In short, there is not a grain of evidence to show that Science would not have found as capable and imaginative workers if thinkers had recognised from the very beginning — which was of course historically impossible [1] — that they were labouring and must labour on one side only of the veil of sense-impressions.

On the other hand, much testimony can be adduced to prove that the molecule and the ether are still

[1] Geometry, for example, was first a real γῆς μετρια before it developed into a pure theory of conceptual space relations. Physics throwing aside its earlier purely descriptive phases, is becoming a generalised theory of motion. Even biology passing from the field to the laboratory manifests a tendency in recent advances to become a science of exact conceptual notions. The reader must not for a moment suppose that a science when it is recognised as conceptual ceases to be related to phenomena, but the relation is not of the material nature postulated by Mr. Balfour. It is a relation of description not of identity.

occupying the attention of by no means chilled and depressed thinkers, although their recognition as descriptive concepts, created by the human mind, is superseding the belief that they are *Dinge an sich*, actively functioning on the other side of the veil of sense-impressions. Finally, it is needless, perhaps, to remark, that it does not follow because scientific progress has been assisted by men who postulated a material molecule, that men of science must now adopt materialistic beliefs. We might as well argue that because Kepler was an astrologer, and may have had doubts as to whether his mother was or was not really guilty of witchcraft, it is necessary that modern astronomers should hold an astrological faith.

We have probably said sufficient to convince the reader that the materialism which Mr. Balfour would thrust upon Science, and which, in his opinion, is "practically accepted without question by all instructed persons," is not only without any weight of scientific authority behind it, but that the arguments Mr. Balfour uses in its favour are simply the product of confused thinking. In particular, the insufficiency of the agnostic standpoint, *i.e.* its limitation of our knowledge to the "circle of impressions and ideas"—to satisfy his individual needs, or indeed to satisfy the needs of all mankind, could prove nothing as to its intellectual correctness. The fact, however, that many men of high culture and careful mental method have found their individual needs satisfied within the "circle of impressions and ideas," might at least have hindered a philosophical thinker from propounding any theory of satisfaction of relative needs as a criterion of the absolute reality of existence.

Part II

If we have now shown that the foundations of Science are not the materialistic postulates of Mr. Balfour, it still remains for us to indicate what those foundations really are, and how their soundness and coherency completely upset the comparison Mr. Balfour makes with the admittedly difficult if not wholly incomprehensible premises of Theology. In doing this we shall have completed our critical examination of Mr. Balfour's first two theses. The third, as involving a very serious social imputation upon Rationalism, demands a more independent investigation.

At the outset we must free our minds from two ideas of the market-place. Science, in the first place, is not going to explain *everything* within the "circle of impressions and ideas"; and, in the next place, it is not going to *explain* anything at all. The field of possible knowledge, if not in Mr. Balfour's eyes, yet in those of most men of science, is immensely wide, and but the fringe of it has yet been worked. It is no reproach to Science to discover a few square feet of unturned soil and cry, "Ah! you can't explain that." There are admittedly acres and acres of untouched prairie land. The rationalist's case against the theologian and the metaphysician does not lie in the statement that behind the veil of sense-impression there are many things theology and metaphysics cannot explain, but in the obvious fact that they cannot formulate a tolerable, to say nothing of an adequate idea about what they assert they do know. In the next place, the mission of Science is not to *explain* but to *describe;* to discover a descriptive formula which will enable men to predict the nature of future perceptions; such descriptive formulæ are, in the only consistent sense of the word, knowledge, they form that "economy of thought," which is the name happily devised by a philosophical physicist to describe and define Science.

We cannot better illustrate the true character of Science, with which Mr. Balfour seems so little acquainted, than by a reference to geometry. The process in this case is to extract from ideas ultimately based on perpetual experience, conceptual limits. This method of limits gives us concepts of continuity, boundary, infinite extension, and so forth; it gives us our notions of lines, planes, surfaces. These correspond to nothing whatever in actual sensatory experience; they are concepts, intellectual ideas, and it is our reasoning about *them* which leads to knowledge. Simple experience is not knowledge; classified experience is a step towards knowledge, but not knowledge itself; knowledge only comes in when the process of reasoning is applied to concepts drawn from classified experience. Once the fundamental concepts are clear, then, as in geometry, unique results only can follow by the application of the reason. Men of science may come to different conclusions, because they start from different, albeit perfectly definite fundamental concepts, or they may differ because their fundamental concepts are not clear and adequate. For example, two geologists may draw from their experiences of a glacier the perfectly definite, but different concepts, viscous fluid and plastic solid. The conceptual models they build up of the glacier will differ totally in character. The moment we have reached clear physical conceptions of viscosity and plasticity, our knowledge of the model glacier, if our analysis be powerful enough, is in either case unique and complete. But two geologists may start from the conception of plastic solid, say, and reach different conclusions, because they have not formed, we will "not say any adequate, but even any tolerable idea" of plasticity. In this case they resemble Mr. Balfour's theologian. Once form consistent and in themselves adequate concepts, and reason will build up a unique theory, the conclusions of which are knowledge.

The reader will best bring this before his mind by thinking of lines, triangles, circles—and propositions about them. Geometry is a knowledge, not of "things-in-themselves," nor even of their sensuous side, but purely of conceptual limits drawn from our experience; its symbols have no reality outside the mind. Now, a careful examination will show that all scientific knowledge is of this character. It is a knowledge of conceptual limits, drawn ultimately, it is true, from our sensatory experience, but these limits are never identical, often not even congruous with experience. If we pass from geometry to physics, we shall find all our knowledge depending upon our concepts of motion, but the modes of motion are just as conceptual as the modes of partitioning space; they are, indeed, based on geometry. Even the most old-fashioned physicists are now admitting that force is a mode of *describing* conceptual motion and not a cause of perceptual motion. Still more is the conceptual character of a "gas," a "fluid," an "elastic solid,"[1] or a "viscous liquid," fully recognised. In these cases we are dealing with conceptual limits, and not with real sensational groups. Then in the borderland of physics and chemistry we find particles, molecules, and atoms, which are essentially conceptual in character. We have a complex kinetic model based on conceptual limits of form and motion, by aid of which we mimic and describe our sensational experiences.[2] The physicist, who projects his concepts into the unknowable beyond sense-impression, is as unphilosophical and as dogmatic as the metaphysician or theologian. It is, indeed, easy for Mr. Balfour to show that this materialism is as inadequate and as incoherent as his foundations of belief themselves. It would only weary the reader to go through the whole list of sciences from astronomy to sociology, and show how their essential contributions to knowledge are conceptual and not materialistic in character, but such is, indeed, the case. Even biology, which seems at first such a purely classificatory and

---

[1] Mr. Balfour hardly realised the doubly-deep pit into which he precipitated himself, when he first identified the ether with an "elastic solid," and then argued that it must on that account be material!

[2] In the same sense that a portrait describes and mimics an individual for us. We may learn many things from a study of the portrait, but we shall not assert that it is the reality behind the individual of our experience. The form and tones of the portrait are symbols, not equivalents, of the actual phenomenon.

descriptive science, is approaching the conceptual stages of growth. On the one side, in its treatment of protoplasm, we find it taking unto itself concepts analogous to those of physics; on the other, in its treatment of evolution, conceptual limits as to continuity, growth, variation, heredity, panmixia, and correlation are being reached which will convert it into an exact, *i.e.* a true conceptual branch of science.

If, then, as I feel assured, this — the reasoning on conceptual limits — is the essential characteristic of Science, the true foundation of all knowledge, how is Science related to the phenomenal world? Simply as providing comprehensive descriptive formulæ—so-called laws—summed up in a conceptual model which more or less completely figures past and rehearses future experience. The symbols of Science are not "things in themselves," nor are they perceptions—nay, as a rule, they do not even stand as equivalents for concrete and actual phenomena. They are conceptual limits to actual experience, and when the results deduced from reasoning upon them are to be made use of in the phenomenal sphere, they require cautious interpretation and careful discounting.

It is true that Mr. Balfour and other "commonsense" philosophers may at once seize upon this modest statement of the function of Science. They may say, if Science does not deal with what they are pleased to term the "reality of things," what is the value of its claims either to practical service or to exclusive authority in the field of knowledge? To the first part of this question the only reply needful is the homely proverb: "The proof of the pudding lies in its eating." If no great bridge be constructed, if no ironclad can be built, nor being launched can be guided across the seas, if no great engineering work can be attempted, still less achieved, without—to take but a small point—the purely conceptual notions of geometry, then is the practical value of this reasoning on conceptual limits established. If from our conceptual model we can predict with surprising accuracy future experience, and no one who has any acquaintance with the physical or biological sciences can for a moment contradict this, then we are not compelled to argue *à priori* upon the practical value of Science. We merely state that those, be they nations or individuals, who disregard its conclusions, will waste unlimited intellectual and physical energy, if they do not ultimately meet with a catastrophe. Our symbols, our conceptual limits, may not be the exact equivalents of any actual group of sense-impressions; that they enable man to largely regulate his own future is sufficient test of their practical validity. It is, indeed, the limiting character of our concepts which gives them their great generality, and enables them to act as a real economy of thought.

Mr. Balfour indulges on pp. 119-132 in a characteristic "screed" on the law of causation. Removed from its verbal prolixity we believe his argument amounts to the following. No proof of the law of causation can be obtained from experience, because we never find exactly the same antecedents, and therefore never the same consequents. It may be that Mr. Balfour goes further and personally believes that absolutely identical antecedents, were they possible, would not be followed by the same consequents. He writes :—

> But when we come to the more complex phenomena with which we have to deal, the plain lesson taught by personal observation is not the regularity, but the irregularity of Nature. A kind of ineffectual attempt at uniformity, no doubt, is commonly apparent, as of an ill-constructed machine that will run smoothly for a time, and then for no apparent reason begin to jerk and quiver ; or of a drunken man who, though he succeeds in keeping to the high road, yet pursues along it a most wavering and devious course. But of that perfect adjustment, that all-penetrating governance by law, which lies at the root of scientific inference, *we find not a trace*.[1]

Now this is a most grossly exaggerated statement of our experience, yet the exaggeration flies entirely wide of its purpose, because the law of causation is like any other formula of science a *conceptual limit*, and is not a something working amid the unknowable *Dinge an sich*. It is the fundamental conception of our model which gives it only a single degree of freedom ; it is the principle which leads from adequate concepts to *unique* results. The law of causation gives to knowledge its unique character, *i.e.* prevents intellectual truth from having that ambiguity with which Mr. Balfour seeks to credit it.[2] But if the necessity and universality of our scientific judgments apply only to the conceptual model, does it not follow that Mr. Balfour is correct in asserting that the law of causation does not necessarily hold for

---

[1] Pp. 130, 131, the italics are ours.
[2] See especially his chapter on "Beliefs, Formulas, and Realities." The argument contained therein seems to me thoroughly pernicious. For the sake of "co-operative unity" we are to be satisfied with half-truths, we are to accept formulæ, conscious that our neighbours and we believe something entirely different by them.

Nature? Quite correct, if he asserts that there is no rational argument by which we can demonstrate a future uniformity in Nature. No amount of argument will demonstrate that the sun will rise to-morrow; no "law of nature" can compel it to do so. No reasoning whatever can *prove* that future experience will follow the same routine as past experience. The test of the law of causation is the same as that of any other conceptual limit drawn by Science. Does it enable us adequately to rehearse future experience, to prophesy the future from the past, by aid of our conceptual model? The test is a purely utilitarian one. It is satisfied, and satisfied notoriously well by human experience, of futures which have become pasts. But, we hear Mr. Balfour objecting, you are not bound by the law of causation, you might use another category, and, perhaps, with better results. That is the cry of the boy in the street to the craftsman at his bench, the maker of knowledge. "You could smooth that plank with another instrument than a plane." "Perhaps so, but before you so glibly suggest that I throw away my tools, you must not only invent new ones, but show by a little hard work yourself that you can turn them to profitable account."

To the reader who has an acquaintance with natural phenomena, be they simple or complex, Mr. Balfour's remarks on the irregularity of Nature must seem strikingly wide of the mark. In branches of Science which are at all fully developed, those jerks and quiverings of the machine, to which he compares the action of Nature, can be as adequately described and prophesied as the perturbations from elliptic orbits of the planets; it is only ignorance which could assert that no account of them can be rendered. Even in less developed branches of Science, where slighter variations of antecedents or adjuncts escape our powers of observation, we are still able to predict the magnitude and frequency of deviations from the normal consequents by aid of branches of Science especially devoted to this end.[1] In complete contradiction to Mr. Balfour, I assert that we do find that "that perfect adjustment, that all-penetrating governance by law which lies at the root of scientific inference"—*i.e.* is a fundamental concept of our "model" —does satisfy all the conditions necessary for describing not only the regularity, but also the "irregularity" of Nature.

Mr. Balfour asserts that we do not deduce the law of causation from experience—that is, draw it as a conceptual limit from our perceptions. He believes that we bring it ready made "to the interpretation of our sense-perception," and he ultimately takes this as evidence that other faiths may be given *à priori*, and are as incapable of rational justification. The rational justification of the law of causation is as we have seen its transcendent utility, Science asserts nothing as to its being an essential element of "things in themselves," or an unchangeable law of an independent material universe.[2] There is further no evidence at all that it is given to us *à priori*. The power of association from

---

[1] The statistical theories of Variation and Correlation.
[2] Its utility might arise, for example, owing to some special characteristic of our own perceptional faculty—of its mode of co-ordinating groups of sense-impressions.

which the idea of this conceptual limit ultimately arises is far weaker in the savage and the infant than in the intellectually developed adult. The savage will over and over again repeat the same superstitious ceremony intended to produce a certain effect, although this effect can never once have resulted from his performance. The infant will place one brick upon the top of another in precisely the same manner, and will ultimately cry at the repeated consequential collapse of the structure. The mother who thought *one* contact of infantile fingers and kettle would teach cause and effect, was surprised—although the association might have been considered particularly close in this case—to find the burnt knuckles wandering soon after the same road. That like causes are followed by like effects is only a gradually learnt truth, and the conceptual limit which we term "the law of causation" is only reached after prolonged experience and some intellectual exercise. While, therefore, we are in perfect agreement with Mr. Balfour when he asserts that "the law of universal causation can never be proved by a mere repetition, however prolonged, of similar sequences," and that because "we *can* apply the law of causation, we are not *bound* to apply it," we hold that these assertions are not of the slightest consequence; for the only test of the validity of our rationalistic conclusions based on the law of causation is their capacity for adequately representing the sequences of our sense-impressions—this test is completely satisfied by experience.

The law of causation stands to science as the laws of motion to physics, the latter cannot be proven by any amount of repeated experience, nor because we *can* apply them, are we *bound* to. But the man who does not apply them will sooner or later find their practical validity amply demonstrated by contact between his head and a stone wall. There is no proof of the law of causation. It is valid because of its strength and sufficiency in use.

Thus while knowledge is unique truth flowing from adequate and consistent concepts, the validity of these concepts—apart from their intellectual worth—depends on practical utility. We can assert nothing as rationally demonstrated of "an independent material world," we cannot assert any necessity *per se* in routines of perception. We *believe* that routines of the past as summed up in the formulæ or scientific laws of our conceptual model will repeat themselves in the future. This belief is not knowledge, but it is, like all beliefs of any operative value, based on a high degree of probability deduced from our statistical experience of the repetition of routine. To sum up, then: Science is based on no statements whatever as to the nature or mode of action of a material world of "things-in-themselves"[1]; nor does it assert any laws as holding

[1] It is hardly necessary to do more than refer, in a footnote, to Mr. Balfour's misstatement concerning the views of Science as to "primary and secondary qualities of matter." He asserts that Science finds it necessary to postulate qualities like solidity and extension in things-in-themselves exactly resembling our impressions and ideas, while in colour and warmth there is no resemblance between quality and sensation. He discusses at some length the nature of colour, and tells us, *inter alia*, that degrees of brightness are no part of reality, and that this is a truism of science. The theory of light makes the degree of brightness depend on the energy of vibration; the kinetic theory of pressure would, I presume, also reduce the resistance, we term hardness, to a motion of the cohering particles. Why the energy measured by one nerve is to be real and that measured by another "no part of reality," I fail to understand. At any

of necessity even for the world of sense-impressions. From our experience of this world it forms concepts by the method of limits, and when these are adequate and consistent, a unique theory—knowledge—flows from them. Congruity between phenomena and conceptual model is not a necessity, but a test of practical validity. This congruity may not exist as in the case of the higher theory of form and number, but our concepts ultimately drawn as limits from sensatory experience may still lead us to intellectual truths. In this case they have intellectual but not·phenomenal validity. The practical side of Science lies in the continual improvement and enlargement of the conceptual model so as to give greater congruity between experience and theory. The justification for the application of the results drawn from past experience to future experience is a probability based upon statistics of repeated routines. This is the basis of scientific belief as distinguished from knowledge. We thus see the distinct parts played by experience, knowledge, and belief in the rationalistic philosophy; experience is given and we are agnostic as to its sources, knowledge is a term which can only be accurately used of intellectual conclusions, belief is based on the statistics provided by experience of the past congruity between scientific concepts and phenomena. In the account which we have, perforce briefly, given of the foundations of Science we have answered our reader's supposed ques-

---

rate, a distinction between "primary and secondary qualities" may be Locke, or Spencer, or Balfour, it is neither critical philosophy nor sound science. It is idle, therefore, to point to this distinction as a paradox in the "philosophy of science."

tions as to the practical service of Science, and justified its claims to unique authority in the whole field of knowledge, by endeavouring to give a clear and consistent meaning to the word knowledge itself.

If this account be correct, the unsoundness Mr. Balfour finds in the basis of Science has existence only in his own imagination. His first thesis is incorrect, and with it, as we will now briefly show, falls to the ground the whole of his rational theology. It is in this section of his work that Mr. Balfour's obscure mode of thinking becomes singularly conspicuous.

Mr. Balfour's argument is of the following kind:— Materialism is the necessary basis of Science, but it is a conviction apart from or in excess of proof. Upon this basis, however, "the loftiest creeds and the most far-reaching discoveries ultimately lean." We step with easy assurance in Science and everyday life, although the ground is "not less hollow beneath our feet than the dim and unfamiliar regions which lie beyond." Having by this neat little confidence trick palmed off on Science as unsound a basis as he admits for Theology, Mr. Balfour tells us that this recognition of general unsoundness "must revolutionise our whole attitude towards the problems presented to us by science, ethics, and theology. It must destroy the ordinary tests and standards whereby we measure essential truth." There is an exquisite irony, unperceived by Mr. Balfour, in the leader of the Conservative party, thus becoming in intellectual matters the champion of revolution and destruction, it is a veritable casting out of the devil by aid of the devil.

But let us see precisely whither a comparison of scientific and theological ideas leads us, if we start from a sound philosophical basis. Take the case of the rational deduction of the deity, which is one of Mr. Balfour's own selection. We must first have some sort of experience, and then from phenomenal existence follows the extraction by the method of limits of a purely intellectual concept. The experience in this case is undoubtedly our experience of mankind. The essential attributes of his deity, Mr. Balfour extracts from man, they are reason, goodness, beauty,—characteristics which he asserts are either non-existent in, or unappreciated by other forms of life. The deity is thus a conceptual limit drawn from our experience of man. He may differ as much from man as a conceptual circle from its phenomenal prototypes, he is a limiting idea not a reproduction. Now this concept, to be at all parallel with those of Science, must be adequate, self-consistent, and when reason is applied to it, it must lead to unique results. Two scientists who start with a triangle or with philosophically expressed laws of motion arrive at the same conclusions by the same rational process, *e.g.* the sum of the internal angles is two right angles, or motion in an ellipse round the focus is accompanied by an acceleration to the focus varying as the inverse square. But experience shows us that no two theologians will necessarily arrive at consistent and unique results by reasoning as to the concept God. Mr. Balfour tells us that we cannot even form a tolerable idea of his mode of action. It is absurd, therefore, to compare the theological idea of God with a scientific concept.

But admit for a moment that they may be paralleled, and see how the practical validity and the social utility of the concept is to be tested. Is our conceptual model congruous with phenomena? Then with what special groups of sense-impressions is it to be compared? Or shall we classify this conceptual limit, the deity, with those valuable scientific limits, which although ultimately drawn from the field of sense-impression, have yet no phenomenal congruity, and only pure intellectual value—such concepts, for instance, as space of negative curvature, or alternate numbers, or kinetic energy of motion in elliptic space? Allow it to be a conceptual limit of this kind, incongruous with the phenomenal world, and we shall still find that it differs from the same class of scientific concepts in the fact that rational processes cannot be applied to it. And lastly, if it were even admitted to be a conceptual limit akin to those of Science, what follows? That it is merely an intellectual symbol, and, no more than a circle, a molecule, or a perfect fluid, has it any claim on real existence. As Science cannot philosophically project its intellectual concepts into the Unknown behind sense-impression, so Theology could find no rational justification for doing so either.

We do not think theologians when they realise the quagmire into which Mr. Balfour leads them, will at all thank him for asserting that Theology and Science are on the same platform. As a matter of fact, scientific truths—the product of reasoning on consistent concepts —and scientific belief—the probability based on statistical experience of congruity between conceptual model and phenomena—are of a totally different order to theological truths and theological beliefs. In Theology we assert something and believe something not of ideas, but of an independent, supersensuous existence behind sense-impression. In Science we assert something of a conceptual world and believe something of its relation to the dependent and sensuous. It is almost inconceivable that any one with a claim to the title of thinker should nowadays have succeeded in confusing his own mind and have proposed to moither his readers with such "rational theology" as this.

For, after all, what we are here dealing with is Natural Theology, the old Bridgewater stock-in-trade, refurbished by Sir G. G. Stokes, and hawked afresh by Mr. Balfour. Now it is true that the latter objects to the terms "rationalist orthodoxy" and "natural theology" as paradoxical. Yet he still appears to be skilfully balancing on the fence with regard to these branches of investigation, much as he is in the matter of inspiration.[1] He tells us in the same paragraph with regard to the arguments of Paley, first that—

My personal opinion is that, as far as they go they are good. The argument, or perhaps I should say *an* argument from design, in some shape or another will always have value;

and then—

They may not be technically defective, but they are assuredly practically inadequate (p. 178).

---

[1] On one page he argues that inspiration is to be confined to no age, country, or people—a crumb to broad-minded theologians. On the next he does not desire to deny that the word inspiration may with advantage be confined to one or more of the modes in which belief is assisted by Divine co-operation—a whole loaf to the strictly orthodox Christian.

An argument good enough personally for Mr. Balfour, but practically inadequate, throws him indeed on to the horns of a dilemma. If "good" means sound, it gives him a monopoly of reason; if "inadequate" means unsound, it throws a strange light on Mr. Balfour's estimate of his own logical capacity. Rational orthodoxy, on the one hand, "will survive the consequences of critical assaults," and on the other, since it attaches Theology to Naturalism by so slender a tie, "the weak and artificial connection which has been so ingeniously contrived will snap at the first strain to which it shall be subjected by the forces either of criticism or sentiment." What Mr. Balfour's real view is can hardly be ascertained from such Gladstonian utterances, but as he immediately proceeds to play the part of the rationalising theologian, we suppose he is content to let his beliefs dangle from his intellect by so weak and artificial a thread. Let us witness the spectacle.

God having been postulated to satisfy the "deepest needs" of man, although the divine existence is beyond rational demonstration (precisely as in the case of Science (!) the material world is postulated in excess of proof to satisfy the "almost animal instincts" or the needs we share with our brute progenitors), it becomes necessary to deduce rationally the divine characteristics. Now it is hard to realise, but none the less it is a fact, that Mr. Balfour having shown how futile is the reason, how much larger a part is played in human development by authority, habit, or even instinct,[1] and how consistent

[1] "Nor is the comparative smallness of the *rôle* thus played by reasoning in human affairs a matter for regret." It is not the difficulty of reasoning nor of determining data, but the idea that "reasoning is a force most apt to divide and

Rationalism is rationally incompatible with conscience or morality, yet proceeds to deduce reason as the first and foremost attribute of his deity! We suspect, indeed, that deity is as much the grand incarnation of reason in Mr. Balfour's opinion as in that of most human theologians; but the Chief Rationalist is to be allowed absolute goodness and absolute beauty, while any remains of these qualities in the terrestrial rationalist are parasitic survivals! There is something so precious about this naïve postulating of reason as a first attribute of the deity, although we are told that it is neither the quality in which we most notably excel the brute "creation," nor is it as efficacious in action as habit! We are inclined to prefer the consistency of the canine theologian, who should instinctively realise that "physiological co-ordination" must be the chief attribute of the unknowable, although the dog would be merely yelping his feelings, and the man would be reasoning on his "deepest needs." At any rate, he gives to the deity of his best.

What is, however, the exact proof by which Mr. Balfour deduces a reason at the back of phenomena? It lies simply in the statement that it would be impos-

---

disintegrate," which influences Mr. Balfour's estimate, and he finally assures us that "though it may seem to savour of paradox, it is yet no exaggeration to say that if we would find the quality in which we most notably excel the brute creation, we should look for it, not so much in our faculty of convincing and being convinced by the exercise of the reasoning, as in our capacity for influencing and being influenced through the action of authority." It is true Mr. Balfour does not define authority, but uses the word almost indifferently for animal instinct, tribal or social custom, tradition, and the *de facto* spiritual or secular human powers. But this statement is peculiarly significant as with his pre-Copernican, man-as-the-centre-of-the-universe tendency he attributes to "physiological co-ordination" in the lower animals, results which are the product in man of conscious mental processes.

sible to reason about things if they had not a rational basis. That in order to reason it is needful for both reasoner and subject-matter to be the product of another reason. Let us pause for a moment to apply this type of argument all round. Because the clock keeps time with the stars, there must be clockwork at the back of the universe; because the loom sends the shuttle flying through the maze of warp, the raw wool itself must be the product of loom and shuttle; because the chaos of rubble comes out of the stone-sorting machine cleaned, sized, and sorted, there must be such a machine ultimately creating rubble; because "physiological co-ordination" enables brute nature to guide itself through the phenomenal world, instinct and reflex action must have created brute and universe; because we can digest a whole round of vegetable and animal matters, organic life must be the product of a Transcendental Stomach; because human hands have learnt the art of delicate design in wood and metal, forest and lode are undoubtedly specimens of a supernatural Engraver's skill; because futilities can be multiplied indefinitely, the material for them, as well as the minds which rejoice in them, must alike be the creation of a Gigantic Trifler. Not one of these statements seems a whit more ridiculous from the standpoint of logic than the argument of Mr. Balfour with which we have prefaced them. If the fingers of man have in long course of development reached a marvellous dexterity in the use of tools, how can the natural theologian with consistency appeal to the head rather than to the hands of man when searching for the sources of phenomena?

Yet, strange to say, Mr. Balfour appears content to allow manual dexterity to be "explained" as the product of evolution, while mental dexterity could, he is quite sure, never on the basis of selection have reached a point beyond that which enabled man "to kill with success and marry with security." It is, perhaps, pertinent to ask whether manual dexterity still remains at this level. Or is, indeed, Mr. Balfour, like Lord Salisbury, prepared to deny the adequacy of natural selection all round?

At the risk of wearying the reader we must cite Mr. Balfour's views, because he tells us that by simply changing the word "reason" into "morality" or "beauty," we are able to find a stable basis for our morals and æsthetics:—

> When once we have realised the scientific truth that at the root of every rational process lies an irrational one; that reason from a scientific point of view is itself a natural product; and that the whole material on which it works is due to causes, physical, physiological, and social, which it neither creates nor controls, we shall (as I showed just now [1]) be driven in mere self-defence to hold that behind these non-rational forces, and above them, guiding them by slow degrees, and, as it were, with difficulty to a rational issue, stands that Supreme Reason in whom we must thus believe, if we are to believe in anything.

As we have seen, the argument from the "ineffaceable incongruity between the origin of our beliefs, in so far as these can be revealed to us by science, and the beliefs themselves" may be applied all round. Mr. Balfour does apply it in the first place to ethics. "It

[1] I presume Mr. Balfour refers to his previous chapter. The only argument there used is that of a necessary congruity between the source of the irrational and the mental machine, if the latter is to co-ordinate its raw material.

is easy to trace back our ethical beliefs to sources which have about them nothing that is ethical." We require to seek behind phenomenal sources "for some ultimate ground with which they shall be congruous; and as we have been moved to postulate a rational God in the interests of science, we can scarcely decline to postulate a moral God in the interests of morality." Now, Mr. Balfour finds Nature's contrivances for protecting the species of "some loathsome parasite" to be "most cruel and most disgusting." We presume, therefore, as Mr. Balfour has beliefs as to the cruel and the loathsome, which can be easily traced back to sources having nothing cruel or disgusting about them, he is prepared to seek behind phenomenal sources for some ultimate ground with which they shall be congruous. We do not find him, however, attributing cruelty and loathliness to his deity. Perhaps he gets out of the difficulty, as a good many others have done, by postulating a devil to satisfactorily account for the necessary congruity. This might explain the difficulty which, according to him, the Supreme Reason has in guiding the non-rational forces to a rational issue. He cannot get quit of his "loathsome parasite," however much he might desire to do so, by telling us that "if in the region of causation it is wholly by the earlier stages that the later are determined, in the region of design it is only through the later stages that the earlier can be understood." For the loathliness [1] is a result of a late rather than an

[1] As I have before pointed out, "disgusting" and "loathsome," like "good" and "beautiful," have validity only in relation to man. To the naturalist not dealing with the individual or social welfare of man, disgusting and loathsome are idle terms.

early stage of parasitic development. Regression and degeneration are as much factors of evolution as advance to more complex organisation, a fact here slurred over by Mr. Balfour, although he appears fully conscious of its weight when he speaks of the Rationalist's morality as a parasitic growth.

Of course Mr. Balfour might tell us that no stage whatever of design is "late" enough for us to understand anything of the whole, a conclusion with which Science might well agree. But he has no business to pick out special stages as "late" or "early" to illustrate the moral tendency he finds in the universe; if he appeals to evolution at all, he must accept the order laid down by competent biologists, or give reasons for differing from their views on the succession of living forms. Mr. Balfour, however, like more than one recent natural theologian, is quite content to make use of natural selection, when it can possibly tell in his favour. It is insufficient, according to him, to account for man's success in reasoning about phenomena. That success demands a Supreme Reason behind it. But having deduced that Reason, it is necessary to show that it is moral, and evolution may be dragged in again to achieve this end. "Preferential action," Mr. Balfour tells us, is the essential sign of moral qualities, and we cannot believe in a moral being who exerts no "preferential action." Here the man of science, Mr. Balfour asserts, is better off than the metaphysician, and triumphantly points to evolution as evidence of the "preferential action" which morality and religion alike compel us to attribute to the deity. The struggle for existence which gives the battle to the strong in limb and the cunning in head may lead, and indeed has led, to a more highly developed race, but to point to this as evidence of the "preferential action" of a deity, without which we could not conceive him as having moral qualities, is perhaps the crowning paralogism of Mr. Balfour's work. "He delighteth not in the strength of the horse; he taketh not pleasure in the legs of a man," may after all be but a pious opinion of the Psalmist, yet it will come nearer to most men's ideas of the preferential action of a deity who maintains "an eternal and absolute distinction between right and wrong," than natural selection.

It is, perhaps, unnecessary to follow Mr. Balfour further.[1] His treatment of absolute beauty is as futile as that of absolute reason or absolute morality. If,

[1] As a matter of fact he deduces—to his own satisfaction—rational grounds for the chief Christian verities. As an example, take the doctrine of the Incarnation. Mr. Balfour tells us that the growth of natural knowledge "has glutted our imaginations with material infinities." As our knowledge of phenomena increases, the Deity retreats "from all realised connection farther and yet farther into the illimitable unknown." By the aid of this Christian doctrine "we are saved from the distorting influence of our own discoveries." In other words, man and his earth as centre of a pre-Copernican notion of the Universe are restored to their old supremacy by the Incarnation. "And the change is not only morally needed, but is philosophically justified." Moral excellency is shown to be infinitely more important to God than material grandeur—"the stability of the heavens is of less importance than the moral growth of a human spirit." If this statement proves anything, which may reasonably be doubted, it shows that there ought to have been a separate incarnation on every one of the starry host—and the number of such may well be myriad—which has passed through the zoic stage; nay, for every pre-Christian nation, and charitably for many post-Christian ones, before the days of newspapers and press-agencies. Meister Eckhart, it is true, did not fear the consequences of such consistency—and taught that the chief occupation of the Father lay in the constant rebirth of the Son. Mr. Balfour is probably hardly prepared to accept this view. It may indeed be philosophical, but it is difficult to reconcile with historic Christianity. Mr. Balfour, notwithstanding his rationalising orthodoxy, is not likely to kick over the traces in order to feel the whip as Eckhart did.

indeed, only those who have studied Mr. Balfour's rationalising about theology can fully appreciate why he classes Rationalism so low, still the reader of this essay may have attained to some appreciation of Mr. Balfour's intellectual grasp. I have shown that his first two theses are completely unsound; I have left his third thesis for another occasion, because the relation of morality to Rationalism is an important problem and cannot be satisfactorily discussed at the end of an already too lengthy paper. It touches, too, the personal probity and social spirit of a group of men who have laboured as hard for the intellectual freedom and moral progress of our generation as many a body of immensely greater numerical strength; and their hope has been, and is, that others may take up and spread their evangel. As Mr. Balfour is not content with the influence of their teaching as exhibited in their lives, it will be necessary to show him that Rationalism has an ethical system, stable because it is bound to no decadent tradition, consistent because it is reasoned, and adequate because it does not fear to face the problems of changing social status and the needs of modern intellectual growth.

My object on the present occasion, however, has been rather to point out the futile character of Mr. Balfour's rationalising, than to compare the true features of Rationalism with his caricature of it. In doing this I have had mainly in view the grave catastrophe which may befall a nation whose leaders not only disparage rational processes, but at the same time can themselves with apparent complacency put forth for public consumption such paralogisms as those in which *The Foundations of Belief* abounds. The simple-minded and devout theologian may return with a sigh of relief to what John and Paul have revealed, but what of the country which has established Mr. Balfour in power? Does the country yet grasp that it is not numbers, nor bone and sinew, but calculating brains, which tell nowadays in the battle of nations? The people which wins in the struggle for existence, is the people whose leaders can think consistently and adequately, and can, in addition, most successfully arouse the intellectual energies of their fellow-countrymen.

We live in an age when neither authority nor tradition can carry a nation internally nor externally very far. It is an age of new problems, of new social and new foreign policies; they demand new methods, and such are the product of brain, and brain only. I do not desire to underestimate the part which habit, custom, and tradition (confusedly classed together under the misleading title of "Authority" by Mr. Balfour) play in the social and political life of a nation; intelligent appreciation of them, I admit, is needed in every statesman. They are forces to be reckoned with, but none the less forces which the leader of brain must control, utilising and readjusting them in the calm light of his own reason. Was the victory to national emotion or to national reason in the Franco-German struggle? Which nation had at the instigation of its leaders planned and thought and reasoned beforehand? Why has Germany proved such a formidable rival to us in trade? Is it not because its traders and manufacturers, in the first place, use their brains? Trade supremacy, maritime supremacy, military supremacy, leadership in arts and letters—all that goes to make a nation great and give it elbow-room and influence on earth—is the product of more adequate brain-power, of more steady and consistent reasoning, and not a little of the success of reasoning is due to the clearer and more efficient ethical code which necessarily accompanies the application of reason rather than precedent to ever-changing social problems.

If we attempt to make a scale of nations in the rank of their weight and influence, we find it practically identical with the scale of their intellectual achievements, and whatever may have been the case in the past, and whatever co-operative factors may still be of high value, it will not, we think, admit for a moment of dispute, that the race of life is now to those who educate and foster thought—to the reasoners among the nations. Mr. Balfour tells us that "none of the influences, reason least of all, by which the history of the race has been moulded, have been productive of unmixed good." If this cannot be at once stamped as sophistry, it is because the word reason is often allowed to cover abuse of reason, bad reasoning, or reasoning from incorrect data. Was it Mr. Balfour's hydra-headed authority, habit-tradition-custom, which proved a better national fulcrum than reason, when Japan met China? And when our modern statesmen term the reason antisocial, will they venture to recommend the policy of China to the inhabitants of Great Britain? Consciously or unconsciously Mr. Balfour teaches this policy philosophically, and preaches it emotionally. His own want of logic, accompanied by no counterbalancing respect for reason as the chief factor of modern national progress must inevitably react on his statescraft, and if his future failure as a politician be not so conspicuous as his present failure as a theologian, it can only be because others supply brain, or chance saves him from the strain of a national crisis. Had the Liberal press but appreciated at its true value Mr. Balfour's *Foundations of Belief*, it is hard to conceive that a doubtful philosopher would have reappeared as a so completely triumphant politician. Liberalism rejoiced in his theology, it will now have a surfeit of his statesmanship.

> Schon hier erwachte in ihm Misstrauen gegen einen Philosophen, der mit *de omnibus dubitandum* begonnen und mit ausschweifender Speculation geendet hatte (Du Bois-Reymond, *Maupertuis*).

VII

WOMAN AND LABOUR[1]

The social revolution which is impending in Europe is chiefly concerned with the future of the workers and the women. It is for this that I hope and wait, and for this I will work with all my powers.—IBSEN.

THERE are two, and we might almost say only two, great problems of modern social life—they are the problem of woman and the problem of labour. Interwoven in a remarkable and hardly yet fully appreciated manner, they are the ground-tones of modern thought, and disguised under many varied forms the chief factors in modern social and political changes. Vaguely expressed under ill-defined terms like the "emancipation of woman" and "socialism," they are regarded, on the one hand, as the Scylla and Charybdis upon one or other of which, according to professors of social and political science, the vessel of the State is sure sooner or later to be wrecked; while, on the other hand, they are for a younger generation the sole motors in life and the only party cries which in the last years of our

---

[1] *Fortnightly Review*, May 1894. It is necessary to draw special attention to this date, as more than one passage from this paper is substantially reproduced without acknowledgment in Mr. H. Dyer's *Evolution of Industry*, published in 1895.

century can arouse enthusiasm, self-sacrifice, and a genuine freemasonry of class and sex.

Fifteen years ago our professors of social science almost condescended to dally with socialism and to coquet with sex; they were for granting women certain university privileges, and ventured to mildly criticise the Manchester school. They had no eyes, however, to see beyond the then tone of trades-unionism, and the apparent apathy of the great bulk of womanhood. They thought it possible to plant their academic chairs on the beach and stem the irresistible tide. Now they are sorrowfully compelled to admit, what was indeed clear enough in 1879,[1] that our country would be among the first to make crucial experiments towards the solution of labour and sex problems; they are now quite certain that the state which makes the first great venture to the new world must be shipwrecked. They do not yet grasp that the channel between Scylla and Charybdis is navigable after all, and leads to calmer social seas. Recognising the necessity of the passage, they find it more congenial to play the prophets of disaster than to take their turn at the oar—nay, so inevitable does disaster seem to them, that if they get a seat at the rowlock they endeavour to hold the boat up rather than pull her steadily along.

Lifeless, hopeless, barren as the views of the older generation of statesmen and writers about the problems of to-day may be, they unluckily find an element of

---

[1] "In England the first attempt at solution will be made—in England where we have hardly yet felt the pangs of labour!"—Article on "Anarchy," written 1880.

justification in much that passes under the names of socialism and emancipation. It is well for us that the social instinct is still strong in our race, but, like other instincts—without training and knowledge—it is apt to be blind to facts, unreasoning in its manifestations, ready with a light heart to handle forces of unknown potency, and to summon spirits from the vasty deep which it may well fail hereafter to exorcise. On the one hand, the worst type of prejudices can only be combated by a ridicule which it is easy to call flippancy.[1] On the other, the essential gravity of our modern problems of sex and labour is not always sufficiently recognised, to say nothing of emphasised. We are caught by a cry of suffering, by an urgent plea of wrongs to be righted, and we become socialists and emancipators without the least knowledge of the history, the complexity, and the delicacy of the social machine. We call upon politicians—possibly as ignorant as we are—to carry out heroic remedies, at the bidding of a class as yet poorly educated, and but half-disciplined. Looked at from this standpoint, whence only the illogical, the sentimental, the semi-hysterical aspects of modern social changes are visible, the future may undoubtedly appear dark—at any rate to the older generation. But these manifestations are only very superficial evidence of a deep undercurrent of social revolution, which is not even voiced, much less controlled by the Social Demo-

---

[1] The best, indeed the only, argument for the man who believes in Jonah and the whale is assuredly a picture of the prophet disporting himself inside the cetacean.

cratic Federation or the Central Society for Women's Suffrage.

Human societies cannot be symbolised as rigid structures of stone and iron; they are plastic forms, yielding and accommodating themselves, if sound, to almost every form of internal and external stress. The rate of change may vary from century to century, from nation to nation, but it is ever continuous, ever developing new phases, ever startling the old and inspiring the young. Social stability can never be synonymous with stagnation; it is, on the contrary, identical with steady and continuous, as distinguished from abrupt change. To grasp the present direction of social growth is the function of the statesman; his duty is to foster that growth, to clear away what may impede it and prevent it from being unduly and unnaturally forced. Here it is that education, political training, and historical knowledge are essential. These are not, and cannot till our society is completely altered, be characteristic of the great mass of electors. The democracy which chooses measures and not men is foredoomed to failure; the hope of democracy is not in the people framing their own social reforms, but in a sound folk-instinct, which in the long run enables the people to distinguish between the charlatan and the statesman. Self-interest and class-prejudice, however cleverly disguised at the hustings, however skilfully manipulated in the House, are recognised at last, and there is a limit to the patience of the people with the political jobber and with the cant of the party politician. The limit may be a wide one. Again and again both labour and woman have been deceived, first by one politician and then by another; first one party makes tools of them, and then the other; but one day Nemesis will come in the form of a strong Independent Labour Party, and an equally strong Independent Woman's Party, and then the political jobbers will disappear right and left.

It may seem strange to bracket Labour and Woman together in this way, and to look to them for the safety of democracy in the future, yet the bonds which unconsciously link them together are very close, and have been close throughout all history. Nor is the reason hard to seek—the status of woman and the status of labour are intimately associated with the manner in which property is held and wealth inherited. During the years of child-bearing and child-rearing, the woman in any but the most primitive stages of civilisation (when ownership is scarcely known [1]) must be dependent upon the owner of property for subsistence. She may, indeed, be the owner herself, or it may be that the group, or the commune, or an individual man is the owner. In all these cases her status will be a different one, but the status of labour will in each case be a different one too. Turn, indeed, to the most primitive Aryan civilisation as evidenced in the fossils of philology and folklore, to the Greeks of the Periclean age, to the Germans of Tacitus, to the feudal civilisation, to the mediæval town in 1500, to the post-Reformation individualism closing the

---

[1] When she could gather fruit, or dig roots, or hunt for shells, or catch fish without danger of infringing the "rights of property." The mediæval privileges of the pregnant woman—her right to game and fish from the lord's preserves, her right to rob orchards and steal from the fields—are in this respect deeply significant.

nunneries, destroying the guilds, and culminating in the commercial epoch of the present century, and the same result will invariably be found. The position of woman is in closest correlation with that of labour, and both vary with the nature of ownership. There has never been a Labour Question without a Woman's Question also. The rape of Lucretia and the death of Virginia are attached in legend not without significance to far-reaching democratic changes.

Even to-day the parallelism is close, however little grasped. Both labour and woman are seeking to throw off the slavery arising from economic dependence; both are demanding—it may be in different spheres—that education shall be free; both desire equality of opportunity, yet have not fully recognised that it can only be rendered possible by unequal legislation; both alike are in danger of underrating their special social functions, of disregarding the national importance of their peculiar activities, because they have been reared under a system which crushed their individualities in order to give a machine-like certainty to their activities. The too great emphasis laid on the relationship to an individual has sadly obscured the social value of the work done. The woman has borne and reared children to her husband; the labourer has hewn coal and hammered metal for the capitalist and the manufacturer. What woman feels in the *first* place that she is bearing a child to the State—a new citizen to assist the common social growth? What artisan thinks of his work doing aught but putting money into his own or his employer's pocket? What miner realises that his labour helps to send our ships over the seas, to make our nation prosperous, and so one of the chief factors in general human progress? Both woman and labour have been forced into narrow grooves, where, no more than pins in a slot, could they grasp the essential value of their functions to the machine as a whole. What wonder if in their common revolt they have occasionally overestimated the claims of individuality and forgotten the real importance of their social activities? What statesman has thought it worth while to appeal to other than stomach and pocket arguments when urging the importance of a Parish Councils Bill, or supporting an Eight Hours Act? What advocate of "woman's rights" has once and for all thrown John Stuart Mill's *Subjection of Women* overboard, and measured woman's as well as man's "rights" by the touchstone of general social efficiency?

What surprise ought we not to feel that the socialistic instinct is so strong as it actually is among all classes, when politicians and publicists almost invariably appeal to the separate interests of individual groups? Why should it appear in the least anomalous that the leaders of the woman's suffrage movement, consciously or unconsciously, are out-and-out individualists? The confusion of thought in this respect is, indeed, widespread. We hear repeatedly the assertion made that woman is only seeking equality of opportunity[1] with man, that she demands only the right to enter any calling or profession, and to succeed or fail according to her capacity.

[1] By "equality of opportunity" we are here to understand equality in all political and social rights, the removal of all sex and class disabilities, whether professional or educational. It does not denote the handicapping of superior natural capacity, be it physical or mental.

On the other hand, we find demands for special treatment and protection, even to the quite serious suggestion that a wife should be legally entitled to the absolute control of half her husband's income. Now this "equality of opportunity" is as fallacious in the case of woman as "freedom of contract" in the case of labour. Freedom of contract is idle, in the first place, while there is not equality of means, and, in the second, while there is not equality of brains. Labour has recognised this, and its recognition of it is, at the same time, its conversion to socialism. The social value of labour is in reality determined less by its numbers than by the physique and general efficiency of its units. It is now a commonplace of all schools that social stability largely depends on the legal protection of labour, on State provision for its efficiency and public regard for its physique. This protection can only be realised by reducing the interest on capital and decreasing the wages of "ability." After all, it is not a very wild nor a very revolutionary assumption that a Stephenson, an Arkwright, or a Baker may be bought at the same price as a Newton or a Darwin. Whatever our personal wishes may be, we may take it indeed as a foregone conclusion that during the next quarter of a century labour will be securely, and on the whole with increased social stability, protected from the crushing individualistic claims of both capital and "ability." It is further to be noted that, with the modern as distinguished from the mediæval socialistic movement, the protection of labour has ceased in the first place to be a moral duty impressed by a Catholic Church more or less efficiently on the individual conscience; it has become a legislative principle based on social expediency.

Hitherto, however, the leaders of the woman's movement do not seem to have appreciated the lessons which may be learned from a study of the kindred labour movement. They have neglected to organise themselves for a single object, independently of party and, if necessary, in opposition to both parties. They have contented themselves with a claim for equality of opportunity, without seeing its futility even if granted. They have not recognised that the very formulation of this claim has hastened the decay of what protection existed in a few remnants of mediæval chivalry. They have not sought security, as labour has done, in a transition from a protection based on the moral conscience of the individual to a protection based on social legislation. They do not understand how social efficiency may depend as much on their special protection as on the special protection of labour. They have scorned what a large class of the male community has not hesitated to accept—nor is the reason far to seek. The leaders of labour have been the product of the trades-union movement; they have voiced the mass of their fellow-workers without standing mentally head and shoulders above them. Their influence has depended principally on the organisations that were behind them, not on their being intellectually superior to those who resisted their claims. Taken altogether, there has been a marvellous solidarity in the labour movement; it has not been the consequence of individuals of special capacity seeking to remove class disabilities because they themselves found their position insupportable. The emancipation of labour has been conducted on lines calculated to benefit the rank and file—not in the interest of the specially endowed; indeed, it may be said to have occasionally sacrificed the latter in order to bring the great mass of labour into line. Similar as are the needs, like as are the general features, of the woman's movement, it has differed very widely in its course from that of labour. It has been very largely the product of highly gifted and cultured women revolting against the conditions under which they had to work. Without much self-conceit they could recognise their superiority, intellectually and morally, to the majority of males who opposed them on the platform or criticised them in the press. They felt conscious that it would be quite possible for them, granted equal educational and professional training, to at least hold their own with the average man. They did not stay to compare the needs, the capacity, the social functions of the *average* woman with those of the average man; they stated what ought to have been an obvious truism — that some women would be more efficient than some men, and therefore they urged, and rightly urged, the social expediency of throwing open all careers to women. Thus arose their watchword, "Equality of opportunity."

Unlike the labour leaders, they were not backed by the masses, the αἱ πολλαί were not behind them. The αἱ πολλαί were not interested in the throwing open of higher education or the professions to women; they already had equal privileges at the Board School—the inspector had his eye on the girl in the street during school hours quite as much as on the boy; while they could obtain the right of following any industry by demonstrating to the capitalist—nearly always an easy matter—that their labour was quantitatively cheaper than that of men. As to the vote, it was hardly yet brought home to their husbands and brothers that trades-union and non-party organisations could make it a thing of value; how then could the women of the people, more listless, more helpless even than the men, learn to appreciate its importance? The energy did not yet exist among them which would have led to organisations for obtaining and manipulating the vote. The preaching of female suffrage has not been a thing of the street corners; it has not been, like the spread of trades-unionism, a product of the workshops and factories. It has been a subject for conventicles in Bayswater drawing-rooms, it has smacked too much of tailor-made gowns, ephemeral novelettes, and somewhat invertebrate members of Parliament.

The leaders of the movement were, as we have remarked, exceptional women, but they were women of one class and with one outlook in life; they fought against what they felt cramped their own individuality, and they did not fully realise the solidarity of their sex. Behind them they had practically women of a single type—cultured women of the middle class, who were restless at the old restrictions, eager for self-development and a more intellectually active life. For a time it seemed as if the chief result of the movement would be to produce, and to some extent find work for, an intellectual proletariat among middle-class women—numerous as compared to the posts which could be found for it, insignificantly small as compared with the bulk of womankind. For such picked women—much above the average of their class, not to say of their sex—the average male was not a subject of overwhelming interest, and matrimony was not a prominent factor of their thoughts. For them "equality of opportunity" seemed to solve the problem of woman's emancipation. With this sort of solution—the increased power of self-realisation in a narrow class of picked women, chiefly unmarried women of the middle class—the movement would have to culminate were equality of opportunity to remain its watchword.

But the remarkable restlessness which so clearly and forcibly expresses its needs in one narrow class of women is by no means confined to that class. It is spread widely and deeply through all the strata of womankind, if it has yet to be consciously formulated as a demand for far-reaching changes in the conditions under which women live and work. The organisation of female labour has only just begun. When comprehensive unions of female shop assistants, of female clerks, and, above all, of female domestic servants have been established, then the woman-question will begin to pass into a new phase, and the demand for special legislation and special protection will entirely replace the cry for equality of opportunity which has marked the earlier stages of the present emancipation movement. Then, perhaps for the first time, we shall realise that woman's emancipation is only possible during a socialistic as distinguished from an individualistic stage of society—we shall learn, what history abundantly demonstrates to its students, that the position of woman rises and falls with that of labour; and that the need of both is neither equality of opportunity nor freedom of contract, but protection.

As freedom of contract is idle when one party owns the means of subsistence, so equality of opportunity is idle when one party has alone to bear a peculiarly heavy part of the social burden. Women who abstain from marriage and have not the sex-impulses strongly developed, women whose potentiality of child-bearing is not a trouble to them, may welcome equality of opportunity and compete with men on equal terms. The woman with strong physique or strong intellect may, under these conditions, excel in any pursuit whatever her average male compeer. But this type of woman cannot become the prevalent type, nor indeed would it tend to social efficiency, if it could. Such women cannot transmit the asexualism which fits them for competition with men to a numerous offspring; they leave the women whose maternal and sexual instincts are strong to be the mothers of the coming generation, and to transmit those instincts to the women of the future. Indeed, it can hardly be doubted that the throwing open of professions and employments of all sorts to women, accompanied as it is at present by a superabundance of women, must lead to a considerable development of the sex-instinct in woman. In the old days, when the proportion of the sexes was more nearly one of equality, and when marriage was practically the one career open to a woman, there was a much smaller selection by sex-instinct. Now, with the many possibilities of independent subsistence, the duty of maternity is not thrust so forcibly upon all women, whether inclined thereto or not, and the result must be a developed sexual instinct in the women of the future. These remarks apply especially to the women of the middle classes, where we are frequently told that the sex-instincts of man and woman are very unequal. A like inequality among the hand-working classes can hardly be asserted by any careful observer. We may be quite certain accordingly that the movement among women which is in progress is unlikely to be accompanied by a decreased sexual instinct in woman.[1] In this respect we may associate the maternal with the sexual instinct, for the fundamental law of inheritance will hardly allow of the one surviving without the other, if society as a whole is to survive.

We may take it, therefore, that the great bulk of women in the future will be as amply endowed with sexual instinct, will be craving as much to be mothers, and be longing as much to be surrounded by child-life as they have ever been in the past. Nor is it well for society that it should be otherwise. To differentiate off what is mentally and physically strong in womanhood as

[1] It is noteworthy that most primitive communities of *socialistic* type are marked by great female license, and the restraint of this license was a chief cause of the survival and superior stability of patriarchal systems. In this respect it is interesting to observe that with our increasing socialistic trend have arisen two quite diverse movements: the one to restrain the sexual freedom of men; the other—of course, less outspoken and manifest, but very active in many quarters—to give greater sexual freedom to women. The social development of the future will largely depend on which of these movements obtains the upper hand, or, at any rate, on how they are harmonised.

a new type—able, indeed, to seize equality of opportunity, but unable to follow instincts which are likely to be as strongly developed in it as in its male competitors, or indeed to reproduce its own selected self—is clearly not to satisfy the legitimate demands of woman, nor to establish a stable and automatically regulated social equilibrium. We do not for a moment underrate the social importance of giving to women with special aptitude and power the freedom of entering any career where their capacity can be of service to society, but this is only an offshoot of the greater problem of woman's emancipation. That problem is summed up in the words: How can woman follow her sexual and maternal instincts?—how can she do freely what she alone can do for society, and yet have full power to control her own special activities, and develop her own individual life; in short, feel herself a free citizen of a free state? The answer to this problem does not lie in "equality of opportunity"; it lies in special protection, in the socialisation of the State. The advanced woman of the near future will be as thorough a socialist as she is now an out-and-out individualist.

A woman of the upper middle classes can take a great part to-day in social and political life, but it is only by hiring others to rear the children whom she cannot hire others to bear for her. The woman doctor or schoolmistress in whom the maternal instinct is strong must be at a disadvantage as compared with their unmarried sisters. This disadvantage can only be compensated by obviously superior ability or by increased exertion. When once the professions now opening to women are fully stocked, the premium on spinsterdom will be immensely increased; the present scarcely recognised opposition of single to married women will be markedly emphasised, and in the struggle of woman against woman the increased activity and exertion demanded from child-bearers must be anti-social in its effects on future generations. Still more will this tell in the struggle of married woman against man, while to a lesser extent the physiological life even of the unmarried woman will handicap her for the contest with man.

We are not here considering the question of professional earnings—the married woman may be quite independent of these—but solely the possibility of her maintaining, during the period of child-bearing, her professional activity and her professional position in competition with unmarried women or with men. It is only in the case of exceptional and picked women that the intellectual worry and ceaseless anxiety of modern professional life, the physical and nervous strain of its many demands, will not be detrimental to the growth of the young life. The restful mental, the moderately active, but not overstrained physical life, which is so essential to many women during pregnancy, is not compatible with the wear and tear of the modern competitive system. Descending in the scale to the hand-worker, the same remarks apply with even more force. The race must degenerate if greater and greater stress be brought to force woman during the years of child-bearing into active and unlimited competition with man. Either a direct premium is placed upon childlessness, upon a crushing out of the maternal instincts on which the stability of society essentially depends, or woman has a double work to do in the world, and she can only do it at the cost of the future generation. Are we then thrust back on the old solution? Is woman's sole field to be the home, and her chief activity maternity? Must she be content for the future with that dependence on the *individual* man which has been her fate in the past? Some may content themselves with fondly imagining this to be the only solution, if they resolutely shut their eyes to every sign of the times, if they try to believe that the great awakening among women of the last twenty-five years has been limited to a small class, and if they content themselves with the idle dogma that the status of woman is an eternal necessity of her nature and not a factor varying with each phase of civilisation.

If, on the other hand, we open our eyes to facts, we must recognise that society is steadily and surely becoming socialistic, that womankind from high to low is gradually perceiving its solidarity, and that women are organising in such a way that they will in the near future become a great power in the State; if, in addition, we note that in all history great changes in the status of woman and in the status of labour have been correlative and often contemporaneous; if, shortly, we throw aside our prejudices and seek merely to understand what is taking place—then assuredly we must admit that the old is passing irrevocably away, and that the woman of the future will have aspirations and, what is more, a power in the State to realise them, which was hardly even dreamt of by her warmest champions a decade ago. It is almost idle to say what we *wish* woman's future to be; the scientific attitude consists in endeavouring merely to trace the changes that are taking place, in sympathising with the difficulties and struggles of our fellow human beings under them, and finally, in trying so to direct, for we cannot possibly check, the revolutionary forces at work that they shall tend to the greater rather than the less stability of the body social.

That history repeats itself is a truth at once of the highest importance, and yet endlessly fallacious in application to details. The use that has been made by certain socialistic writers of the analogy between the present socialistic movement and primitive socialist communities is a striking instance of this kind. The present movement is essentially an outcome of capitalistic methods of production, of large states, and of highly complex municipal, political, and social conditions. It is not, as so often is supposed, a revolt against all these, but simply their evolutionary outcome, the goal towards which they have led us and the end for which they have trained us. Its success must depend on the extent of area, the magnitude of population to which it is applied. Men and women stand now on an entirely different intellectual plane to what they did in the days of primitive socialism. They are no longer the rude creatures of appetite, unconscious of the strong social instinct within themselves; they no longer need to the same extent the old supernatural sanctions to induce them to sacrifice self for class or for society.[1] Selection has developed and early training strengthens a tribal conscience, to which democratic institutions and a free press give ample voice. Man is recognising the biological laws under which he has reached his present state of fitness, and largely conscious now of the forces under which he must live, and of the conditions under which alone he can advance; he is likely in the future to turn the laws of life to his own social profit, much as he has applied and not opposed physical laws in the immediate past. Under such changed conditions the history of the primitive socialist communities can never repeat itself; nay, we are already almost as far beyond even the ideas involved in the communistic socialism of Fourier.

Yet the analogies between primitive socialism and the tendencies of to-day are still suggestive, if they be not pressed into details, and if we merely follow the general results which must inevitably flow from a transfer of the chief means of production from the individual to the State. In such a society the care of the weak, of women during child-bearing, of children and of the aged falls, not on the individual, but on the community at large. The tendencies in a like direction are very obvious to-day; few people, perhaps, realise the large proportion of babies which are brought into the world even now at public expense, or by the aid of

[1] A movement so intense and so widespread as the late coal strike would have needed a religious basis in the Middle Ages. The actions of the individual are now largely controlled by the needs of his class, and it is only one step from this to their control by the needs of society at large. The missing link at present is the conception that all activity, all labour is undertaken for society and not for the individual employer. But this conception will in time be realised.

some form of local or semi-public charity. The compulsory and free education of children, the existing factory legislation concerning them, likely to become still more complete and stringent in the near future; the various local and public provisions for their apprenticeship and technical education; the watchful eye which widely-supported societies of one type or another keep on the action of the individual parent; the growing army of children reared in orphanages and industrial schools—all these mark how strong is the present tendency for society or the State to interfere with the individual in the management and nurture of children. Already the question of old-age and invalid pensions has been seriously raised, partly settled, in Germany; it will be a test political question within the next few years in our own country. Here the essential, the all-pregnant feature of the reform lies in the fact that it once for all recognises that the labourer works for society at large and not for the individual. It elevates his labour, and replaces the false basis of pauperism by an essentially social principle. It is very unlikely that the idea involved in national insurance against old age and illness will be lost sight of when united womanhood begins to formulate its wants and realise its power. Lastly, we may note the provisions already made for the care of the sick at the public expense: besides parochial infirmaries, public asylums, hospitals and dispensaries, there are semi-public charities dealing with increasing numbers of the lower middle class either freely or as "paying patients." It probably would be no exaggeration to affirm that two-thirds of the sick of this country are already treated either in public institutions almost entirely at the public expense, or in institutions, like the London hospitals, whose municipalisation is only a question of time.

We have not mentioned these matters in order to emphasise the growth of socialism in this country—for that we must refer the reader to Mr. Sidney Webb's paper in the *Fabian Essays*—but solely to emphasise the fact that the central feature of modern social evolution is not "equality of opportunity," but legislative protection and State support for those who are temporarily or permanently disabled from protecting or supporting themselves. It limits within healthy bounds the crushing effect of competition within the community itself. It does this by considering the work done by the individual as *pro tanto* work done for the community at large, and renders the community and not the individual responsible for the general welfare of the worker, and for the conditions of his life being such that he can work with the maximum efficiency for the maximum period. In all this, society is acting in its own interests, is increasing its own stability, and placing itself in a better condition to compete with external rivals and to master the opposition of hostile physical nature.[1]

[1] It is scarcely necessary to point out the dangers to which all forms of socialism are liable; how essentially their success depends on the maintenance of high social spirit, on still more stringent regulations and still stronger social feeling against the idler and the waster of public resources than exist at present. Yet more important is the principle that society shall reproduce itself from the best and not from the mentally and physically poorest stock, as is so largely the case now, when the middle classes and the better working classes are marrying later, and, largely owing to the spread of neo-malthusianism, having fewer and fewer children. The limitation of population has indeed begun where it was

Now the tendency of the age in all these respects is extremely unlikely to be lost on womanhood seeking its own salvation. Occupied even more than man is at present in social works and social duties, more often than he undertaking work not for pay but for its social value, woman is hardly likely to miss the great principle that all labour, all activity, has social value, and demands from society at large that recognition and protection which the individual employer cannot or will not give. Still less is woman likely to disregard the part the State has played and is playing in regulating the conditions of labour, so as to make the worker an efficient healthy member of society. Shortly, at the very time she is learning to organise and assert herself, she will perceive that the whole drift of modern socialistic legislation is to protect one class against another, to provide for the individual during disablement, and to ensure that one class or individual shall not profit at the expense of another to such an extent as seriously to injure the stability and efficiency of the social body as a whole. The return for this protection and assistance is simple and obvious: work done to the extent of power and ability for the social advantage.

From the social standpoint, the problem whether woman has the brain or the arm of man is as purely idle as the question whether Jones or Robinson is intellectually or physically the superior. It is obviously

socially undesirable, and the manner in which what we may perhaps term Mr. Booth's "Class B" reproduces itself is one of the chief difficulties of our present transitional social state, and one which will have to be directly faced by the socialism of the future. The population question will be the legacy, and no enviable one, which past individualism hands down to the socialistic future.

the best social policy to get the maximum of efficient work out of *both* Jones and Robinson, and to render their mental and physical surroundings such, that this maximum is easily reached and effectively maintained. For the woman of the hand-working classes there has never been any question of whether she should contribute to the labour of the community or not. She has had, however, to work under conditions which did not get the maximum of efficient work out of her, nor in the least recognise the primary social importance of her maternal activity. On the other hand, the woman of the middle classes has, until quite recent times, been unduly restrained from contributing her quota to the fund of socially valuable labour; she has had unceasingly impressed upon her that her chief function is maternity, but this function has not been regarded as primarily of social value, but associated essentially with her dependence upon an individual. To complete the crushing mental and physical influence of this extreme individualism on the middle-class woman, the phrase "social duties" has been applied to an ultra-social, if not anti-social, form of activity which has been devised as an occupation for her idleness. The reawakening of middle-class woman is now, however, altering all this. Her desire to take part in work of social value is accompanied by economic conditions and a social opinion which convert the desire into a command. At the same time, "equality of opportunity," untempered by special protective legislation, must, under the fierce struggle of the competitive system, reduce her ultimately to a position like that of the women of the hand-working classes, who are far from working under conditions which enable them efficiently to perform double social duties. For the first time in the history of civilisation there is, arising from these causes, a strong feeling among women of the solidarity of their sex; there is a strong desire to organise themselves for the protection of their common interests, and there is a growing possibility of an independent woman's party, which may ultimately become a decisive factor in social progress. There is a union of interest and feeling between women workers with the head, women of ability, and women workers of the hand, women of the people, which has hitherto been almost impossible among men, because "ability" in the latter sex has been chiefly used as a means of obtaining inordinate profit from those pursuing the more physical forms of labour.

Let us endeavour to draw the threads of our argument together. A womankind seeking in all ranks of life to take part in social labour and social activity; a society so economically constituted that it demands labour as a social duty from all its members, but at the same time offers special protection for peculiar disabilities; a generation of women which—to judge from historical experience and the selective processes at present at work—is likely to have increased rather than decreased sexual and maternal instincts; a race having an increasing knowledge of the healthiest physiological life for both sexes, and of the physical and sanitary conditions under which child-bearing can best be undertaken; a race conscious of the vital importance of the problems of heredity, and for which the problem of population, the question of who shall be the parents of its children, will, with the growth of the socialistic tendency, become one of the chief problems of the State; a race regarding its actions and its activities less and less in relation to individuals, and more and more in relation to society and to the State; a religion quietly and unobtrusively burying its god, in order to devote itself to the present welfare of mankind; a religion ready to accept the moral as the social, the immoral as the anti-social, and conveniently reticent as to supernatural dogmas and transcendental ethical codes. In short, an organisation of society turning essentially on capacity for work, on the provision of the best conditions for efficient activity, and on the replacement of individual dependence and personal control by State protection and State regulation. Granted these things, as things of the present or of the near future, things which are independent of our hopes or fears, which we may slightly guide or modify, but can in no manner oppose with success, what course is organised womanhood likely to take amid them? Has not labour already given the clue in its demands for national insurance against old age and for the eight-hours day?

The duty of woman to labour is becoming as clearly recognised as her right to labour; neither one nor the other can be withdrawn now; the door has once been opened, and it cannot again be shut. The home, whether we approve it or not, has ceased for ever to be the sole field of woman's activity. Will woman be content with "equality of opportunity"? We cannot for a moment believe it will be so, if she recognises the power organisation can confer upon her. Equality of opportunity can only help a picked class, and only the picked women of that class, unless they all forego instincts which, taken from every side at once, are as strong in them as in men. Rather the woman of the future will demand such conditions for her labour as shall practically handicap the competition of the unmarried with the married woman, and of man with woman. The justification for this will not be sought in chivalry towards the "weaker"; it will not be looked upon as furthering the interests of one class at the expense of another; it will be simply based upon the recognition that woman's child-bearing activity is essentially part of her contribution to social needs; that it ought to be acknowledged as such by the State; that society at large ought to insist, exactly as in the case of labour, that the conditions under which it is undertaken shall be as favourable as possible, and that *pro tanto* it shall be treated as part of woman's work for society at large.

Once this aspect of child-bearing and rearing becomes general, once maternity is considered essentially as citizen-making in the first place, and not as the accidental result of the private relation to an individual, then the similarity between the woman's movement and the labour movement will be again complete. The demand for the franchise is not a first stage to equality of opportunity, but to legislative protection of women and to State regulation of her labour. Women naturally object to State interference with women's labour at the present stage. Without a voice in the State, they, reasonably or unreasonably, suspect that the cry, "We must protect the child-bearers whether they wish it or not," is called forth, not so much by men's regard for the future generation as by their fear of the market being flooded by the cheaper labour of their wives and daughters.[1] But with the franchise and a wider conception of the social value of maternity, woman will demand, as she can then demand in safety, special protection and special provision for the child-bearer. As in Germany there already are societies for insuring women against the presumably unproductive and penniless condition of spinsters—the very condition in which the society of the future will consider them most capable of providing for their own support—so we may expect in the near future national insurance against motherhood to be as much a feature of woman's political programme as national insurance against old age will soon be a feature of the programme of labour. The provision of such insurance will for the first time allow of efficient regulation of the labour of married women during the child-bearing years—a regulation which will come none too soon to stop the degeneration of physique which is going on in certain classes of the labouring population.[2]

---

[1] If it can be done without detriment to the children, it is much better for both man and woman, as free human beings, that the man should earn twenty shillings and the woman fifteen shillings a week, than that the woman should earn nothing and the man thirty-five shillings for the same piece of work. But if the competition of women means that two women each at fifteen shillings *replace* the man—as is frequently the case—then the male fear of woman's effect on the labour market may be selfish, but it is at the same time perfectly reasonable.

[2] It may even be doubted whether insurance and regulation will not have to go further. The anæmic condition of many women to-day—for example, among domestic servants—is probably due to the hard work they are put to at a critical period of their growth, for instance, in the case of girls who are "general servants" at the age of fifteen.

The idea of a national insurance against motherhood may appear absurd enough at first, but it is hard to see in what else the present woman's movement can end. There is a demand amongst women for self-realisation, for liberty to work and to develop the powers, great or small, with which they may be endowed; there is a revolt against women's lives being devoted to a single activity and to their absolute dependence on a fellow human being. It is a revolt in which labour has preceded woman and is using the franchise to demand special protection and special provision for disablement. So deep have been the feelings aroused in woman's case that more than one advocate of her emancipation has seemed to see woman's freedom in the development of an asexual type, regardless of the fact that such a type could not reproduce itself, and its differentiation from the rest of womanhood would only emphasise the maternal instincts in the woman of the future. Yet this crude standpoint was the not unnatural, if exaggerated, expression of dissent from those who asserted that maternity was the chief function of woman, and her dependence upon the individual man an unchangeable law of nature.

To reconcile maternal activity with the new possibilities of self-development open to women is *par excellence* the woman's problem of the future. It is not one which can be solved by "equality of opportunity," but solely by the recognition of maternity as an essentially social activity, by the institution of some form of national insurance for motherhood,[1] and by the

---

[1] It is perhaps unnecessary to point out that this insurance has nothing to do with the parental responsibility to provide for the maintenance of children.

correlated restriction and regulation of woman's labour. We may be far distant at present from any such solution, but the growing feeling of solidarity among womankind, the gradual but steady organisation of women to give expression to their needs, and the training which even party organisations are giving to women in political methods, can in my opinion only culminate in precisely the same way as the similar movement has done in the case of labour, namely, in the cry for special protection and special provision for the essential conditions of efficient activity.

It is true that a long education both of man and woman will have to be undertaken before woman reaches the standpoint of the Roman matron, and recognises maternity as a social activity. But this education has at least commenced. A study of the more advanced woman's journals, both in this country and in America, shows how deeply thinking women are interested in the problems of heredity and of the parental responsibility for producing and rearing healthy human beings. The population question is essentially a woman's question; the social value of one side of her activity is essentially determined by the need for good citizens. For woman a high birth-rate and a high infant mortality can never be the last word of biological science, its principal recipe for an efficient human society. Sexual rather than natural selection must inevitably be the means by which woman will seek to make her maternal activity of the highest social value. To the most careful sexual selection the woman advocates of woman's emancipation are incessantly urging their sisters. These are indeed the first signs that woman is beginning to realise that maternity is a social activity, which not only demands serious thought on her part, but at the same time gives her special claims on the community at large. The unlimited reproduction of bad stock is not only an injury to the community at large; it is a peculiar injury to woman, in that it lessens the value of maternity, and throws her into competition with man without any claim to special protection or to special provision during the years of child-bearing.

These are the new features of the woman's problem of the near future—the steps which are converting it from the cry of the unmarried for equality of opportunity to the cry of the married for the reconciliation of maternity with the power of self-determination. Labour and woman meet on the same ground and turn to the same remedies. Will they be successful or not? The answer in both cases largely depends on whether the socialistic state of the future can solve the population question: Can it maintain a fair state of social efficiency without a ruthless destruction of individual life, is a low birth-rate compatible with a high standard of individual fitness? That is at once the final problem of woman and the final problem of labour.

VIII

VARIATION IN MAN AND WOMAN

> The method of investigating truth commonly pursued at this time therefore is to be held as erroneous and almost foolish, in which so many inquire what others have said, and omit to ask whether the things themselves be actually so or not.—WILLIAM HARVEY, 1651.

1. *Introductory*

IN a recently-published volume dealing with the secondary sexual characters of man and woman, the following wise sentences occur :—

> A precise knowledge of the actual facts of the life of men and women forbids us to dogmatise rigidly concerning the respective spheres of men and women. It is a matter which experience alone can demonstrate in detail. If this is not exactly the result which we set out to attain, it is still a result of very considerable importance. It lays the axe at the root of many pseudo-scientific superstitions. It clears the ground of much unnecessary verbiage, and fruitless discussion, and enables us to see more clearly the really essential points at issue.[1]

Unfortunately the writer of these very sentences has done much to perpetuate some of the worst of the pseudo-scientific superstitions to which he refers, notably that of the greater variability of the male human being.

[1] H. Ellis, *Man and Woman*, p. 386.

Thus he sums up the data presented in his book with the following paragraph : [1]—

> Yet there are certain general conclusions which have again and again presented themselves, even when we have been occupied in considering very diverse aspects of the physical and psychic phenomena of human life. One of these is the greater variability of the male; this is true for almost the whole of the field we have covered, and it has social and practical consequences of the widest significance. The whole of our human civilisation would have been a different thing, if in early zoological epochs the male had not acquired a greater variational tendency than the female.

Now there are several points to be noticed here. (i.) The greater variability of the male, the conservatism of the type in the female, is assumed as one of the best demonstrated of the author's conclusions; (ii.) it is, or has been, one of the effective causes in determining the drift of the whole of our human civilisation; and finally (iii.), this assumed law is stated to have social and practical consequences of the widest significance.

The object of this essay is to lay the axe to the root of this pseudo-scientific superstition. It will not be necessary to prove that the male is either more or less variable than the female, but merely to show that when the proper statistics are considered and are dealt with scientifically there is no evidence to show a preponderating variability in man.[2] Nor is this a result which

---

[1] H. Ellis, *Man and Woman*, p. 387.

[2] The law of the greater variability of the male was, I believe, first stated by Darwin. It appears as an explanation of what Darwin thought a greater tendency to polydactyly in men, *i.e.* in a greater tendency to a certain abnormality. It may be doubted whether wider statistics on the subject even justify the statement that men are more often polydactyle than women. The passage is only introduced in the second edition of the *Animals and Plants under Domestication* (vol. ii. p. 457), and I do not think the matter is again referred to by

à priori would be unexpected by any one who has thought closely on the problem of evolution by natural selection. According to this theory, the more intense the struggle the less is the variability, the more nearly are individuals forced to approach the type fittest to their surroundings, if they are to survive. This conclusion is amply verified by the variability of civilised races being greater than that of savage races, when both are compared with regard to the same organs. Some, out of the large amount of evidence available on this point, will be given in the sequel. Now the one sure test of the intensity of the struggle for existence is the mortality table rightly studied.[1]

Darwin, or that he gives elsewhere evidence in favour of greater male variability. Darwin's words are as follows:—

Both these facts can be explained on two principles, which seem generally to hold good: firstly, that of two parts the more specialised is the more variable, and the arm is more highly specialised than the leg; and secondly, that male animals are more variable than female.

My statistics do not appear to confirm either of these principles of Darwin. There appears to be no sensible preponderance in variation in arm measurements over leg measurements (see our p. 305), nor of man over woman.

Darwin has been followed by a great variety of lesser authorities, for example:—

It is a universal law of animal life that, owing to sexual selection and other causes, the males of a species vary considerably more than the females.—J. JACOB, *Studies in Jewish Statistics*.

As a general rule in the evolution of the human race, as well as of the lower races, the female is less subject to variation and is more constant to and conservative of the type of the race than the male.—EDWARD CARPENTER, *Woman*.

On the other hand Tennyson, as pointed out to me by Mr. Francis Galton, appears to have held the opposite view:—

> For men at most differ as Heaven and earth,
> But women, worst and best, as Heaven and Hell.
> *Merlin and Vivien.*

[1] The mortality of the artisan classes is greater than that of the middle and upper classes. We find, accordingly, that they are less variable; and, what is more, that their sons and daughters are more closely correlated.

This test shows us that man in civilised communities has a harder battle for life than woman. We should therefore expect that the variability of adult men and women would be relatively more equal among savage races, where the struggle for existence is more nearly identical for both, and alter in an increasing ratio for the women as we pass to civilised communities. Consequently the difference in variability of unselected men and women would have to be considerable, if the balance in favour of man is to be at all large in anthropometric statistics of civilised communities. But the variability of unselected men and women is, in the first place, determined by biparental inheritance. If women are to be more conservative in type than men, they must take more after their mothers than after their fathers, or at least less after their fathers than their brothers do. Common experience would certainly not justify any dogmatic statements on this point.[1] Thus *à priori* we might feel grave doubts as to this assumed law of the greater variability of man, simply on the ground that the general theory of evolution by natural selection combined with heredity does not seem in accordance with it.

General and *à priori* conclusions, however, are

[1] So far as I am aware, the only attempt hitherto made to deal with the problem of relative parental influence is in a memoir on *Regression, Heredity, and Panmixia* (*Phil. Trans.* vol. clxxxvii. p. 253). The statistics of stature, all that were available when that memoir was written, seem to show that both sons and daughters take sensibly more after their fathers than after their mothers, but that daughters inherit less from their parents than sons. On the other hand, mediocre fathers have more frequently sons and exceptional fathers daughters; a result making the ultimate variability of the two sexes very nearly the same.

very liable to be erroneous, and we ought accordingly to trust solely to statistics of actual variability. Now it will be urged that the law of greater variability has been founded on statistics, and surely some weight must be given to these. In order to approach the problem safely, then, we must seek answers to the following questions: (i.) What are the most suitable organs or characteristics for measuring the relative variability of man and woman? (ii.) How is variability to be scientifically measured?

2. *On the Material suitable for testing the Relative Variability of Men and Women*

Our first question really involves a definition of variability, and the definition given may be so vague as to beg offhand the solution of the problem we propose to discuss. If we are to test whether different degrees of variability are secondary sexual characters of human beings, we shall only be arguing in a circle if we test variability by statistics of organs or characteristics which are themselves characteristic of sex. For example, gout and colour-blindness, without being confined to one sex, are peculiarly male diseases; and their frequency can no more be used as an argument for greater variability in man than the prevalency of hysteria or cancer of the breast among women could be used as an argument in the opposite direction. Greater variety of costume must be due to some greater diversity of taste in woman than in man, but this may in itself be as much a secondary sexual character, as possibly greater variety of intellectual productivity in man is. Nor may we use the greater prevalence of idiocy among men and leave on one side the greater frequency of insanity among women. In fact, the whole trend of investigations concerning the relative variability of men and women up to the present seems to be erroneous, for it has been directed by the idea that variability is to be tested by the relative frequency of abnormalities among the sexes. Such frequency is by no means necessarily a measure of that degree of variation from the average which the bulk of either sex enjoys, and yet this is the true field of variation within which natural selection acts, and whence progressive evolution draws its chief materials. The fact is, the investigation of relative variability has hitherto taken the form of a pathological analysis, rather than a statistical inquiry as to normal variation in organs or characteristics not of a secondary sexual character.

The argument that the frequency of pathological variations of a marked character is a measure of what may be termed normal organic variation has been supported by Virchow's statement, that every deviation from the parent type must have its foundation in a pathological accident. Such a statement, however, is really meaningless. When once we have grasped the manner in which a population reproduces itself—by distribution of a fraternity about a regressed mean—we see that the great bulk of normal offspring deviate in various degrees from the parental type, and that the aim or mean of any fraternity of offspring is *not* the parental type at all, but a type lying between the parental type and the race type. Of course it is possible so to widen the conception of "pathological accident" that every individual born is the result of a "pathological accident," but this is not the sense in which the word pathology is used in current medical science.

It may, of course, in many cases be difficult to distinguish between what we have termed normal variation and what a physician would term pathological variation. In fact, the physician's pathological variation is, for the anthropologist, often only an extreme case of normal variation. It is, in fact, the old difficulty of precisely defining what is a "sport" revived under a new form. Statistically, however, the mathematical theory of evolution deals with the pathological variation precisely as the mathematical theory of errors deals with an abnormal set of observations. A physicist in measuring a physical quantity will scarcely record in two experiments precisely the same value. He obtains from a great number of experiments a certain average value or mean, from which individual results deviate more or less. The average of these deviations from the mean he terms the average deviation, and it measures the accuracy of his experimental methods and his powers of observation. Any other deviation which is a fraction or a multiple of the average deviation occurs with a certain frequency, which is large when the fraction is small and very small when the multiple is large. Theoretically it is found convenient to use not the average deviation for our standard, but 1·2533 times it. This quantity is termed the *standard deviation*, and the frequency of any other deviation is known when we know the standard deviation.[1]

If in any sub-group of experiments, or in any repetition of the series on a small scale, the frequency of any deviation is very much greater or less than the value determined from the ascertained standard deviation, then the physicist concludes that this sub-group is abnormal. For example, by throwing 10 coins at once a very great number of times, it has been demonstrated that the frequency of heads, which may be anything from 0 to 10, actually does distribute itself *per* 1024 throws in very close agreement with the following numbers:—

Heads	0	1	2	3	4	5	6	7	8	9	10
Frequency	1	10	45	120	210	252	210	120	45	10	1

Thus the frequency of 9 heads is under 1 *per cent* of the throws. Now suppose in some other series of experiments we find the frequency of this particular throw to be not 1 but 10 *per cent*, say. Then we should class this series of experiments as *abnormal*, and might reasonably conclude that the 10 coins with which they were made were probably "pathological" specimens of the race of coins.

If it can be shown that organic variation has a

[1] The following table gives the frequency F, for a deviation D in a system of which the standard deviation is S:—

D/S.	F/P.	D/S.	F/P.	D/S.	F/P.	D/S.	F/P.
·0	1	·7	·7827	1·4	·3753	2·8	·0198
·1	·9950	·8	·7262	1·6	·2780	3	·0111
·2	·9802	·9	·6670	1·8	·1979	3·2	·0060
·3	·9560	1	·6065	2	·1353	3·4	·0031
·4	·9231	1·1	·5467	2·2	·0889	3·6	·0015
·5	·8825	1·2	·4868	2·4	·0561	3·8	·0007
·6	·8353	1·3	·4286	2·6	·0340	4	·0003

Here unit range of deviation is taken at D, and P is the frequency for unit range at the mean. P is equal to the total number of experiments divided by the root of the product of 6·2832 and S.

distribution of frequency similar to that we have just referred to, then it will be possible to detect "pathological variation" in much the same manner. The fundamental step is to measure the deviations from the mean in as large a general population as possible, and thus to ascertain the frequency of each deviation. This gives us what we may term the law of normal[1] or healthy variation in the population in question. In any special group, or sub-population, in which the frequency of a particular deviation diverges very improbably from that given by the law of normal variation, we may safely conclude that special pathological causes are at work. The elimination of pathological variations from a series may often require very delicate mathematical analysis, often only a certain common sense; but in either case the process is closely akin to that needed in the elimination of anomalous observations by the physicist.[2]

The above remarks may be sufficient to indicate to the reader that it is possible to discriminate between normal and pathological variation, and also that the prevalency of the latter is no necessary test of the extent of the former. What we have to do is to take healthy, normal populations of men and women, and in these populations measure the size of organs which do not appear to be secondary sexual characters, or from which the sexual character can be eliminated by dealing

---

[1] Normal is here used in the sense of the physician and is opposed to pathological, not in the sense in which the mathematician applies the term to a certain type of distribution.

[2] For example, in measuring a population common sense would indicate that we should exclude the halt and the deformed, but given the distribution of frequency we may still have to apply delicate mathematical tests to ascertain whether it is homogeneous, or composed of complete pathological and complete normal variation distributions compounded together.

solely with ratios. We have then to inquire how far the variability in these organs differs in the case of men and women. It is conceivable that pathological variation might be greater and normal variation less in one and the same sex, and this point does not appear to have occurred to those writers who point to a greater pathological variation in man, and then remark that

From an organic standpoint, therefore, men represent the more variable and the more progressive element, women the more stable and conservative element, in evolution.[1]

Such a statement begs one of the most essential and yet difficult problems of the theory of evolution as we approach it to-day. It assumes that progress is the result of the abnormal and pathological variation, which is admittedly infrequent, and not of the small and frequent normal variation. It would suggest that evolution proceeds by leaps and bounds, and not by the gradual selection of ever-present and always frequent slight variations. Now, while it is quite certain that a great deal of evolution must have taken place by the gradual selection of slight normal variations—as, for example, in a continuous change from dolichocephaly to brachycephaly, or in a continuous change from less to greater stature in man—there is, I believe, no well-authenticated case of *natural*, as distinguished from *artificial*, selection having produced a saltatory evolution by means of pathological variation. When we refuse to confine our attention to museum specimens,[2]

[1] H. Ellis, *Man and Woman*, p. 367.
[2] The immense influence of the museum collector and selector is brought to light by comparing the difference in the standard deviations for the same measurement made on skulls of the same race taken from a burial-place and from an anatomical museum.

all the evidence seems to point to a *continuous* series of types, which have successively replaced each other. Even in the case of artificial selection and protection leading to a new species from a sport, it may be reasonably questioned whether this sport was not of the nature of an infrequent normal variation rather than a pathological accident. In short, if organic variation is to be taken as a measure of the tendency to progressive evolution, there are good grounds for believing that this measure must be sought rather in normal organic variation than in any frequency of pathological abnormality.[1] Lastly, we may note that mere frequency of a pathological condition is no true test of variability at all. One sex might be much more subject than the

[1] Even in the treatment of pathological variation great difficulty arises, for we may after all be finding greater frequency in one sex because we are really dealing with a secondary sexual character. Further, such variations are very liable to be hidden by the sufferer of one or other sex even from the medical man. The very inconclusive nature of the evidence adduced in Mr. Ellis's chapter on "The Variational Tendency of Men," has in part led me to publish the present paper. That author deals almost entirely with pathological variation, the one exception on p. 367, where reference is made to stature and brain-weight, is incorrect, for the authors referred to have used no scientific conception of variation in reaching their conclusions. Even in the discussion of the comparative pathological variation of men and women, I cannot find that really scientific methods have been adopted. There has been little, if any, attempt to measure the mean intensity of the pathological feature and the variation about this mean. Statistics of disease are, perhaps, the only materials which are at all copious, or available for calculation, but I do not here find a markedly greater variability of the man. For example, take the case of acquired phthisis, I deduce from Dr. R. E. Thompson's statistics the following values :—

	No.	Mean Age at attack.	Standard Deviation.
Men .	1000	27·255 years	9·46 years
Women .	1000	23·63 ,,	9·16 ,,

The slightly less variability in the age of women is here more than accounted for by the lesser mean age of incidence, which limits their variability on the side of childhood.

other to this condition, and yet really be less variable with regard to it; the less afflicted sex may suffer a much wider range of degrees of intensity, and thus actually have a greater variability. I do not assert that this is so, I merely point out that, in order to prove that men are more variable even in pathological condition than women, we require, in the first place, not statistics of the frequency of the condition in the two sexes, but of its diverse degrees of intensity in the cases where it does occur.

Starting, then, from the principle that the comparative variability of the sexes ought properly to be tested by normal rather than by pathological variation, we may ask : How is it possible to obtain a general population of either sex, and what organs will it be desirable to measure ? We have first to obtain a normal sample of the population as free as possible from pathological abnormalities, and fairly numerous. In many cases the measurement of a large number of individuals can only be undertaken co-operatively and in the face of considerable difficulties. Great numbers of people still have a superstitious objection to being measured ; many others have no regard for science, and seeing no immediate profit to themselves in such measurements, decline in any way to contribute to a statistical collection.[1] In the case of hospitals and museums, where considerable statistical data or materials for measurement accumulate, there is too often a redun-

[1] More than a year ago the author, to test various theories of heredity, started a series of family measurements intended to ultimately include 2000 to 3000 families. Twelve months' urgency on the part of willing helpers has only brought the collection up to between 800 and 900 families !

dancy of pathological specimens, or specimens selected on account of specially extreme variation. Still we cannot neglect hospital returns, as they provide a great deal of the comparatively small amount of material at our disposal. For example, in the matter of brain-weight, the post-mortem room is practically the sole source of information.

Putting on one side measurements on the living and hospital data, perhaps the best source of really normal material is the cemetery or crypt. Death strikes all ages, sexes, and conditions, and the graveyard gives a tolerably fair sample of the general population.[1] It may tend to some extent to give a more aged sample than the hospital, but age here, like pathological condition there, is likely to affect the variability of both sexes equally. In particular the measurement of skulls offers many advantages. They are comparatively easy of definite measurement; they vary markedly with different races; if not in themselves a test of intellectual fitness, they are the seat of the brain, and their variation may be justifiably assumed to be more or less closely correlated with those variations in the brain upon which the progressive evolution of mankind largely depends. Lastly, there already exist large collections of skulls, and a vast series of craniological measurements for a great variety of races. These can be at once used for mathematical calculation, and are more and more available for comparative study as new series are being ever collected and measured. In the statistics given in the

---

[1] A "fair sample" will be a random sample,—one which has not been specially selected, and in which pathological variations will consequently be in a very small minority.

present paper I shall largely, but not entirely, confine myself to skull measurements, and in particular to two characters, capacity and cephalic index.

Some remarks will be proper here as to the nature of my material. It is drawn from a variety of sources, each acknowledged in its place. While considerable diversity exists in the manner in which different scientists have taken cranial measurements, this diversity is of less importance for our present purpose than it is in the case of the comparative study of races. For in every case included in our results the same investigator has measured both sexes, and we are comparing the variability obtained from two series both made in the same manner. Thus while skull capacity has been measured in a great variety of methods, and two observers will differ often widely in using the same method on the same skull, there is no reason for supposing any observer to have had sex-bias in making his measurements; and the relative variability of the sexes may be deduced from them, although it may not be entirely satisfactory to compare, for racial purposes, statistics of English, French, and German skull capacities obtained by different observers and different methods. Much the same remarks apply to the case of the cephalic index. This index may be roughly defined as one hundred times the ratio of the breadth to the length, but the length has been measured somewhat differently by various craniologists. There is the glabello-occipital length adopted by most English and French investigators, there is the ophryo-occipital length of Sir W. H. Flower, and there is the "horizontal" length adopted by the Germans in the so-called *Frankfurter Verständigung*. These differences may affect comparisons based on statistics formed by different scientists, but they do not seem of importance when we test relative sexual variability in the same series.[1] I have confined my craniological statistics almost entirely to capacity and cephalic index,

[1] As a matter of fact, I do not think they sensibly affect the values of the variation constants as calculated from *different* series. I hope, however, shortly to publish the results of measurements made in a variety of ways, and of the same method of measurement applied by different observers, upon a sample series of skulls, in order to show how far degrees of racial variation may be determined from data due to different observers. The following table shows the divergencies in the case of cephalic indices. I have to express my gratitude on the one hand to Mr. A. Martin Leake for the measurements on which these results are based, and on the other hand to my colleague Professor G. D. Thane for permission to publish here and elsewhere in this paper data concerning his splendid Whitechapel collection, before his own measurements and researches are completed.

COMPARISON OF THE ENGLISH AND GERMAN METHODS OF MEASURING THE CEPHALIC INDEX OF SKULLS

Measurements made by A. Martin Leake on 115 skulls taken from excavations at Gower's Walk, Whitechapel, E.C.

(i.) *English Method.*—The callipers were used and the glabello-occipital length taken.
(ii.) *German Method.*—The skull was placed in Prof. Ranke's craniophor, the horizontal plane found, and the horizontal length as laid down in the *Frankfurter Verständigung* ascertained.

The cephalic indices as obtained by the two methods were only identical in the case of six skulls.

Number.	Constant.	English Method.	German Method.
63 Male Skulls	Mean Variation	75·39 3·005	75·30 3·006
53 Female Skulls	Mean Variation	74·68 3·173	75·33 3·043

Thus the English and German methods gave results practically identical for the male skulls, and the German method gave results practically identical for both sexes. The English method, however, appears to have slightly emphasised the dolichocephaly and the variability of the female skulls.

because these are the quantities to which I have, in the first place, applied mathematical treatment. The arithmetic involved has been of a very lengthy and laborious character, and would hardly have got as far as it has already done, had it not been for the hearty assistance of my very zealous helpers, Miss Alice Lee and Mr. G. U. Yule.

One further point must be noticed before we pass to our second question. While in observations made on the living, or in the case of hospital data, the sex can be at once distinguished, the determination of sex from the skull is not of so straightforward a character. In a considerable series of skulls, however, the trained craniologist has not the same difficulty as arises in the case of a single skull. A comparative study will enable him to distinguish a large group of males and a large group of females, with a residue about which he may only have slight, or in some few cases absolute, doubt. All cases of great doubt have been excluded from our data, and where the series was fairly considerable even cases of slight doubt. It is quite possible that occasionally a male or female skull has been really included in the series attributed to the opposite sex, but this will not sensibly affect the maleness or femaleness of the great bulk of either series, the more so, as there is no reason for supposing that errors which may have crept in owing to the judgment of many individual observers have, on the whole, any definite sex-bias. Exception may, of course, be taken to the smallness of some of the series, and very little weight would be due to these individually, but statistics of this kind are not to be had for the mere asking. We must be content with what are available and taken as a collected whole, they suffice to do more than lay the axe at the root of a great pseudo-scientific superstition.

3. *On the Scientific Measure of Variability*

If we agree to confine our attention to normal organic variation, and select stature, weight,[1] brain-weight, skull capacity, cephalic index, etc., as quantities not directly sexual characters, of which we can fairly easily ascertain the normal as distinguished from the pathological variation, we must next inquire, what is the nature of the distribution of variation, and how is it to be scientifically measured? In a previous essay[2] the reader has been introduced in general terms to the theoretical frequency curve. Now it has been found for a great variety of anthropological measurements, that in adult mankind the frequency distribution has a very small skewness, and the mode sensibly coincides with the mean. Accordingly for such measurements the frequency is fully defined by a knowledge of the mean and of the standard deviation.[3] This approach to symmetry when a large series of measurements is dealt

---

[1] Even with regard to variability in the weight of various vital organs, the sex-life may lead to a consequent sexual character in the amount of variation. It is usually stated that cardiac hypertrophy occurs in association with pregnancy, and there may be like hypertrophy in the case of other organs. Even the stature of nulliparous and multiparous women may vary differently. Thus the measurement of organs belonging in part to parous and in part to nulliparous women may lead, owing to this heterogeneity, to a higher value of the variation than occurs in the case of man.

[2] *The Chances of Death*, see p. 15.

[3] It may interest the mathematical reader to know that in all series of less than forty the standard deviation was found by the method of squares from the individual observations without grouping.

with is of such importance that it deserves to be illustrated graphically and arithmetically. I have accordingly selected from data at my disposal one series for stature and one for cephalic index. A curve is obtained by dividing a horizontal line into equal elementary lengths, each of which represents, say, a selected unit of stature or of cephalic index. At the centre of each of these units is set up a line which measures by its length the frequency in the given population of individuals whose stature or ·cephalic index falls within the given unit. If the tops of these lines be joined we obtain a frequency polygon, which represents for us graphically the frequency of each group of individuals whose organs fall within a selected unit of variation from the average or mean organ of the entire population. The shape of this frequency polygon approaches very closely to that of the frequency curve, which gives the distribution of deviations from the mean in a series of physical measurements, or very approximately the frequency of various draws, tosses, or throws in diverse games of chance.[1] The distribution of variation in any population is accordingly defined by a certain theoretical frequency curve fitted to an observation frequency polygon. When the distribution is symmetrical, and mode and mean coincide, this curve can generally be defined by one constant, the standard deviation, which as we have noted is a deviation 1·2533 times the mean deviation. For practical purposes we may say that the entire range of variation of an organ or characteristic lies between nought and three times the standard deviation taken on

[1] See the diagrams on p. 13.

either side of the mean. The standard deviation is in fact a scientific measure of the concentration of the variation of the population about its average or mean.[1] Until either a theoretical frequency distribution has been fitted to the observation frequency polygon, or at least the standard deviation calculated, we are not in a position to make any definite scientific statements with regard to the magnitude and extent of organic variation for a population. A very common error of those who have dealt with the comparative variation of sex is to take the highest and lowest sizes of an organ, and treat their difference as a measure not only of the range, but of the total quantity of variation. The fallacy of this method of dealing with variation will at once appear, if we consider that for the problem of evolution the frequency of large variations is the important point. A population in which 98 per cent differed from the mean stature by less than 2 inches, and 2 per cent differed by 5 inches, would not from the standpoint of evolution be as *effectively* variable as one in which 50 per cent differed by less than 2 inches and 50 per cent differed by more than 2 inches, no individual differing by more than 4 inches from the mean. For the problem of evolution the question is, what is the *bulk* of large variation upon which natural selection can act? The existence of isolated cases of giants or dwarfs is no test of effective variation at all, unless it can be shown that, not the death-rate, but the

---

[1] Considered as the "radius of gyration," it still remains a scientific measure of this variation, if the distribution of frequency be of any character whatever. Hence the conclusions of this paper do not really compel us to assert that Gauss's law of frequency is true of organic variation.

selective death-rate, which is a very different thing, will ultimately leave those isolated cases in a majority. What we really require as a test of effective variation is the degree of concentration of variation about the mean, and this degree is accurately measured by the standard deviation. The range from maximum to minimum size observed is no safe test and often leads to most fallacious conclusions. For example, in the accompanying figure three distributions of frequency about the mean O are given by the continuous line $A\alpha aB$, the dotted line

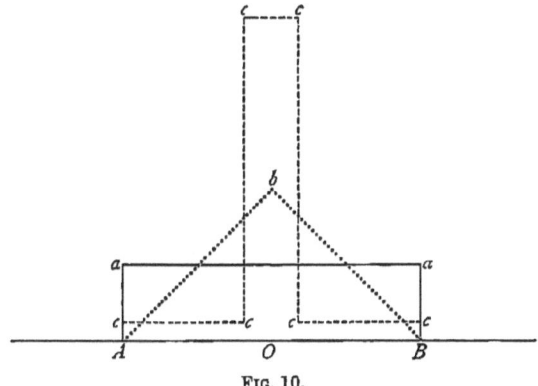

FIG. 10.

AbB, and the dashed line $AcccccB$. All three have the same range AB, but the reader will observe at once that the bulk of large variation is greatest for the continuous line, less for the dotted, and least for the dashed line. The mean deviations of the three series are in fact in the ratio of $\frac{1}{2}$ to $\frac{1}{3}$ to $\frac{1}{8}$ nearly. Clearly the mean deviation is here the correct test of effective variation and not the mere length AB of range. It is this judgment by range and not by mean deviation which is the source of some of the fallacious conclusions drawn by Weisbach, Marshall, and others with regard to sex-variability in stature and brain weight.

If we compare the observation polygon and the theoretical frequency curve in the accompanying diagram, which represents the variation in stature of 25,878 United States recruits,[1] we notice a close accordance. The mean height is here 67·701 inches, and the standard deviation 2·5848 inches. This latter fully suffices to enable the mathematician to construct the theoretical curve, and so to describe the distribution of variation. The following table gives the observed and theoretical frequencies of each height:—

Inches.	Observed.	Calculated.	Inches.	Observed.	Calculated.
78-79	2	1	65-66	3019	2788
77-78	6	3	64-65	1947	1854
76-77	9	12	63-64	1237	1065
75-76	42	42	62-63	526	535
74-75	118	125	61-62	50	224
73-74	343	325	60-61	15	85
72-73	680	703	59-60	10	29
71-72	1485	1350	58-59	6	7
70-71	2075	2221	57-58	7	2
69-70	3133	3126	56-57	3	1
68-69	3631	3818	55-56	1	0
67-68	4054	3980	Below 55	4	1
66-67	3475	3582			

The close accordance between the two series suffices to show that we have really reached a scientific method of treating frequency and estimating variation.

The next diagram gives the distribution of the

[1] J. H. Baxter, *Medical Statistics of the Provost-Marshal-General's Bureau*, vol. i. p. lxxx. 1875.

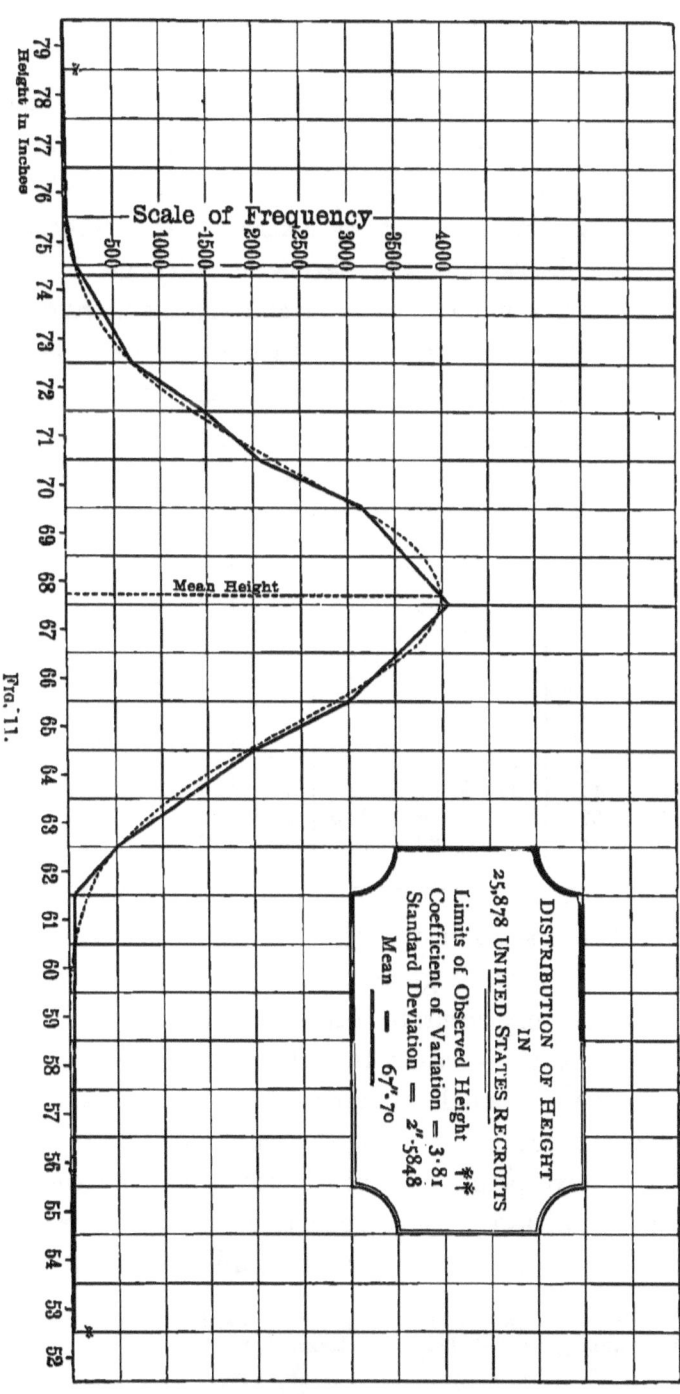

Fig. 11.

cephalic index of 900 modern Bavarian peasant skulls, measured by Professor J. Ranke in the *Beinhaüser* of the Bavarian churchyards.[1] Although much less numerous than the stature statistics, the accordance between observation and theory is very good. The mean cephalic index is 83·0711 and the standard deviation 3·468. From the latter we deduce the following table of observed and calculated frequencies :—

Index.	Number.		Index.	Number.		Index.	Number.	
	Obs.	Calc.		Obs.	Calc.		Obs.	Calc.
70	1	} 1	80	71·5	69·5	90	10	14
71	1		81	82	86	91	8	7·5
72	0	1	82	116	98·5	92	3	3·5
73	2·5	1·5	83	98	103·5	93	1·5	2
74	1·5	3·5	84	107	99·5	94	2	
75	3·5	7·5	85	82	88·5	95	1·5	
76	12·5	13·5	86	74	72	96	0	} 2
77	17	23	87	58	54	97	0	
78	37	35·5	88	34·5	37·5	98	1	
79	55	52·5	89	19	23·5	99	0	

These two special instances must suffice to show that when we measure large normal populations, we are able to obtain a very accurate theoretical measure of the frequency of each variation from the mean, and that the knowledge of a single quantity, the standard deviation, is sufficient to fully describe the variability.

The next point to be considered is how far we may trust a small sample of a general population to give us a fair approximation to the standard deviation, which

---

[1] *Beiträge zur physischen Anthropologie der Bayern*, Bd. i. For a discussion of this frequency, see *Phil. Trans.* vol. clxxxvi. A, p. 388.

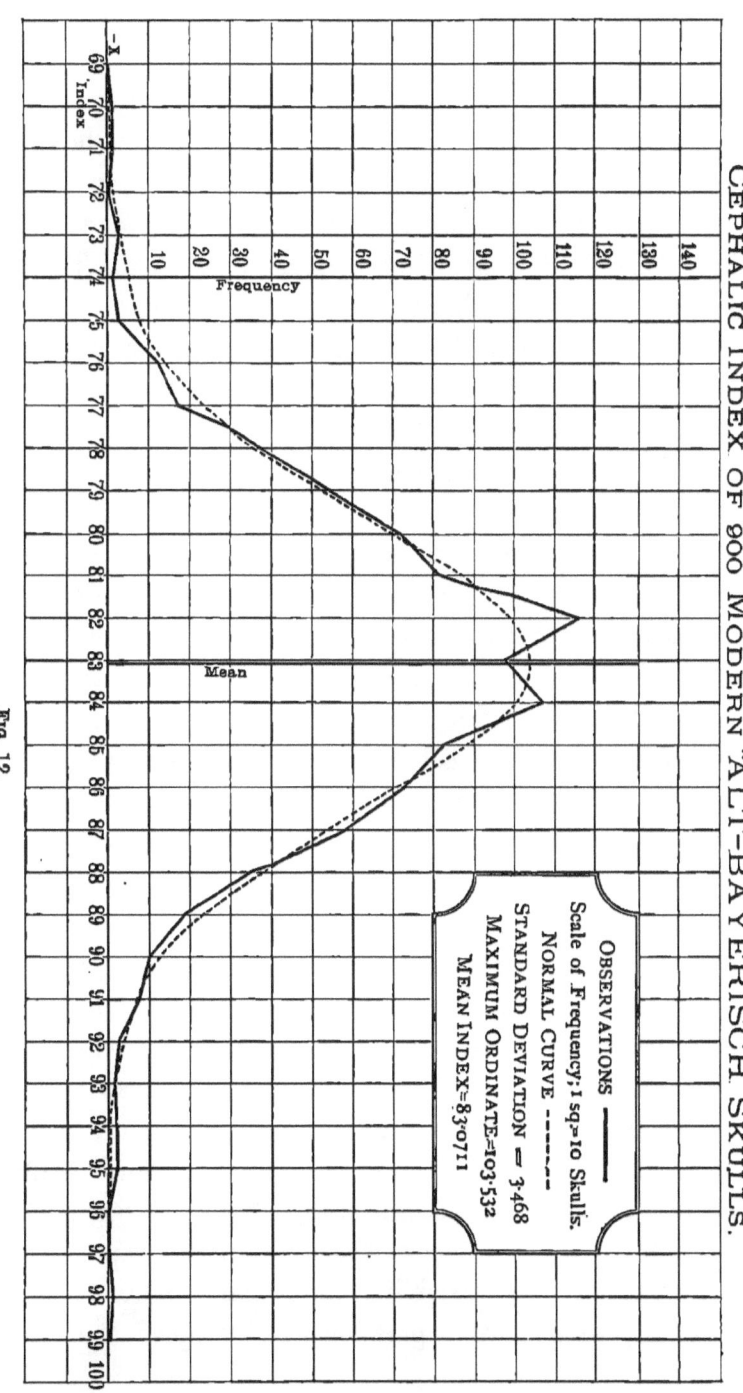

Fig. 12.

would result had we statistics of a great number of individuals at our command. The physicist thinks he has got a very fair approximation to the probable error of his methods if he repeats his experiments twenty or thirty times, and he does not always go as far as that. There can be little doubt that the ideal sample would consist of a thousand or at least several hundred individuals, if the needs of the mathematician could regulate the practical difficulties in the way of the anthropologist and craniologist. But alas! such ideal samples are in most cases practically impossible. The craniologist has often to be satisfied with 20, 30, or 50 skulls of one race and one sex, which are all that are at his command. He is in fact delighted with 50, overjoyed with 100, and the expression of his emotions in the unique case known to me in which more than 1000 are available exceeds all description. With such small series as are indicated above no smooth polygons of frequency like those given for stature and cephalic index in the diagrams can be expected. But a very fair approximation to the standard deviation, upon which the theoretical frequency curve for a large population depends, may be obtained even from small numbers. Thus I divided the male skulls of Professor Flinders Petrie's newly-discovered Egyptian race into two groups corresponding to two different series of excavations, and found for the standard deviation of the first series with 50 skulls $2\cdot82$, while for the second series of 53 skulls it was $2\cdot95$. Thus there is little doubt that $2\cdot8$ to $2\cdot9$ represents pretty closely the variability in cephalic index of the males of the general population who occupied the district near Nagada in Upper Egypt some 5000 years ago.

The general problem of determining a criterion for the amount of error in the standard deviation of a series of observations has already been referred to in the essay on Monte Carlo Roulette.[1] It must suffice here to say that if we took a very great number of samples of 50 to determine the standard deviation of a population, we should make a mean error in its determination of slightly over 6 per cent; a sample of 200 would lead to a mean error of about 3·2 per cent, while one of 30 would give us a mean error of about 8 per cent. Thus, while it would be impossible to base any sweeping conclusion as to relative variability of man and woman on a single small sample of both, we may yet feel quite confident that a large series of small samples will effectively bring out any persistent trend to greater variability in one sex if such actually exists.

As a last point to be considered before passing to the actual statistics, we must consider how *relative* variability is to be measured. So far we have only seen how actual variation round the mean of any organ or characteristic is to be ascertained, but a new problem arises when we have to deal with the relative variation of an organ, the actual size of which is a secondary sexual character. The problem can be well illustrated by considering what would be a practical measurement of the variation in price of a given stock or security. For many purposes of investment, not only magnitude

---

[1] See p. 52. The expression for the mean percentage error is $63{\cdot}7 \times \dfrac{1}{\sqrt{2n}}$, where n is the number of individuals in the sample.

of interest, but, if prompt realisation should be at any time needful, smallness of variation in value may be a recommendation. If now we take any stock, say Great Southern consols, standing at something between 160 and 190 per 100, we shall observe in any stockbroker's share list the current price on a certain day and the maximum and minimum prices reached during the past month. Clearly such a method is just as fallacious when applied to stocks as when applied to brain weights; it tells us extreme values, but nothing whatever about the frequency of their appearance. If, however, we were to tabulate the value of the stock daily, for as long a period as possible,[1] and then calculate its mean value and standard deviation we should have a very close measure of the nature of its variation in price. Suppose the mean value of Great Southern was 175 per £100 and its standard deviation £6, we should have a very fair means of appreciating the probable limit to our loss, if we invested in Great Southern on the condition that at any time realisation might be necessary. Now supposing another stock, the Mid-Anglian, to stand at an average of 114 per £100 and have a standard deviation of £5, we may inquire which is relatively less variable in value. Clearly it would not be instructive to say that their relative variations are measured by their standard deviations of six and five respectively, and this for the very simple reason that the deviation of six is on a much larger amount. £175 invested in Great Southern would clearly have a less average

[1] The period must depend of course on the rapidity of any secular change in the value of the stock or in the value of money. The consideration of such secular changes is all-important in dealing with temporal fluctuations in prices.

fluctuation in value than the same amount in Mid-Anglian. What we require is the *percentage* fluctuation in order to measure the weight of the stock as a stable-valued security. Such a measure of relative variation is the percentage of the standard deviation on the mean. This value has been termed the *coefficient of variation*, and this coefficient serves as a test of relative variability when the variable quantities to be compared are of different magnitudes.[1] Till we have reached some conception of this kind, it seems purely idle to attempt any comparison of the relative variability of different species or indeed of different sexes. Is the leg of a pony or a horse the more variable? If we merely mean by the question: Is the average deviation of the horse's leg from the leg of the mean horse greater than the average deviation of the pony's leg from the leg of the mean pony? there can be practically no doubt about the answer, for the horse may be looked upon roughly as a magnified pony, and all the deviations will then be magnified also. There appears scarcely more sense in such a question than the question of whether there is greater variation in the weights of elephants or in the weights of men, when we deal in both cases with the deviations from the mean weights as absolute weights. There does, however, seem a real biological problem to be answered when we ask: Is the elephant more true to its type than man to his type? and inquire whether, *size*

---

[1] The probable error of a coefficient of variation is $\cdot 6745 \times \frac{1}{\sqrt{3n}}$ of its value, n being the number of measurements in the sample. The use of this result will enable the reader to judge how far the variations of men and women are sensibly different.

for size, one is relatively more or less variable than the other. Are the percentage fluctuations, the coefficients of variation, greater or less in the one or other case?

A fallacious method of answering the problem of the relative variability of the sexes has often been adopted, based upon an investigation of absolute variabilities. The stature of man and his brain weight are both greater than those of women; we should expect, and we find, that the absolute deviations of man for either organ are greater than the corresponding absolute deviations of woman. But to assert that man is therefore more variable than woman seems to be comparable with the statement that the larger is always more variable than the smaller, or that Great Southern, with a standard deviation of six, is more variable than Mid-Anglian with one of five, although the percentage variation is actually less. Some conception of this difficulty has indeed been reached by writers on the brain, who, noticing that on the general average the size of the brain as the size of other organs increases with the size of the body, have taken the weight of the brain relative to stature or to body weight as the basis for sexual comparison. But here again confusion may easily creep in. It does not follow that the sexual factor or ratio in brain weight is the same as that for stature or body weight, and should these factors be different the value of the method is not beyond criticism. It does not appear that the writers who have used these methods have justified them *à priori* by an investigation of the constancy of the sexual factor for the organs under consideration; nor is it at all certain that such an investigation if carried out would have justified their procedure.[1] I hold that the only useful sense in which we can study *relative* variability is by endeavouring to answer the problem: Is one sex closer to its mean, more conservative to its type than the other? and that the only scientific answer to this lies in the magnitudes of the percentage variations of the two sexes for corresponding organs. To accept as an obvious and fundamental fact an absolute sexual difference in the size of organs, and not recognise a corresponding sexual difference in the size of deviations in these organs, appears to me precisely like recognising a difference in absolute weights between man and the elephant, and yet considering absolute deviations in these weights may be directly compared before any attempt has been made to reduce them to a common scale. Accordingly, in order to test the relative variability of the sexes in the case of the *absolute* size of any organ, I shall in the sequel compare their coefficients

[1] The following values of the sexual factor for various organs have been calculated from statistics published by Ranke, Bischoff, Boyd, Manouvrier, and others. The body weights have been taken for adults under 50, although weight varies much with age, because the brain weights are for adults in general. In each case the results are based on series of several hundred individual measurements.

SEXUAL RATIOS.

Organ.	English.	German (Bavarian).	French.
Stature . . .	1·081 (Pearson)	1·078 (Bischoff)	1·069 (Manouvrier)
Brain Weight .	1·120 (Boyd)	1·117 (Bischoff)	1·125 (Parchappe) (Manouvrier)
Skull Capacity .	1·179 (Pearson)	1·126 (Ranke)	1·164 (Broca's Registers)
Body Weight .	1·170 (B. A.)	1·197 (Bischoff)	1·157 (Quetelet)

Thus for three different races the sexual ratios for brain weights lie between those for stature and body weights, and the factor of reduction requisite to reduce a male brain or skull capacity to its female equivalent is by no means identical with the factors required to reduce male stature or body weight to their emale equivalents.

of variation. Such coefficients of variation are I believe the true criterion for relative variability in both sex and race.[1] At any rate, anthropologists and brain students have now rejected absolute deviations as tests of relative variability in sex. In place thereof they have taken tests which assume the sexual factor to be the same for different organs, an assumption not justified nor probably capable of justification; the coefficient of variation avoids this difficulty, and seems in and for itself far more satisfactory than any measure hitherto proposed.

4. *On the Cephalic Index as a Test of Variability*

At the same time it is very unlikely that the sexual factor changes considerably in the case of two nearly allied organic measurements, and while it does not seem to me satisfactory to test the variability of the ratio of brain weight to stature,[2] I think far less objection can be raised in the case of the ratio of two measurements of like type[3] made on the same organ. For example, the ratio of the length to the breadth of the skull, or the cephalic index.[4] This ratio, or index, possesses the

---

[1] Their value for racial investigations I hope to return to in another paper.

[2] Whether women or men are the more variable for the ratio brain weight to stature is, I think, quite undetermined, for the considerations of the late Professor Marshall (*Journal of Anatomy and Physiology*, vol. xxvi. p. 445, 1892) are not based on any adequate conception of variation, but suffer under the kind of fallacy I have noted on p. 284.

[3] For example, two lengths, two volumes, or two weights, but not a weight and a length, etc.

[4] Thus while the sexual factor varies from 1·16 to 1·07, or about 9 per cent, if we pass from the brain weight to the stature of Parisians, it only varies from 1·05 to 1·07, or about two per cent, if we pass from maximum length to breadth of skull in the same people. The latter ratios are based on statistics kindly extracted for me from the MS. registers of the late M. Broca by M. Manouvrier. The ratio of the mean skull heights (basio-bregmatic diameters) for the same

additional advantage of only differing very slightly in the two sexes,—evidence, *pro tanto*, for what is also directly demonstrable, that the sexual factors for length and breadth of skull are nearly equal. Accordingly, in this case the relative variability can at once be tested by a direct comparison of standard deviations, and we do not need to consider the coefficients of variation. It is on account of this advantage that the cephalic index has been largely used in the statistics which follow. But there are other advantages associated with the cephalic index which ought to be noticed. It is not only a quantity which is capable of being determined with a high degree of accuracy, a much higher degree than the capacity for instance, but it appears to be a quantity closely associated with degrees of civilisation and capacity for racial survival in the struggle for existence. It is a measure of round-headedness, and in a certain rough sort of way round-headedness gives the maximum of skull capacity for the same amount of material.

The accompanying figure places before the reader typical long and round heads, the cephalic index of the *dolichocephalic* skull being 70, and of the *brachycephalic* skull 85.

series of male and female skulls is 1·055. Or, we see a fair amount of constancy for the sexual ratio of measurements of the same type on the same organ. If we desired to form an index independent of this sexual ratio for skull capacity or brain weight, it would seem more correct to divide these measurements by something of the nature of a volume rather than by a linear quantity like the stature. If we take the cube of the stature, the sexual factor=1·22, if we take the product of the three chief skull diameters, the sexual factor=1·185, both larger than the factors for brain weight and skull capacity in the same people by 3 to 6 per cent. Such an index, therefore, does not, *à priori*, promise as good results as the cephalic index, if used as a test of comparative sex-variability.

Now, although we cannot demonstrate that in any case an intra-group struggle has gone on in which the brachycephalic individuals have been the successful variation;[1] although we cannot show in any particular race brachycephaly replacing dolichocephaly — for we find skulls of both types in the earliest burial mounds

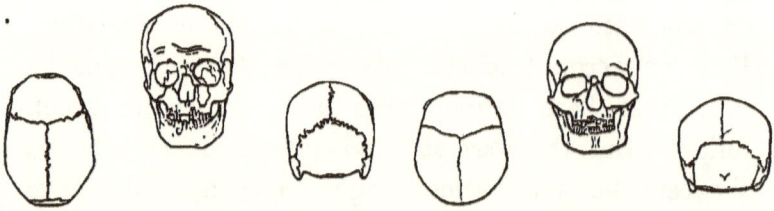

Typical Dolichocephalic Skull.   Typical Brachycephalic Skull.

FIG. 13.

—still we may state generally, although not without duly noticing exceptions, that on the whole the extra-group struggle for existence does seem to have gone in favour of the brachycephalic races. In most continents we find the mainland occupied by such races, while its promontories, outlying borders and islands, are occupied by dolichocephalic races, apparently driven out before victorious brachycephaly. In larger parts of Germany now preponderatingly brachycephalic, the old graves of more than a thousand years ago show a mixture of two races, the dolichocephalic, however, being to the brachycephalic as four to one. Various authors have endeavoured to show that town populations are more brachycephalic than country populations. It would seem that in general — not, however, without excep-

[1] The attempt of O. Ammon to demonstrate it for the Germans appears to me, for reasons given elsewhere, to be a failure.

tions—the higher the caste in India the greater the cephalic index,[1] and a class distinction of the same kind can possibly be noted in European countries.[2] The following table, however, taken from statistics of various observers, but with means and standard deviations calculated for this paper, will bring out one or two important points. The races, so far as cephalic index goes, were selected at random, and solely because a sufficiently large series of skulls were available. Many of the results usually cited are based on even smaller series, and are quite untrustworthy :—

[1] For example, in the head-indices tabulated by Risley I find Brahmans, 78·86; Mahomedans of Eastern Bengal, 77·775; Sonthals of Western Bengal, 76·17; Lahore Chuhras, 73·31. Further, the Chuhras are the most, and the Brahmans the least, conservative of their type, *i.e.* on the whole the higher castes have the more variability.

[2] Whitechapel skulls—it is true some 200 years old—give a cephalic index some two or three points lower than that of the middle classes of to-day. Over 200 years ago the poorer classes, however, congregated in Whitechapel.

[TABLE

TABLE OF CEPHALIC INDEX, MEAN AND STANDARD DEVIATION OF MALES

Race.	Number	Mean.	Standard Deviation.
Native Peruvians (1)	47	89·15	8·25
Mediæval Jews	12	84·74	4·35
Bavarian Peasants	100	83·41	3·58
,, Townsfolk (2)	56	83·39	5·42
"Alt-Bayerisch" Peasants	900	83·07	3·47
Baden Recruits (3)	6748	81·15	3·63
Ancient British (Round Barrow)	25	80·92	3·83
Modern and Mediæval Jews	28	80·59	5·07
Andamanese (4)	12	80·56	2·63
French Peasants (5)	56	79·79	3·84
Parisians (West End)	77	79·53	3·27
,, (City)	67	79·25	4·46
Chinese	82	78·96	4·84
Ancient Scandinavians (6)	20	78·90	3·51
,, Swiss (7)	62	78·89	6·36
Etruscans	84	78·53	3·31
Ancient Gauls (8)	36	78·36	4·44
,, Swedes	35	77·86	3·97
,, Friesians	83	77·75	3·57
English, Upper Classes (9)	1000	77·70	3·03
Ancient Scandinavians (6)	43	77·51	3·35
Romans	36	77·31	3·41
Ancient Britons (10)	114	77·30	5·51
Brahmans of Bengal (11)	100	76·86	3·65
Aino	87	76·50	2·41
Mahomedans of Bengal (11)	100	75·77	3·37
Egyptian Mummies	336	75·08	3·35
Anglo-Saxons	35	75·00	3·14
Whitechapel English	107	74·73	3·31
Sonthals (11)	100	74·17	3·50
Negroes	54	73·28	2·77
Libyans (?)	89	73·16	2·88
Ancient British (Long Barrow)	60	71·77	3·89
Bushmen and Hottentots (12)	54	70·91	4·66
Panjab Outcaste Tribes	79	70·66	2·98
Australians	29	70·34	2·99
Fijians	6(!)	65·86	2·14

Remarks.—(1) The cephalic index of some of these Peruvians exceeded 100, and the high value of the mean is undoubtedly due to artificial deformation of the skull, a practice known to have been in vogue among this people. The immense amount of variation is also due to the same source. Hence the Peruvians must be excluded from any general argument based on a consideration of this table.

(2) These are skulls of the Munich town population, the great variability as compared with the peasant skulls, even when collected from a considerable range of churchyards, as in the case of the "Alt-Bayerisch" peasants, is due not only to the mixed character of a town population, but to the fact that the skulls are a collection formed for an anatomical museum.

VARIATION IN MAN AND WOMAN

(3) The cephalic index has been deduced by subtracting two units from the head-index, and therefore is only an approximation to the true value.

(4) The skulls here are far too few in number to give trustworthy results, as may be readily tested by taking 12 skulls at random out of a larger series of 100, and noting the differences of means and variation-constants. It would also be interesting to know how far skull deformation is fashionable.

(5) Skulls of captive French soldiers who died at Munich during the Franco-German war. The soldiers belonged to a regiment recruited among the peasantry.

(6) The first series of Ancient Scandinavians was from the chambered long barrows in the islands of Falster and Moen, the second series was a stone-age series measured by Virchow in Copenhagen, *Die altnordischen Schädel zu Kopenhagen.*

(7) Taken from His and Rutimeyer, *Crania Helvetica*, but the series involves at least three distinct races, one of which was very brachycephalic and one very dolichocephalic. This mixture accounts for the high value of the variation.

(8) Probably a mixture.

(9) From the head-index of Cambridge students.

(10) Ancient Britons and Romano-Britons, again a mixture.

(11) Deduced from the head-index measured on the living subject.

(12) Most certainly a mixture. The data were drawn from a variety of sources, and in one or two catalogues the skulls were simply grouped together as Bushmen and Hottentots.

Now let us divide this table into two arbitrary and approximately equal portions, say below the second group of Ancient Scandinavians, since 77·5 may be taken as midway between the beginnings of the brachycephalic (80 and upwards) and dolichocephalic (75 and under) populations. In this case we find that the following general conclusions may be drawn:—

(1) *The dominating and most highly-civilised peoples of the world, together with the races from which they have sprung, fall into the brachycephalic portion of the table.*

The rule is not without exceptions and important exceptions. If we exclude the Peruvians as having artificially deformed skulls, the Andamanese still form a noteworthy exception on the one side, and the Anglo-

Saxons and Whitechapel English on the other. How far, noting their wide difference from the Friesians, these early Anglo-Saxons had a mixture of Ancient Long Barrow British among them, a very dolichocephalic race, is, indeed, a moot question. The Whitechapel English will still, however, remain a striking anomaly.

(2) *The more highly-civilised races, besides being more brachycephalic, are the more variable.*

Here, again, there are individual exceptions, but if we take the mean-value of the standard deviations of the first portion of the table (omitting the Peruvians as anomalous and the Ancient Swiss as undoubtedly mixed), we find its value to be 3·87, as against the 3·49 of the second portion of the table.

Accordingly it appears reasonable to conclude—with all due reservations—that brachycephaly and greater variability are characteristics of the races which have been successful in the struggle for existence, and at the present time are the dominant races of earth. While, therefore, no stress must be laid on instances occurring in individual races, it does seem to me that if it can be shown that one sex is on the whole more brachycephalic than the other, or one sex is more variable than the other, then there might, at first sight, be some scientific ground for speaking of the inferiority of that sex. At the same time the greater variability of the more dominant and civilised peoples admits of being interpreted as a result of the lesser severity of the struggle for existence among them. Thus greater variability would be an effect not a cause of the higher state of civilisation, and with due regard to the facts as to relative variability in men and women as we pass from the lower to the higher races, this is how I should be inclined to interpret it.

Having now discussed how variation is to be scientifically measured, and what is the general significance of brachycephaly and variation in the cephalic index, I will pass to those statistics of sex-variation which, with the help of my indefatigable assistants, I have up to the present calculated out.

5. *Statistics of the Relative Variability of the Sexes*

In considering the statistics below, I would ask the reader to remember the following points :—

(*a*) The relative weight to be given to a series depends upon its extent. A series of 900 ought to carry three times as much weight with the reader as one of 100; relative weights being in fact as the square roots of the numbers of individuals included.

(*b*) Very little stress must be laid on individual anomalies or exceptions, especially in small series, or series very far from homogeneous. It is the general trend of the statistics as a whole to which attention should be directed.

(*c*) There has been no attempt whatever to select statistics more or less favourable to one sex, but so far as sex is concerned, they were taken entirely at random.

(*d*) Whenever an absolute measurement is made, the test of the relative degree of variability is the size of the *coefficient of variation*. When an index or ratio has been measured, the test is to be sought in the greater or lesser value of the *standard deviation*.

My material will be dealt with in the following order :—

A. *Body measurements*—(*a*) Stature and Span, (*b*) Long Bones, (*c*) Weight, (*d*) Chest Girth, (*e*) General Anthropometric Data of Physique, (*f*) Vital Organs. B. *Head measurements*—(*a*) Brain-Weight, (*b*) Facial Measurements, (*c*) Skull Capacity, (*d*) Cephalic Index. The bulk of my material falls into B (*c*) and (*d*), which are the skull measurements to which I have chiefly paid attention.

A (*a*). *Stature and Span*

English.—The following statistics cover 1000 cases of heights of men and women taken out of the Family Measurement Data I have collected for the problem of heredity. All were adults under sixty-five years.

	No.	Mean.	Standard Deviation.	Coefficient of Variation.
Men . . .	1000	172·81 cms.	7·04 cms.	4·07
Women . .	1000	159·90 ,,	6·44 ,,	4·03

We conclude accordingly that English women so far as stature goes are slightly less variable than English men. Mr. Galton's stature statistics (see p. 311) make them, however, slightly more variable.

German.—The following statistics are reduced from

returns for Bavarian men and women published by Bischoff.[1]

	No.	Mean.	Standard Deviation.	Coefficient of Variation.
Men . . .	390	165·93 cms.	6·68 cms.	4·02
Women . .	266	153·85 ,,	6·55 ,,	4·26

The stature of German women is thus more variable than that of German men.

French.—The following data are based on statistics given in the *Mémoires de la Société d'Anthropologie de Paris*, 1888, t. iii.

	No.	Mean.	Standard Deviation.	Coefficient of Variation.
Men . .	284	166·8 cms.	6·47 cms.	3·88
Women	135	156·1 ,,	6·79 ,,	4·35

Thus French women are very sensibly, both absolutely and relatively, more variable in stature than French men.

American Children.—The following results are based upon details published by Porter in his *Growth of Saint Louis Children*. Unfortunately he does not give the raw material, and the standard deviations had to be calculated from results given by him, and obtained by a method which I do not consider wholly satisfactory.

[1] *Das Hirngewicht des Menschen*, Bonn, 1880.

	Age.	No.	Mean.	Standard Deviation.	Coefficient of Variation.
Boys	6	709	108·94 cms.	5·041 cms.	4·63
Girls	6	780	107·67 ,,	5·070 ,,	4·71
Boys	7	1850	114·03 cms.	5·352 cms.	4·69
Girls	7	1791	112·95 ,,	5·560 ,,	4·92
Boys	8	2223	119·13 cms.	5·767 cms.	4·85
Girls	8	2193	118·36 ,,	5·486 ,,	4·64
Boys	9	2205	124·35 cms.	5·560 cms.	4·50
Girls	9	2122	123·67 ,,	5·678 ,,	4·59
Boys	10	2087	128·87 cms.	5·901 cms.	4·58
Girls	10	2053	128·43 ,,	6·019 ,,	4·69

For the next three years the girls have a greater variation than the boys, but we exclude these from our consideration, because in the three years preceding puberty girls develop with great rapidity and so exhibit greater variation. Similarly in the years fifteen, sixteen, and seventeen boys exhibit greater variation, owing to the rapidity of growth in the years just preceding puberty. The difference of the ages of puberty in boys and girls renders it in fact impossible to make any comparison from about the age of ten to an adult age. Considering, however, the years from six to ten, we see that in four years out of five girls are more variable than boys with regard to stature, and we may very well question whether the greater variability of boys in the eighth year is not anomalous,—an exception peculiar to these statistics. Thus generally in regard to stature we conclude that woman is more variable than man. There is not, however, anything like that preponderating variation in woman which has sometimes been claimed for man; it is, perhaps, nothing more than might be reasonably accounted for by a slightly less intense struggle for existence.

Indeed stature suggests a very difficult problem for those who claim a preponderating variability for man, and in doing so would propose to measure "effective" variation[1] by absolute and not percentage variation. Let us admit for the sake of argument that the absolute variation of man is greater, and that this absolute variation is a measure of effective variation, then we ought to find in the space of several thousand years a continuous change in the sexual ratios. The more effectively variable male will have been more progressively changed than the less variable female. No such change in the sexual ratios can, however, be definitely demonstrated,—at least in the matter of stature. The means of both sexes have altered considerably, but the sexual ratio has remained curiously constant. This is hardly consistent with a preponderating absolute variation in man being the measure of his capacity for progress. It is quite consistent with the small deviations from equality which are characteristic of the male and female coefficients of variation. If the coefficient of variation be the true measure of effective variation, then we are in a better position to grasp why the sexual ratios for stature have remained so persistently constant.

Take, for example, the case of neolithic man. M.

---

[1] By "effective" variation, I understand that measure of variability which is significant of capacity for progressive change of type.

Manouvrier has reconstructed the stature of neolithic man from the measurement of bones found in the *Cave aux Fées* at Brueil, Seine-et-Oise. The discussion of his method of reconstruction will be found in the *Mémoires de la Société d'Anthropologie de Paris*, t. iv.[1] His measurements of the *Cave aux Fées* bones will be found in a memoir entitled, "Étude des crânes et ossements humains recueillis dans la Sépulture néolithique," published in the *Mémoires de la Société des Sciences Naturelles . . . de la Creuse*, t. iii. (1894). He compares the Brueil bones with others found at Mureaux, and they give these results:—

		Number of Bones of Diverse Individuals.	Mean Stature.	Sexual Ratio.
Brueil	Men	43	161·2 cms.	1·075
	Women	22	150·0 „	
Mureaux	Men	49	163·8 „	1·062
	Women	22	154·3 „	

The mean of the two gives a sexual ratio, 1·0685, sensibly identical with the modern French, 1·069. The modern Frenchman may not have been evolved by natural selection from neolithic man, but the constancy of the local value for the sexual ratio for stature, notwithstanding change of means, for, perhaps, 4000 years, is certainly not an argument in favour of absolute variation as a test of effective variation.

Closely allied to stature is span. The following

[1] I hope shortly to publish a paper on the reconstruction of stature from the measurement of long bones, as the point is one of great interest for the problem of secular evolution. I am not satisfied that the methods of reconstruction hitherto adopted give the best, or, in many cases, even good, results.

results are taken from my Family Measurement cards, and are for adults under sixty-five years of age:—

ENGLISH

	No.	Mean.	Standard Deviation.	Coefficient of Variation.
Men	1000	69"·09	3"·172	4·591
Women	1000	62"·20	2"·881	4·632

The women are thus very slightly more variable in span than the men. This result is in agreement with Mr. Galton's measurements (see the table, p. 311), and further with Mr. Porter's observations on American boys and girls.

A (b). *Long Bones, etc.*

I had hoped that it might be possible to obtain a fairly accurate conception of the relative variability of the long bones in man and woman from the 400 skeletons of the Libyan race of 4000 B.C., brought to this country by Professor Flinders Petrie. Unfortunately, in many cases there were several interments in one grave, and the identification of the bones with the skulls and with each other has often proved impossible. A fairly accurate determination of sex chiefly from the skulls could only be made in something over 100 cases. The whole of the measurements on these bones have been undertaken by Mr. E. Warren, Demonstrator in Comparative Anatomy, University College, and will, no doubt, be ultimately published by him. I have to express my gratitude to him for the numbers on which the following results are based:—

Left Femur (Libyan)

	No.	Mean.	Standard Deviation.	Coefficient of Variation.
Men	56	45·114 cms.	2·277 cms.	5·05
Women	55	42·536 „	1·899 „	4·46

Left Tibia (Libyan)

	No.	Mean.	Standard Deviation.	Coefficient of Variation.
Men	65	36·054 cms.	2·199 cms.	6·10
Women	71	33·832 „	1·674 „	4·94

Left Humerus (Libyan)

	No.	Mean.	Standard Deviation.	Coefficient of Variation.
Men	36	31·475 cms.	1·639 cms.	5·21
Women	51	29·424 „	1·504 „	5·11

Right Radius (Libyan)

	No.	Mean.	Standard Deviation.	Coefficient of Variation.
Men	23	25·406 cms.	1·189 cms.	4·68
Women	29	23·230 „	1·225 „	5·27

To judge by these returns, man is more variable than woman in both femur and tibia, but less so in the radius; there is no sensible difference in the humerus. The frequency polygons, however, while fairly smooth for the long bones of the women, present a very double humped character in the case of the men, and suggest that the male Libyans are really mixed. To test the above conclusions, I accordingly searched for other material, which is, however, very sparse. I found data for the femur of neolithic man in a paper by J. Rahon, "La taille préhistorique" (*Mémoires de la Société d'Anthropologie de Paris*, t. iv. p. 452, 1893). This gives:—

FEMUR (NEOLITHIC MAN)

	No.	Mean.	Standard Deviation.	Coefficient of Variation.
Men . .	110	44·327 cms.	2·098 cms.	4·73
Women . .	45	40·156 ,,	1·813 ,,	4·51

The only other data which I have been able to draw from M. Rahon's memoir—which gives, as a rule, only the means and the range for, it is true, a great series of prehistoric long bones—are the following:—

FEMUR (ANCIENT INHABITANTS OF THE CANARIES)

	No.	Mean.	Standard Deviation.	Coefficient of Variation.
Men .	163	45·006 cms.	2·088 cms.	4·64
Women .	124	41·155 ,,	1·937 ,,	4·71

A much more valuable series of long-bone measurements, in which the sex was definitely known, is that due to Dr. E. Rollet, in a paper entitled "De la mensuration des os longs des membres," published in the *Bibliothèque d'Anthropologie Criminelle* (Lyons, 1889). The measurements were made on modern French subjects in the Anatomical Laboratory at Lyons. From these measurements the following results have been calculated :—

Left Femur (French)

	No.	Mean.	Standard Deviation.	Coefficient of Variation.
Men . . .	49	45·371 cms.	2·293 cms.	5·05
Women . .	50	42·342 ,,	2·135 ,,	5·04

Left Tibia (French)

	No.	Mean.	Standard Deviation.	Coefficient of Variation.
Men . . .	46	36·548 cms.	1·818 cms.	4·975
Women . .	48	33·381 ,,	1·791 ,,	5·365

Left Humerus (French)

	No.	Mean.	Standard Deviation.	Coefficient of Variation.
Men . . .	48	32·642 cms.	1·5997 cms.	4·89
Women . .	48	29·246 ,,	1·641 ,,	5·61

Right Radius (French)

	No.	Mean.	Standard Deviation.	Coefficient of Variation.
Men . . .	48	24·398 cms.	1·189 cms.	4·87
Women . .	49	21·490 ,,	1·125 ,,	5·23

Another good series of long-bone measurements are given in the *Mittheilungen aus der medicinischen Facultät der k. Japanischen Universität*, Bd. ii. Tokio, 1894. They refer to that extremely interesting race the Aino.

Right Femur (Aino)

	No.	Mean.	Standard Deviation.	Coefficient of Variation.
Men .	44	40·770 cms.	1·899 cms.	4·65
Women .	25	38·204 ,,	1·598 ,,	4·18

Right Tibia (Aino)

	No.	Mean.	Standard Deviation.	Coefficient of Variation.
Men .	38	33·89 cms.	1·669 cms.	4·92
Women .	22	31·86 ,,	1·434 ,,	4·50

Right Humerus (Aino)

	No.	Mean.	Standard Deviation.	Coefficient of Variation.
Men .	45	29·50 cms.	1·342 cms.	4·55
Women .	28	27·39 ,,	1·279 ,,	4·57

Right Radius (Aino)

	No.	Mean.	Standard Deviation.	Coefficient of Variation.
Men .	39	22·91 cms.	1·117 cms.	4·88
Women .	24	21·08 ,,	1·009 ,,	4·79

The right bone was always taken, except in a few cases where only the left was available. Here we notice, on comparison with the French and Libyan results, several instances of the general rules, that the more primitive and savage a race the less will be the variation of both sexes, and the greater will be the approach to equality of variation between the sexes.

To these results I may add the length of the left forearm extracted from my Family Data cards :—

LEFT FOREARM (ENGLISH)

	No.	Mean.	Standard Deviation.	Coefficient of Variation.
Men	1000	18″·384	0″·964	5·24
Women	1000	16″·534	0″·848	5·13

Now considering all these results together we note that there is, on the whole, a very striking agreement about them. We may safely say that the coefficient of variation for any long bone in man or woman for any race is very approximately five. If the Libyans have the male more variable in femur, tibia, and humerus than the female, and the Aino the male more variable in femur, tibia, and radius, French women are equally variable in femur with French men, and sensibly more variable in tibia and humerus. As to the radius, both French and Libyan women are more variable than their men. The French returns, however, for both tibia and humerus are far more reliable than the Libyan, owing to our knowledge of the sex being complete. The results for the ancient inhabitants of the Canary Islands make the female femur more variable than the male, and tend to confirm the view that the male Libyans are a mixture of at least two races. The neolithic results although they give a preponderancy to male variability, are still opposed to the high values of male variability found for the lower long bones of the Libyans.

To sum up, then, I believe that when larger series of

long bones have been measured, it will be found that man is more variable than woman in the case of the femur and tibia. In the case of the humerus and radius, woman is probably somewhat more variable than man.[1] A preponderating variation of either sex is, however, a view which finds absolutely no confirmation in such measurements of the long bones as have hitherto been made.

From the standpoint of secular evolution, it is interesting to note that if modern French men have slightly longer femurs, tibias, and humeri than the ancient Libyans, they have shorter radii. French women, however, are singularly close to Libyan women, thus illustrating a point to which I shall return later—*e.g.* the greater physical equality of the sexes in the older matriarchal civilisations.

A (c). *Body-Weight*

English.—The following returns are deduced from statistics published by Mr. Francis Galton on p. 200 of his *Natural Inheritance*.

Age 23-26.	No.	Mean.	Standard Deviation.	Coefficient of Variation.
Men . . .	520	64·86 kgs.	4·54 kgs.	10·37
Women . .	276	55·34 ,,	4·60 ,,	13·37

We conclude that English women are both absolutely

---

[1] The means of the variations for the whole series are as follows:—

	Femur.	Tibia.	Humerus.	Radius.
Men	4·82	5·33	4·88	4·81
Women . . .	4·58	4·93	5·10	5·10

and relatively more variable than English men with regard to weight.

German.—The material from which the data were calculated were taken from Bischoff in the volume already cited for stature. All the individuals were adult.

	No.	Mean.	Standard Deviation.	Coefficient of Variation.
Men . .	535	50·171 kgs.	10·38 kgs.	20·67
Women . .	340	41·922 ,,	10·51 ,,	25·07

Thus German women are sensibly more variable than German men with regard to weight. It would, of course, have been more satisfactory to have had data for only a few years' range of age. I have not been able to find such German data. The weights are less clothes; the lowness of the means and the highness of the coefficients of variation are accounted for not only by the range of age, but by the fact that the weights are those of bodies coming to the post-mortem room.

French.—M. Manouvrier, in reply to my inquiries, kindly informs me that there are no reliable French data of the body-weights of the two sexes.

American Children.—My source is again the work of Porter referred to above, and the data are accordingly not quite so satisfactory as if the raw material had been available. I find—

	Age.	No.	Mean.	Standard Deviation.	Coefficient of Variation.
Boys	6	707	19·75 kgs.	2·120 kgs.	10·73
Girls	6	798	18·93 „	2·135 „	11·28
Boys	7	1814	21·67 kgs.	2·491 kgs.	11·49
Girls	7	1714	20·82 „	2·787 „	13·39
Boys	8	2188	23·78 kgs.	2·906 kgs.	12·22
Girls	8	2147	22·88 „	2·891 „	12·64
Boys	9	2188	26·06 kgs.	3·099 kgs.	11·89
Girls	9	2055	25·08 „	3·306 „	13·18
Boys	10	2064	28·32 kgs.	3·306 kgs.	11·67
Girls	10	1947	27·49 „	3·425 „	13·99

Later years are omitted as in the case of stature, because the influence of puberty is felt at different ages in the two sexes.

These figures show us that girls between the ages of six and ten are much more variable in weight than boys of the same ages.

We may carry the investigation back to babyhood. Thus I have calculated the following numbers from statistics given by Quetelet in his *Anthropométrie*, p. 355. They are for the weights of new-born infants:—

	No.	Mean.	Standard Deviation.	Coefficient of Variation.
Male	63	3·289 kgs.	·482 kgs.	14·66
Female	56	3·053 „	·538 „	17·62

Thus, both absolutely and relatively, Belgian female babies are at birth more variable in weight than male babies.

I sought to test this result from the statistics of weight of new-born infants given in the *Report of the Anthropometric Committee of the British Association for* 1883. I found—

	No.	Mean.	Standard Deviation.	Coefficient of Variation.
Male . . .	451	3·230 kgs.	·508 kgs.	15·74
Female . .	466	3·152 „	·481 „	15·28

Here the male babies are slightly more variable that the female, the coefficients of variation both falling between the values previously found for male and female. Notwithstanding the much greater number of babies in this case, I hardly trust these statistics, for we are told that the babies were weighed at Queen Charlotte's Lying-in Hospital, London, and the Royal Maternity Charity, Edinburgh; in other words, we are dealing with a mixture of English and Scottish babies. The results for stature show a marked racial difference between the English and Scottish, and therefore this is probably true for weight also. The greater variability of the male baby in weight is, however, in accord with the results to be deduced from Elsässer's measurements (*Zeitschrift für die Stadtsarzeneikunde,* Bd. xlii. 1841). I find for Stuttgart babies—

	No.	Mean.	Standard Deviation.	Coefficient of Variation.
Male . . .	500	3·238 kgs.	·439 kgs.	13·567
Female . .	500	3·151 „	·418 „	13·278

The means are in striking agreement with the

English-Scottish series, and the reduction in variability is in accordance with the mixed character of the latter measurements.

In order to settle this question, I sought for a large and homogeneous series of English babies. By the courtesy of Dr. J. D. Rawlings I was able to obtain from the registers of the Lambeth Lying-In Hospital measurements of nearly 2500 babies. From these I selected for weight the children of *married* women born at the *normal* time. These statistics gave the following results:—

	No.	Mean.	Standard Deviation.	Coefficient of Variation.
Male	861	3·335 kgs.	·512 kgs.	15·65
Female	770	3·225 „	·466 „	14·44

Clearly London male babies are sensibly more variable than females. It would seem therefore that Teutonic (English and German) males are more variable at birth than females, but that the reverse holds for Belgian infants.

Summing up in general our conclusions for weight, it would appear that, except at birth, man is not more variable than woman. On the contrary, at several ages woman is markedly more variable than man. Here again the relative intensity of the struggle for existence may be an all-important factor.

A (d). *Chest Girth*

Mr. Porter gives results for American children for chest girth midway between expiration and inspiration, *i.e.* he takes the mean of the measurements at full inspiration and full expiration. I deduce the following table :—

	Age.	No.	Mean.	Standard Deviation.	Coefficient of Variation.
Boys	6	677	59·05 cms.	3·29	5·56
Girls	6	741	58·34 „	3·67	6·29
Boys	7	1708	60·62 cms.	3·52	5·81
Girls	7	1631	59·47 „	3·66	6·15
Boys	8	2095	62·18 cms.	3·48	5·59
Girls	8	2040	60·81 „	3·55	5·84
Boys	9	2120	63·90 cms.	3·71	5·81
Girls	9	1966	62·51 „	3·74	5·99
Boys	10	1997	65·59 cms.	4·02	6·14
Girls	10	1893	63·02 „	3·95	6·27

Thus girls are relatively more variable than boys in chest measurement in all five years, and absolutely more variable than boys in all but the tenth year. This preponderance of variability in girls goes on with the exception of the sixteenth year (probably anomalous) from six to eighteen. I have omitted years after ten, however, to avoid any special influence due to rapid development just before puberty. Variability in chest girth certainly ought to be a factor which would be seized by progressive evolution. I may note further, without giving the actual statistics, that in span of arms girls are uniformly more variable than boys.

A (*e*). *General Anthropometric Data*

Mr. Francis Galton obtained a series of measurements at his Anthropometric Laboratory in the International

Exhibition of 1884, which, although expressed in percentiles, admit of reduction to the form adopted in this paper. They are given on pp. 200, 201 of his *Natural Inheritance*, from which I have already extracted the weight statistics.

Subject of Measurement.	Sex.	No.	Mean.	Standard Deviation.	Coefficient of Variation.
Stature, Age, 23-51	Men	811	67″·9	2″·55	3·75
	Women	770	63″·3	2″·40	3·79
Height, sitting, Age, 23-51	Men	1013	36″·0	1″·41	3·91
	Women	775	33″·9	1″·21	3·58
Span, Age, 23-51	Men	811	69″·9	3″·06	4·38
	Women	770	63″·0	2″·77	4·39
Breathing capacity, Age, 23-26	Men	212	219 in.^{3}	36·3 in.^{3}	16·6
	Women	277	138 ,,	28·1 ,,	20·4
Strength of pull, Age, 23-26	Men	519	74 lbs.	11·10 lbs.	15·0
	Women	276	40 ,,	7·73 ,,	19·3
Strength of squeeze of strongest hand, Age, 23-26	Men	519	85 lbs.	11·47 lbs.	13·4
	Women	276	52 ,,	11·10 ,,	21·4
Swiftness of blow, Age, 23-26	Men	516	18·1 ft. p. s.	3·51 ft. p. s.	19·4
	Women	271	13·4 ,,	2·29 ,,	17·1
Keenness of sight, distance of reading diamond test-type, Age, 23-26	Men	398	25″	5″·92	28·68
	Women	433	24″	7″·73	32·21

Thus we see that women relatively are slightly more variable in stature and span, much more variable in breathing capacity, strength of pull, squeeze of hand, and absolutely are much more variable in keenness of sight. They are less variable in sitting height, and much less variable in swiftness of blow. These results have been substantially confirmed by the measurements taken by the British Association Anthropometric Committee at successive meetings of the Association. The reports of that Committee also go to show that woman is *absolutely* more variable than man in length of thigh, length of hand, cephalic index, nasal index, and face index. Until complete results are published by the Committee, it does not seem desirable to discuss the small returns for the annual series in order to ascertain how far for these small numbers woman is *relatively* more variable than man in the case of other organs. We can, however, confirm Mr. Galton's results for strength of pull by some given by Quetelet in his *Anthropométrie*, p. 365. The units are those of Regnier's dynamometer. From Quetelet's statistics I find—

	No.	Mean.	Standard Deviation.	Coefficient of Variation.
Men	90	144·11	23·61	15·32
Women	197	75·74	17·13	22·62

It will be noticed that the ratio of the means is very similar to that of Mr. Galton's returns, while the coefficients of variation are much like his.

I have procured another most interesting series of anthropometric data from Cambridge.[1] Unfortunately the women students of suitable age for comparison with the men are somewhat few in number, but as an anthropometrical laboratory is now being established at Newnham College, we may hope that this will speedily be rectified.

[1] By the courtesy of the Cambridge Anthropometric Committee I have been allowed copies of the measurements of all the women and about 1000 men on their registers.

Nature of Measurement.	Sex.	No.	Mean.	Standard Deviation.	Coefficient of Variation.
Stature	Men . .	1077	68"·93	2"·506	3·636
	Women .	135	63"·82	2"·419	3·790
Weight	Men . .	1071	154·044 lbs.	16·514 lbs.	10·721
	Women .	137	126·590 ,,	13·990 ,,	11·051
Strength of pull .	Men . .	1066	84·438 lbs.	13·152 lbs.	15·580
	Women .	134	49·127 ,,	8·217 ,,	16·725
Strength of squeeze, left hand	Men . .	1056	81·152 lbs.	11·706 lbs.	14·550
	Women .	134	53·298 ,,	10·012 ,,	18·785
Strength of squeeze, right hand	Men . .	1058	85·214 lbs.	11·616 lbs.	13·640
	Women .	133	56·293 ,,	10·372 ,,	18·424
Eyesight,[1] left eye	Men . .	1041	58·438 cms.	19·430 cms.	33·249
	Women .	130	59·246 ,,	19·513 ,,	32·935
Eyesight,[1] right eye	Men . .	1035	61·213 cms.	20·218 cms.	33·249
	Women .	132	60·303 ,,	20·946 ,,	34·735

Thus, with the exception of the sight of the left eye, women are in all cases sensibly more variable than men. When comparison is possible, these results are in complete agreement with Mr. Galton's conclusions given in the previous table. The agreement is particularly noteworthy as the age of the Cambridge students—nineteen to thirty, with comparatively few under twenty—differs somewhat from Mr. Galton's. The two series also probably belong to somewhat different classes. The practical constancy of the coefficients of variation, even for divergent means, is a satisfactory test of the usefulness of this constant for the problem of racial variation.

Further confirmation of the greater variability of the female in strength of squeeze, and her lesser variability

---

[1] Distance of reading test-type. I am not, however, very well satisfied with the method of measurement adopted, as, to judge from the returns, the type was only placed at a series of fixed distances in geometrical progression.

in height sitting may be found in Mr. Porter's measurements on American children. Thus we have—

HEIGHT SITTING

Sex.	Age.	No.	Mean.	Standard Deviation.	Coefficient of Variation.
Boys	6	714	61·31 cms.	4·174	6·81
Girls	6	751	59·45 ,,	3·004	5·03
Boys	7	1853	63·32 cms.	3·907	6·22
Girls	7	1727	61·80 ,,	3·241	5·18
Boys	8	2239	64·74 cms.	3·345	5·18
Girls	8	2120	63·97 ,,	3·019	4·74
Boys	9	2258	66·73 cms.	3·463	5·18
Girls	9	2071	66·16 ,,	3·123	4·74
Boys	10	2118	69·25 cms.	3·582	5·18
Girls	10	2037	68·19 ,,	3·241	4·74

We may thus safely assert that less variability in height sitting is a secondary sexual character of woman.

SQUEEZE OF HANDS

Sex.	Age.	Hand.	No.	Mean.	Standard Deviation.	Coefficient of Variation.
Boys	6	right	626	6·09 kilogs.	2·087 kilogs.	34·34
Girls	6	,,	687	5·14 ,,	2·057 ,,	39·96
Boys	6	left	629	5·59 ,,	2·116 ,,	37·89
Girls	6	,,	686	4·77 ,,	2·176 ,,	45·58
Boys	7	right	1551	7·69 kilogs.	2·250 kilogs.	29·30
Girls	7	,,	1493	6·53 ,,	2·472 ,,	37·89
Boys	7	left	1550	7·15 ,,	2·546 ,,	35·67
Girls	7	,,	1488	5·70 ,,	2·398 ,,	42·03
Boys	8	right	1880	9·38 kilogs.	2·886 kilogs.	30·78
Girls	8	,,	1873	8·11 ,,	2·768 ,,	34·19
Boys	8	left	1882	8·76 ,,	3·078 ,,	34·34
Girls	8	,,	1882	7·52 ,,	2·960 ,,	39·37
Boys	9	right	2002	11·35 kilogs.	3·626 kilogs.	31·97
Girls	9	,,	1829	9·23 ,,	3·123 ,,	33·89
Boys	9	left	2007	10·43 ,,	3·937 ,,	37·74
Girls	9	,,	1828	8·47 ,,	3·108 ,,	36·70
Boys	10	right	1878	12·83 kilogs.	3·937 kilogs.	30·64
Girls	10	,,	1801	10·42 ,,	3·360 ,,	32·41
Boys	10	left	1886	11·72 ,,	3·804 ,,	32·41
Girls	10	,,	1798	9·38 ,,	3·300 ,,	35·22

Thus girls are persistently more variable in squeeze of hands than boys.

Another interesting anthropometric comparison, namely, of sensitivity at the nape of the neck (as measured by the just-perceptible distance apart of the points of a pair of compasses), has been made by Mr. Galton (*Nature*, vol. l. p. 40). His results, expressed in terms of our constants, give—

	No.	Mean.	Standard Deviation.	Coefficient of Variation.
Men .	932	13·8 cms.	4·82	35·70
Women . .	377	11·8 „	5·49	45·75

Thus women, both absolutely and relatively, are far more variable in respect to this sensitivity than men.

To sum up, it would seem that under our present conditions of civilisation the physique of woman is, anthropometrically considered, considerably more variable than that of man. Man has probably at present a more uniform physical training. As this training for women becomes more widespread and more uniform in character, we may expect a rise in several of women's anthropometric means and a fall in her variability. Until, however, the selective mortality is practically the same for both sexes, *i.e.* the struggle for existence equal, it will still be difficult to determine whether unequal variability of the sexes for any organ results from (1) a difference in nurture, (2) an inequality in selective mortality, or is really (3) a secondary sexual character.

A (f). *Weights of Various Internal Organs*

(i.) *The Heart.*—My only data are in this case English. We have post-mortem measurements of the healthy heart by Clendinning,[1] Reid,[2] and Peacock.[3] The latter gives two series. In the first he excludes all hearts over 12 ozs. in weight as unhealthy, but in the later series he includes many such hearts, apparently having meanwhile convinced himself that such hearts can really be normal. I have worked out separately the series of Reid and the later series of Peacock, and find them in substantial agreement as to means and coefficients of variation; I have accordingly had no hesitation in combining them to form one series. Clendinning's means are not in accord with those of Reid and Peacock, and as he only gives 28 available males under fifty-five years of age, I have neither included his returns nor worked them out separately.

Heart.—Adults twenty to fifty-five years of age.

	No.	Mean.	Standard Deviation.	Coefficient of Variation.
Men . . .	181	10·699 ozs.	2·121 ozs.	19·825
Women . .	110	8·927 ,,	1·848 ,,	20·701

Thus the hearts of both men and women are extremely variable, but those of women slightly more so than men. The effect of excluding any organ as "unhealthy," not on account of pathological characters,

---

[1] *Medico-Chirurgical Trans.* vol. xxi. 1838.
[2] *London and Edinburgh Monthly Journal of Medical Science*, 1843.
[3] *Ibid.* 1846, 1854. Reprint, 1861.

but simply on account of size, is well illustrated by taking Peacock's first series of heart measurements, and calculating out the coefficients of variation for 100 cases of male and female adults under fifty-five years of age.

	No.	Mean.	Standard Deviation.	Coefficient of Variation.
Men . . .	100	9·52 ozs.	1·578 ozs.	16·58
Women . .	100	8·88 „	1·478 „	16·64

The women are still more variable than the men, but the manner in which the means and the variations are reduced is noteworthy. As a matter of fact, an examination of the plotted frequency distributions shows a sudden fall from a very great number of male and female hearts between 11 and 12 ozs. to none between 12 and 13. This discontinuity is quite contrary to our experience of the gradual change in frequency with size which occurs in all organs, and we may safely conclude that Peacock has either included many unhealthy hearts between 11 and 12 ozs., or, what is much more probable, has cut off a considerable tail of really healthy hearts weighing over 12 ozs.

(ii.) *The Liver.*—My statistics are here again extracted from the works of Reid and Peacock previously referred to.

I find for adults from twenty to fifty-five years—

	No.	Mean.	Standard Deviation.	Coefficient of Variation.
Men . . .	84	53·48 ozs.	7·658 ozs.	14·32
Women . .	52	47·69 „	10·600 „	22·23

Thus the liver is seen to be again a very variable organ, but woman is, absolutely as well as relatively, more variable in the weight of her liver than man. Although this greater variability is somewhat reduced, if we arbitrarily eliminate one or two large livers from the series for women, *without eliminating the correspondingly large livers for men*, we still find woman absolutely more variable than man with regard to the liver, and the statistics go a long way to showing that this greater variability of liver is a secondary sexual character.

(iii.) *The Kidney.*—My statistics are due to Reid and Peacock in the journals already cited. As there is apparently a persistent difference in average weight between the right and left kidneys, I have selected the former.

I find for adults between twenty and fifty-five years of age [1]—

	No.	Mean.	Standard Deviation.	Coefficient of Variation.
Men . . .	100	5·57 ozs.	1·141 ozs.	20·49
Women . .	61	5·08 ,,	1·145 ,,	22·53

Thus we see that the weight of the kidney is more variable in woman that it is in man.

Summing up our results for the three vital organs—heart, liver, and kidney—whose weights we have discussed and whose variation ought surely to form material for progressive evolution, we see that there exists no

[1] The distribution of weight in kidneys gives a remarkably skew-frequency curve.

preponderating variability in man. On the contrary, in two of the organs absolutely, and in all three relatively, woman is the more variable.

B (a). *Brain-Weight*

The statistics here present certain difficulties. In the first place, the weight of the brain depends largely on the amount of fluid weighed with it, and greatly on the time after death at which it is weighed. Further, the brains of but few healthy individuals find their way into the post-mortem room. It appears also to be still an open question how far various forms of disease influence brain-weight, and how far brain-weight is influenced by age. For example, it is usually assumed that the brain diminishes in weight after sixty; but, as the same brain can never be weighed at two different ages, it is quite possible that the apparent diminution with age is really due to a greater power of survival inherent in persons with lighter brains. We should expect therefore high coefficients for brain-variation, and very divergent results for different observers, according to the class of brains with which they have dealt, their method of weighing, and the particular conceptions they have formed as to what brains are to be considered as "healthy." There is no reason, however, to suppose that one sex rather than another would be particularly influenced by any individual method of treatment. In the following statistics the best has been done with not very satisfactory material.

English.—The most numerous statistics are those of Boyd, but the averages for various age-groups alone having been published, the statistics are of no service for the problem of variation. We have, accordingly, to fall back on smaller series by Reid,[1] Peacock,[2] Sims,[3] and Clendinning.[4] Only the two former give results which seem capable of being at once grouped together. I find, for adults under fifty-five (Reid and Peacock)—

	No.	Mean.	Standard Deviation.	Coefficient of Variation.
Men . .	150	1429 grs.	132·73 grs.	9·29
Women . .	100	1280 „	101·49 „	7·93

The men are thus sensibly more variable than the women. But turning to Clendinning we have,

For adults under fifty-five—

	No.	Mean.	Standard Deviation.	Coefficient of Variation.
Men . . .	90	1282 grs.	108·01 grs.	8·07
Women . .	71	1201 „	127·74 „	10·64

Thus the women are in this series, both relatively and absolutely, remarkably more variable than the men. The same conclusion is still reached if we go so far as to exclude from the women's series two very small brains and one very large brain, although such a proceeding would be entirely arbitrary.

Finally, if to settle whether the Reid-Peacock series

[1] *Monthly Journal of Medical Science,* 1843.   [2] *Ibid.* 1847.
[3] *Medico-Chirurgical Trans.* vol. xviii. 1835.   [4] *Ibid.* vol. xxi. 1838.

or the Clendinning series is to be given greater weight, we appeal to Sims, we find, for all adult brains—

	No.	Mean.	Standard Deviation.	Coefficient of Variation.
Men . . .	100	1295 grs.	132·68 grs.	10·25
Women . .	98	1225 ,,	129·73 ,,	10·59

Here women are slightly more variable, but there has been a great rise in both coefficients of variation, owing to the wider age range taken in order to secure a large series. The great differences between Reid and Peacock on the one hand, and Clendinning and Sims on the other, with regard to means will be noted. The two latter authorities make men and women much more equal in brain weight than the two former, or than continental authorities make German or French women.

Finally if we treat all three series as of equal weight, and take the means of all the results, we find—

	No.	Mean	Standard Deviation.	Coefficient of Variation.
Men . . .	340	1335 grs.	124·48 grs.	9·20
Women . .	269	1235 ,,	118·7 ,,	9·72

We should conclude from this that for brain weight English women are slightly more variable than English men.

French.—My data are based on statistics published in the *Mémoires de la Société d'Anthropologie de Paris*, t. iii.

VOL. I   Y

	No.	Mean.	Standard Deviation.	Coefficient of Variation.
Men . . .	292	1325·18 grs.	121·43 grs.	9·16
Women . .	140	1144·46 ,,	104·56 ,,	9·14

Thus the variabilities in brain weight of French men and women are sensibly equal, the difference being much below the probable error of the determination. The variation is close to the English.

German.—The statistics on which my data are based are due to Bischoff, *loc. cit.* p. 295.

	No.	Mean.	Standard Deviation.	Coefficient of Variation.
Men . . .	559	1361·72 grs.	114·33 grs.	8·40
Women .	347	1219·09 ,,	102·54 ,,	8·41

Bavarian men and women have thus sensibly the same variability in brain weight. The mean weights are of the same order as the English mean weights.

Thus our investigations with regard to brain weight seem to demonstrate no such greater variability in men, as many writers have assumed. These writers have followed brain students like Weisbach and Marshall, who, while great anatomists, have had no true scientific conception of how variation is to be measured. Accordingly writers like Mr. Havelock Ellis, who tells us that: "As might be anticipated, the greater variability of men in mental capacity is, on the anatomical side, connected with a greater variability in the size of the skull and the brain,"[1] are appealing to an anatomical conclusion which would also demonstrate the mental

[1] *Man and Woman*, p. 366.

capacity of the elephant to be greater than that of man. In fact, the existence of a higher average mental power in man, if it can be demonstrated, would not in the least touch the problem of the relative variability of the sexes. The average of the woman might be much less than that of the man, and yet both her absolute and relative variabilities (as we have seen in the cases of the weights of Germans) be much greater than that of the man. The confusion between higher mental power, greater variability, and more capacity for progress, is indeed great in the writers referred to. Equal variability by no means connotes equal average power, although, on the theory of evolution by natural selection, it would, granted equal inheritance, most probably connote equal capacity for progress where the struggle for existence was equally severe for the two sexes. But let us turn to further head measurements to confirm the conclusions already reached.

B (b). *Facial Measurements*

(i.) *Profile Angles.*—My statistics are here not very numerous. I have calculated the following data from results given by Ranke, *Anthropologie der Bayern*, Bd. ii. § 10, for the Munich town population:—

	No.	Mean.	Standard Deviation.
Men . . .	50	85°33'·6	2°·79
Women . .	50	86°52'·8	3°·59
Babies . .	15	86°28'	1°·71

Thus the variation in the profile angle in women is

very much greater than that of men. The skulls of newborn babies were too few in number to allow of any very definite conclusions, but so far as we can say anything at all, we should have to conclude that men resemble babies in being less variable than women. This conclusion is so opposed to that of various medical and popular writers on anthropology, who tell us that "women remain nearer to the infantile state than men," that we will dismiss it as having no weight, until we have collected and analysed statistics enough to determine whether that statement be not also "a pseudo-scientific superstition." Taking now the Bavarian peasants, I find Ranke gives details of profile angle for 101 skulls. Hence I deduce—

	No.	Mean.	Standard Deviation.
Men . . .	40	89°·11	3°·10
Women . .	61	88°·73	4°·12

Here while the women have a slightly more slanting profile, we see that their variation is very much greater.

(ii.) *Alveolar Angle.*—Closely allied with the profile angle is the alveolar angle, which measures the slope of the upper gum or lip to the horizontal. Ranke gives the measurements for 78 skulls. I find, omitting the senile skulls—

	No.	Mean.	Standard Deviation.
Men . . .	30	82°·50	6°·51
Women . .	48	83°·46	8°·73

Thus the Bavarian peasant women have markedly

more variation in their alveolar angle than men. Ranke also gives the measurement for a small number of skulls from Waischenfeld in the Bayreuth Oberland. In 100 skulls from the Ossuarium of Waischenfeld only 26 could have their alveolar angle measured. The measurements give the following results :—

	No.	Mean.	Standard Deviation.
Men . .	15	86°·27	2°·27
Women . .	11	85°·86	2°·58

The women are again more variable than the men, but this Oberfrankish race is clearly as to both sexes far less variable than the old Bavarian folk.

I now pass to measurements of the face and forehead, my material being still drawn from Ranke.

(iii.) *Kollmann's Index.*—This is one hundred times the ratio of the width of the face at the cheek-bones and the distance from the frontal nasal suture to the alveolar rim of the upper jaw. The *Alt-Bayerisch* measurements give—

	No.	Mean.	Standard Deviation.
Men . . .	54	52·37	3·26
Women . .	64	53·23	3·33

(iv.) A second face index is used by Ecker in his *Crania Germaniae*. He takes one hundred times the ratio of the distance between the most projecting points of the cheek-bones and the distance between the *sutura nasalis* and the chin. I find from his numbers for modern Badensians—

	No.	Mean.	Standard Deviation.
Men . . .	62	110·77	8.365
Women . .	33	113·27	12·748

Women are thus much more variable for this measure of facial rotundity.

(v.) *Roundness of Forehead.*—This may be measured by an index equal to one hundred times the ratio of the direct distance from the bregma to the frontal nasal suture and the same distance measured along the surface of the skull. Ranke's measurements on Bavarian peasants give when reduced—

	No.	Mean.	Standard Deviation.
Men . . .	92	87·9	2·88
Women . .	98	87·6	2·68

(vi.) *Forehead-Breadth Index.*— This gives us a means of measuring the pear-shaped character of the forehead. Ranke takes this index as the ratio of one hundred times the least breadth of the forehead between the nearest points of the temporal ridges and the greatest breadth (stephanion to stephanion). I find from his measurements—

	No.	Mean.	Standard Deviation.
Men . . .	72	78·5 [1]	3·01
Women . .	83	78·5	3·00

[1] Ranke, who gives the mean of his measurements, has here, as in several other places, wrong figures, *e.g.* 80·6 (vol. i. p. 75).

(vii.) *Eyes.*—We may take first the eye-index or ratio of height to breadth of eye-socket in skull. From Ranke's numbers for *Alt-Bayerisch* skulls I find—

	No.	Mean.	Standard Deviation.
Men . . .	71	84·66	6·66
Women . .	78	86·75	5·22

To test this superior variability of men in the shape of the eye-socket, I calculated the variation for the Oberfrankish skulls from Waischenfeld; I found—

	No.	Mean.	Standard Deviation.
Men . . .	32	82·74	7·45
Women . .	22	84·28	4·78

It would thus appear that men are sensibly more variable than women in the shape of the eye-socket.

Taking the absolute distances between the inner rims of the eye-sockets for the *Alt-Bayerisch* peasantry, I found from Ranke's measurements—

	No.	Mean.	Standard Deviation.	Coefficient of Variation.
Men . . .	57	23·81 mm.	2·098 mm.	8·81
Women . .	65	23·54 ,,	2·273 ,,	9·23

Thus both absolutely and relatively women are more variable than men in the distance of their eye-sockets apart.

(viii.) *Nose Index.*—Ranke has also measured the

ratio of height and breadth of nose for the same race. I find for the variation—

	No.	Mean.	Standard Deviation.
Men	70	49·18	4·43
Women	72	49·35	4·61

As a somewhat kindred measurement we may note the length of palate for the same race.

(ix.) *Length of Palate.*—This is measured from the point of the *spina* of the hard palate, *spina nasalis posterior*, to the inner side of the alveolar rim.

	No.	Mean.	Standard Deviation.	Coefficient of Variation.
Men	55	44·35	2·848	6·42
Women	57	43·11	2·954	6·85

Women are thus as to length of palate absolutely and relatively more variable than men.

Summing up the last nine series of measurements, we conclude that women are more variable than men in profile and alveolar angles, in the ratio of breadth to height of middle face, in the distance between the eye-sockets, in the shape of the nose, and the length of the palate; they are less variable than men in roundness of forehead and shape of eye-sockets only; they are equally variable in the ratio of forehead-breadths.

B (c). *Skull Capacity*

Modern English.— My data are here based on statistics drawn from Barnard Davis's *Thesaurus Craniorum.*

	No.	Mean.	Standard Deviation.	Coefficient of Variation.
Men . . .	20	1339·2 cm.³	109·6 cm.³	8·18
Women . .	13	1138·1 „	95·5 „	8·29

The absolute measurements must here, I think, be looked upon as quite untrustworthy. Barnard Davis gives his measurements in ounces of Calais sand: men 81·75 ounces and women 69·46 ounces. I have reduced these according to Broca's estimate of an ounce of Calais sand to cubic centimeters, but the results for the means are far too small.

Hunting everywhere, I have only succeeded in finding the capacities of forty English male crania recorded. Of these six in German museums have a mean of 1454 cm.³, fourteen in the Royal College of Surgeons' Museum have a mean of 1510 cm.³, and Barnard Davis's twenty above have a mean of 1339 cm.³ It is impossible to group all these English skulls together. Nor can we reduce Barnard Davis's mean to the Royal College of Surgeons' mean. For, while the former have a coefficient of variation of 8·18, the Royal College crania have a coefficient as high as 9·68. Indeed their standard deviation is as high as 146 cm.³, and shows us only too clearly that we are dealing with "museum" or selected specimens.

The coefficients of variation found from Barnard Davis's measurements are quite in keeping with the French and German results. Very little weight can, however, be attached to this relative variation, it only suffices to show that there exists no very large difference in variability between men and women.

My next English series is from Professor Thane's collection. I find—

The Whitechapel Skulls

	No.	Mean.	Standard Deviation.	Coefficient of Variation.
Men . . .	26	1522·00 cm.³	116·84	7·68
Women . .	32	1298·59 „	105·75	8·15

We therefore conclude that English women are more variable as to skull capacity than English men.

French.—My statistics are here drawn from the MSS. of M. Paul Broca, preserved in the *Laboratorie d'Anthropologie* at Paris, and I have to thank M. Manouvrier for the courtesy with which he has had the details copied and forwarded to me.

Parisians

	No.	Mean.	Standard Deviation.	Coefficient of Variation.
Men . .	144	1546·66 cm.³	113·76	7·36
Women .	83	1329·31 „	94·35	7·10

These statistics show us that the Parisian women as a whole are less variable than the men in regard to skull capacity. The statistics, however, forwarded to me by M. Manouvrier were divided into two groups, entitled respectively *Parisiens de l'Ouest* and *Parisiens de la Cité*. In examining them I was at once struck with the great constancy to type, not only in capacity of skull but in cephalic index, of the women of the *Cité*. It is clear that the skulls of these women must have been drawn from some narrowly selected or very limited class; very possibly it is a class in which the struggle for existence is far more severe than that undergone by the Parisians of the West End, for the male skulls from the *Cité* are also, if to a lesser extent, markedly less variable than those of the West.

Separating the two series, we have the following results :—

PARISIENS DE L'OUEST

	No.	Mean.	Standard Deviation.	Coefficient of Variation.
Men . . .	77	1559·70 cm.³	121·17 cm.³	7·77
Women . .	41	1338·27 ,,	109·35 ,,	8·17

PARISIENS DE LA CITÉ

	No.	Mean.	Standard Deviation.	Coefficient of Variation.
Men . . .	67	1531·63 cm.³	102·57 cm.³	6·70
Women .	42	1320·55 ,,	78·55 ,,	5·95

It is clear from these subdivided statistics, that in one class of Parisians the women are more, and in another class, less variable than the men. This conclusion is identical with what may be deduced from the values of the cephalic indices of the same two series of skulls. I have no further series of skull capacities for French women to test whether the Parisians of the West or the City are to be considered as more truly representing the average French relative variability of the sexes. A series of fifty-six skulls in the Munich Anthropological Museum, which belonged to French soldiers who died of their wounds in Munich during the Franco-German war, give—

Mean, 1473·05 cm.³; Standard deviation, 107·3 cm.; Coefficient of variation, 7·29. The absolute values determined in Germany cannot satisfactorily be compared with those determined in Paris. The coefficient of variation (7·29), however, does not differ very widely from that of the 144 Parisian skulls (7·36), although it is nearer to that of the West Enders than to that of the inhabitants of the City. I shall return to this point when dealing with the cephalic indices of the corresponding groups. The only safe conclusion at present to be drawn is that there is no sufficient evidence to show that French men are definitely more variable in skull capacity than French women.

Italians.—Of modern Italians I have been able to collect the measurements of 101 skulls, principally from the Royal College of Surgeons' Catalogue. I find—

	No.	Mean.	Standard Deviation.	Coefficient of Variation.
Men . .	75	1476·73 cm.³	123·10 cm.³	8·34
Women . .	26	1283·65 ,,	115·35 ,,	8·99

Italian women thus appear to be sensibly more variable than men in skull capacity, while, as we shall see later, they are less variable in cephalic index.

Of several other races for which a fair number of skulls with measured cephalic index could be found, there were not sufficient skulls with measured capacity to render a reduction of any significance. Thus I pass by Ancient Romans (from Italy) and Dutch, and proceed at once to the Germans.

German.—My first statistics are here taken from

Ranke's *Beiträge zur Anthropologie der Bayern*, Bd. i. §§ 79, 80. I find—

	No	Mean.	Standard Deviation.	Coefficient of Variation.
Men . . .	100	1503·75 cm.^{3}	116·45 cm.^{3}	7·744
Women . .	100	1335·50 ,,	109·45 ,,	8·195

Or we conclude that Bavarian women are very sensibly more variable in skull capacity than Bavarian men.

This value about 8 for the coefficient of variation in skull capacity for South German women is very closely reached by the measurements given by Weisbach[1] for Viennese women of German race, a closely-allied Teutonic stem. I find—

	No.	Mean.	Standard Deviation.	Coefficient of Variation.
Women . .	23	1336·6 cm.^{3}	106·6 cm.^{3}	7·98

The coefficients of variation for both men and women are in very close agreement with those for Parisian men and women of the West End.

The only other German series I have been able to discover is a small one for men and women of Saxon race due to Welcker (*Untersuchungen über Wachsthum und Bau des menschlichen Schädels*, 1862). From his tables I deduce—

	No.	Mean.	Standard Deviation.	Coefficient of Variation.
Men . . .	30	1450 cm.^{3}	111·9 cm.^{3}	7·72
Women . .	26	1300 ,,	127·5 ,,	9·81

[1] *Der deutsche Weiberschädel*, *Archiv für Anthropologie*, Bd. iii. § 59 (1865).

Here the women are, both absolutely and relatively, more variable than the men. We may then, I think, conclude that German women are more variable in skull capacity than German men. It does not follow, however, that German women are altogether more variable in the head than German men. We shall see later that, while more variable in capacity and facial measurements, they are less variable in cephalic index.

Indeed, we cannot insist too much on any individual set of measurements, but must be content with the general trend of a great range of data. For example, the 9·81 of Welcker's measurements is very high, and we begin to question whether he is not using "museum specimens." Ranke's series were taken from the *Beinhäuser* of Bavarian village churchyards, and the men and women are undoubtedly of the same race and class. Unluckily we have no other equally good series of male and female skulls to compare them with. As a warning, however, of the danger of using "museum specimens," I will compare Ranke's peasants with skulls from the Munich Anatomical Museum which belonged to men of the same race, but are selected skulls of criminals and others. I find—

	No.	Mean.	Standard Deviation.	Coefficient of Variation.
Men . . .	56	1553·27 cm.³	169·94 cm.³	10·94

This immense variability is unparalleled by any other series of skull capacities I have yet reduced. Some of it, as compared with the male peasant value given above, may be due to the fact that we are dealing with a town, as distinguished from a rural, population—and a great deal of evidence has convinced me that town populations are sensibly more variable than country — but undoubtedly the greater part of the difference is due to the fact that we are taking statistics from an *anatomical* museum. The danger of any argument based solely on museum specimens cannot be too widely appreciated. Macrocephaly and microcephaly are often the reason for a skull being originally included in a museum collection, and these features exercise in the first place a great influence on variability in skull capacity.

Skull Capacity in the races from whom modern English, Germans, and French may be supposed to be in part descended.

Anglo-Saxons.—My statistics are taken from the *Crania Britannica*.

	No.	Mean.	Standard Deviation.	Coefficient of Variation.
Men . . .	33	1521·8 cm.^{3}	114·85 cm.^{3}	7·55
Women . .	14	1340·8 ,,	121·40 ,,	9·06

The series of women is far too few to base any very valid conclusion upon it. So far as it can be trusted, it would show women to be more variable than men both absolutely and relatively.

Ancient Skulls of Friesland and Adjacent Parts. —My statistics are drawn from Virchow, Sasse, and Barnard Davis.[1]

[1] An abnormal skull of Sasse's has been rejected, and a slip of Virchow in quoting Barnard Davis corrected. See Virchow: *Beiträge zur Anthropologie der Deutschen*, 1877, p. 159.

	No.	Mean.	Standard Deviation.	Coefficient of Variation.
Men	27	1462·9 cm.³	119·48 cm.³	8·17
Women	21	1295·0 „	105·82 „	8·17

The series are both sadly deficient in numbers, but no difference in the variability of the sexes is noticeable.

Ancient Swiss.—My material here is taken from the *Crania Helvetica*. This work does not, unfortunately, embrace a "random" collection of ancient skulls, but certain skulls have been selected to represent the arbitrary types insisted upon by the authors (His u. Rutimeyer), and these types have been selected not only from ancient but from modern skulls. The types are obtained by what I think to be a very fallacious process,—that of cutting a frequency curve into vertical strips and supposing each strip to give a different race or type. We thus have a mixture of "historical" and modern skulls; of skulls from the *Beinhäuser* of the German cantons, mixed with Roman and Burgundian skulls of the fifth to ninth centuries and with prehistoric skulls of the pile-dwellings. Omitting one skull, which has been "selected" on account of its great capacity to represent the so-called "Sion type," and the odds against which appearing in a "random" selection of the same number are 277 to 1, we have the following results for the total collection of Swiss skulls in the *Crania Helvetica*:—

	No.	Mean.	Standard Deviation.	Coefficient of Variation.
Men	29	1477·9 cm.³	114·9 cm.³	7·77
Women	21	1374·5 „	108·6 „	7·90

I lay no real stress on this result by itself, but it agrees pretty well with previous results in showing no preponderating variability in the male.

Ancient British.—My statistics here are taken from J. Thurnam's work: *On the two principal Forms of Ancient British and Gaulish Skulls.* They are, however, of very small weight, for we have only eight women's skulls from the Long Barrows and none from the Round Barrows!

	No.	Mean.	Standard Deviation.	Coefficient of Variation.
Men (Round Barrow)	18	1586·7 cm.^{3}	119·34 cm.^{3}	7·52
,, (Long Barrow)	35	1617·1 ,,	130·21 ,,	8·05
Women (Long Barrow)	8	1474·0 ,,	96·19 ,,	6·53

A further series of capacities for "Ancient Britons," only without statement as to the nature of the barrow, is given in the *Crania Britannica,* where ten skulls only are attributed to women. We find—

	No.	Mean.	Standard Deviation.	Coefficient of Variation.
Men . .	56	1585·1 cm.^{3}	121·1 cm.^{3}	7·64
Women . .	10	1406·8 ,,	52·69 ,, (!)	3·75 (!)

It is clear that while the coefficients of variation deduced from the different male series are in fair accord, no reliance whatever can be put on the results for the female series, which are deduced from eight to ten skulls only. I should have omitted the data, would doing so not possibly have appeared to some, who have not considered the small weight due to such series, like the omission of a case in which the males are markedly more variable than the females. It may be placed beside the following data for Ancient Romans and Romano-Britons, taken from the *Crania Britannica.*

	No.	Mean.	Standard Deviation.	Coefficient of Variation.
Men . . .	36	1542·9 cm.^{3}	120·70 cm.^{3}	7·82
Women . .	11	1251·8 ,,	105·04 ,,	8·39

This makes the women of the Romano-Britons more variable than the men, but no weight is to be given to a series of only eleven skulls.

Ancient Civilisations

I have found no good series of ancient Greek or Roman skulls available for capacity, and my data are accordingly limited to four races.

Etruscans.—The skulls were taken from tombs at *Tarquinii*, and their measurements are given in the Leipzig Anthropological Catalogue. We find—

	No.	Mean.	Standard Deviation.	Coefficient of Variation.
Men . . .	71	1444·17 cm.^{3}	138·39 cm.^{3}	9·58
Women . .	33	1321·12 ,,	112·85 ,,	8·54

The men are distinctly more variable than the women, but both are extremely variable as compared with any races we have hitherto dealt with, and possibly the skulls are a mixture.[1]

[1] A division of the skulls into those from *tomba Etrusca* and those from *tomba Romana* made no alteration in the means sufficient to indicate a racial difference.

Egyptian Mummy Skulls.—These skulls are principally from Thebes, and my data are taken from the measurements given in the great catalogue of the German anthropological collections now being published by the German Anthropological Society. We find—

	No.	Mean.	Standard Deviation.	Coefficient of Variation.
Men . . .	283	1383·00 cm.³	112·40 cm.³	8·13
Women . .	154	1254·63 ,,	104·05 ,,	8·29

For craniometry these are both fairly extensive series, and they give a greater variability in skull capacity to the woman.

Here again the variability in both sexes is high.

Libyans (?).—This refers to the "new race" discovered by Professor Flinders Petrie at Nagada in Upper Egypt, and dating some 3000 years B.C. Mr. Herbert Thompson has with great kindness measured for me the capacities of nearly 100 skulls, with the following results:—

	No.	Mean.	Standard Deviation.	Coefficient of Variation.
Men . .	39	1339·03 cm.³	83·37 cm.³	6·23
Women . .	55	1242·82 ,,	103·12 ,,	8·30

Thus both absolutely and relatively the women are much more variable than the men with regard to skull capacity.

Ancient Peruvians.—My statistics are drawn from the Leipzig Anthropological Catalogue. I find—

	No.	Mean.	Standard Deviation.	Coefficient of Variation.
Men	47	1312·08 cm.^{3}	111·32 cm.^{3}	8·48
Women	22	1199·23 ,,	85·54 ,,	7·13

The men are markedly more variable than the women, but the series of the latter is not very large.

Primitive and Uncivilised Races

Aino.—The statistics are due to Koganei, in the work cited p. 302. I find—

	No.	Mean.	Standard Deviation.	Coefficient of Variation.
Men	76	1461·86 cm.^{3}	100·68 cm.^{3}	6·89
Women	52	1306·25 ,,	89·05 ,,	6·82

The men are here very slightly more variable than the women.

Negroes.—The statistics were copied from the records of the *Société d'Anthropologie de Paris*, and I owe them to the courtesy of M. Manouvrier. The individuals were drawn from a considerable variety of African districts.

	No.	Mean.	Standard Deviation.	Coefficient of Variation.
Men	54	1429·63 cm.^{3}	101·1 cm.^{3}	7·07
Women	23	1256·00 ,,	86·7 ,,	6·90

Thus the males are very slightly more variable than the females, the difference, however, being far less than the probable error of the series.

Panjab Tribes.—These are skulls of low or outcaste tribes; my statistics are taken from papers by Professor R. Havelock Charles, entitled "Craniometry of some of the Outcaste Tribes of the Panjab," *Journal of Anatomy and Physiology*, vol. xxvi. pp. 1-25 (1892); and vol. xxvii. pp. 5-20 (1893). In the first paper Professor Charles would exclude 9 skulls of the series, as possibly belonging to the descendants of Mussulman invaders. The reason for excluding them seems to lie not in a consideration of the cephalic indices, but of their comparative macrocephaly. However, the mean capacity of 39 male skulls given in the second paper is 1363 cm.^{3}, with a standard deviation of 106·06 cm.^{3}; while 39 male skulls (including the 9) of the first paper give a mean of 1366 cm.^{3}, and a standard deviation of 91·01 cm.^{3} Hence to exclude the 9 would give unequal mean capacities to the first and second series, and make their standard deviations still more different than they actually are. I think, therefore, they must be included. Indeed Professor Charles speaks in his second paper of all 96 skulls as those of low class Panjabi, but doubts the pureness of blood of these tribes.

We find, including all material available—

	No.	Mean.	Standard Deviation.	Coefficient of Variation.
Men . . .	78	1364·6 cm.^{3}	98·83 cm.^{3}	7·24
Women . .	17	1211·2 ,,	108·88 ,,	8·99

Thus both absolutely and relatively the women are much more variable than the men.

Polynesians.—These statistics are taken from the

Mémoires de la Société d'Anthropologie de Paris, t. iii. pp. 233, 262. I find the following results :—

	No.	Mean.	Standard Deviation.	Coefficient of Variation.
Men . .	110	1588·18 cm.^{3}	130·21 cm.^{3}	8·20
Women . .	55	1397·09 ,,	77·55 ,,	5·55

The men are here markedly more variable than the women. These results for the Polynesians may be compared with a series given by Barnard Davis for Kanakas. The capacities are measured in ounces of Calais sand. I have not reduced them to cubic centimetres, as I do not trust Broca's equivalent.

	No.	Mean.	Standard Deviation.	Coefficient of Variation.
Men . . .	64	77·63 ozs.	5·723 ozs.	7·37
Women . .	47	70·27 ,,	4·695 ,,	6·68

The greater variability of the Polynesian men appears to be thus confirmed.

I have been unable to obtain any female Chinese skull measurements, but it will not be without interest to place here the result for Chinese male skulls. It is strikingly like that for modern Saxons.

	No.	Mean.	Standard Deviation.	Coefficient of Variation.
Men . . .	99	1431·3 cm.^{3}	111·5 cm.^{3}	7·79

It will be seen that the most diverse races exhibit a great constancy in the coefficient of variation for skull capacity.

One other series may be referred to here, although its smallness makes it of very little significance.

Andamanese.—The statistics are given by Sir W. H. Flower in the *Journal of the Anthropological Institute,* vol. ix. p. 108 (1879). I find—

	No.	Mean.	Standard Deviation.	Coefficient of Variation.
Men	11	1244·54 cm.³	62·61 cm.³	5·04
Women . .	12	1127·50 ,,	62·97 ,,	5·59

The women are in this case more variable than the men.

Summary.—Looking at the results of the whole series of skull capacities considered in the preceding pages, we note six races in which the men are more variable with regard to skull capacity and eight in which the women are more variable. There are two in which men and women are sensibly of equal variability. There is thus no marked trend to greater variability in the male sex with regard to skull capacity. It must be noted that this statement is based entirely on the coefficient of variation as a test of relative variability. If we take absolute variation, there are only three races in which women, as judged by the standard deviation, are absolutely as well as relatively more variable than men, namely, among the ancient Anglo-Saxons, the Libyans, and the Panjabi.

We may stay, indeed, to ask whether the statistics of skull capacity do not in themselves give us any information with regard to the superiority of either the standard deviation or the coefficient of variation as a test of that variability which is valuable for progressive evolution.

If we deal solely with the male data, and divide them by order of mean capacity, standard deviation, and coefficient of variation into three lists, we may draw certain general conclusions. Dividing these lists each into three equal parts, and terming these parts high, moderate, and low, we may fairly well draw attention to a race belonging to a particular division with regard to capacity or variation, even if it would be quite futile, considering the diverse methods of measuring capacity adopted by different observers, to base any argument on actual succession in these lists. We note the following points :—

(a) The following races have low capacity and low variation whether we judge by coefficient of variation or standard deviation : Aino, Negroes, Panjabi Outcastes, Libyans, Andamanese.

(b) The following have moderate capacity and low variation, however judged : French peasants.

(c) The following have moderate capacity and moderate variation, whether we judge by coefficient of variation or standard deviation : Ancient Swiss, Anglo-Saxon, modern Saxons, Whitechapel English, and modern Bavarian peasants.

(d) The following have moderate capacity and high variation, however judged : Italians and Friesians.

(e) The following have high capacity and high variation, whether we judge by coefficient of variation or standard deviation : Polynesians, Munich Town Population,[1] and Long Barrow British.

(f) The following have high capacity and high or

---

[1] See, however, a possible reason for this high variation in the series being from an anatomical collection, p. 334.

moderate variation, according as we judge by standard deviation or by coefficient of variation: British and Romano-British, Parisians of the West End.

(g) The following have low capacity and high variation if judged by the coefficient of variation: Ancient Peruvians, Etruscans, and Egyptians. If we judge by the standard deviation, Etruscans retain their high variation, but Egyptians and Peruvians sink to the border of moderate and low variation.

(h) Lastly, the Chinese have low capacity and low or moderate variation according as we judge by the standard deviation or coefficient of variation.

Now, these results certainly do not enable us offhand to say that either standard deviation or coefficient of variation, e.g. absolute or percentage variation, is the better measure of the variability which is a source of "progressive" evolution or of higher civilisation. If we place on one side the remarkable exception of the Polynesians, it would appear that the races which combine a low capacity with a low degree of variability, however this latter be measured, are the non-progressive or "low" races. The coefficient of variation, however, seems superior as a measure of progressive civilisation to the standard deviation, in that it unites ancient and high civilisations, like those of the Egyptians, Etruscans, and Peruvians, in one category, namely, that of low capacity and high variation. In this case it is possible that the low capacity relative to modern German or French town populations is only a sign that a secular evolution in skull capacity has taken place. Judged by the test of the coefficient of variation, we should say that women differ from men in skull capacity, not in the direction of the modern semi-civilised races like Aino, Negro, and Panjabi Outcastes, but as modern man differs from the man of the ancient civilisations of Egypt, Etruria, and Peru. It may be simply a chance coincidence, or it may after all be a deeply significant fact, that those ancient civilisations were very largely the product of matriarchal institutions, *i.e.* were highly developed forms of the primitive civilisation of woman.

The mean coefficient of variation in the case of sixteen races, for which the series are sufficiently large to give to some extent reliable data, is for man 7·74 and for women 7·68. These values are, with due regard to the probable error, essentially identical.

Before we leave the subject of skull capacity we may look at the following table of sexual ratios, and make one or two remarks upon it:—

SEXUAL RATIOS FOR SKULL CAPACITY

Ancient Swiss	1·075	Ancient Friesians	1·130
Libyans	1·077	Anglo-Saxon	1·135
Etruscans	1·093	Polynesians	1·137
Peruvians	1·094	Negroes	1·138
Long Barrow British	1·097	Italians	1·154
Egyptians	1·102	French	1·164
Ainos	1·119	English	1·177
German Peasants	1·126	Whitechapel	1·179
Panjabi	1·127	Romano-British	1·232
Ancient British	1·127		

Now, there are two remarkable exceptions to an obvious general order in this list, namely, the German peasants and the Romano-British. The female skulls found in the Roman tombs in England are very few in number, and possibly no argument of any kind can be based upon them. At any rate, their mean capacity is remarkably less than that of either the Long Barrow British, or what in the *Crania Britannica* appear as Ancient British. There are no skull measurements, so far as I know, of ancient Roman men and women to determine whether the sexual ratio 1·232 is really approximately correct for the Romans. Possibly the Romans in Britain brought Eastern women, hetairae, with them. At any rate, we must for the present exclude this Romano-British ratio from our consideration.

The German peasant ratio, which forms the second exception, cannot be placed on one side in the same manner. In the first place, it is fairly well confirmed by the sexual ratio for Saxon skull capacities (1·115), and by that for the brain weights (1·117) of the Munich population, and in the next place it is not very widely divergent from the sexual ratio for allied races of Ancient Friesians and Anglo-Saxons. It differs, however, in a remarkable manner from the sexual ratios for French and English. The French represent, indeed, a town population, but the large value is confirmed by the sexual ratio (1·158) for brain weights. The English sexual ratio appears trustworthy, although it does not accord well with that for brain weights, nor with those for the Celtic and Teutonic races from which the English may be supposed to have sprung. If it be correct, we should have to lay it down that the English and French males have progressed much more rapidly than the German males on their females. But even this statement would depend upon a comparison of town and country populations.

Putting on one side the Ancient Swiss, a very mixed

series, the Long Barrow British and the Romano-British, we may divide our races into four groups.

I.	II.	III.	IV.
Ancient Civilisations.	Low Races.	Ancient Celts and Teutons.	Modern Celts and Teutons.
Libyans Etruscans Peruvians Egyptians	Ainos Panjabi Polynesians Negroes	British Friesians Anglo-Saxons	English French Italian German
Mean 1·091	Mean 1·130	Mean 1·130	Mean 1·156

It would not be correct to lay too much stress upon this table, but it would seem generally to indicate that the relation of the sexes among our Celtic and Teutonic ancestors was much the same as among the low races of to-day. Modern civilisation tends to give the male preponderating skull capacity, while the ancient civilisations tended to a greater sexual equality. The modern civilisations are largely based upon patriarchal institutions, subjection of the woman, limitation of her struggle for existence, and emphasis of brain-power in that struggle for men. The ancient civilisations were matriarchal, and gave a far greater play to woman's activity. The intermediate groups are those in which physique tells equally with brain-power, and in which we have evidence of transition from matriarchal to patriarchal institutions. Looked at from this standpoint, we might, perhaps, find some explanation for the Long Barrow British according with the matriarchal group, for the Romans according with the modern patriarchal group, and for German peasants of Bavaria according more closely with the intermediate civilisations than with those of the patriarchal group. We may stay to note that whereas in group I. the women are very slightly less variable than the men, in groups II. and III. together they are sensibly equal, and in group IV. the women are more variable than the men.[1] This would accord well with the lessening of the struggle for existence among women as we pass from matriarchal to patriarchal civilisations. On the other hand, the differences are of a very slight and doubtful character. Indeed, the whole table is based upon very limited data, and so far as any conclusions have been drawn from it, they must be considered as merely suggestions for further inquiry and nothing more.

B (d). *Cephalic Index*[2]

I now pass to the last division of the material which

[1] 8·10 to 8·07, 7·58 to 7·59, and 7·78 to 8·11. These are based on the exclusion of the small series of British women.

[2] The following results will be of interest for comparative purposes, although I have failed to obtain equivalent results for the women.

Jews.—I have only succeeded in finding the skulls of twenty-eight Jews in English and German museums. They are those of German, Dutch, Swiss, Italian, English Jews, and vary in date from 1400 onwards! Further, in twelve cases the sex was not given. We should therefore expect to find a high degree of variability. I deduce—

No.	Cephalic Index.	Standard Deviation.
28	80·59	5·07

Taking a much more homogeneous series of head-indices measured on living Jews and given by Stieda (*Archiv für Anthropologie*, Bd. xiv. p. 68), I find—

No.	Head-Index.	Standard Deviation.
67	82·41	2·81

Thus the means are in close accord, for it is a fairly accurate rule that the

I propose at present to consider, namely, the relative variability of men and women with regard to roundness of head. By taking an index we initially free our measurements from any very great sexual influence; and, as the means for both sexes only differ very slightly from each other, it will not be necessary to calculate the coefficients of variation, but we may study relative variation from the size of the standard deviations.

Modern Civilisations

English.—My data are here based on statistics drawn from Barnard Davis, the collections of the Royal College of Surgeons, and various German universities.

	No.	Mean.	Standard Deviation.
Men . . .	50	77·036	3·796
Women . .	25	77·308	4·044

We conclude that English women are more brachycephalic and more variable than English men.

The Whitechapel Skulls.—I owe the measurements subtraction of two units from the mean of the head-index will give the mean of the skull-index,[1] but the standard deviations are, as might be expected, widely different.

Chinese.—My statistics are drawn from the Royal College of Surgeons, Barnard Davis's *Thesaurus Craniorum*, and the catalogues of the German museums. I find—

No.	Cephalic Index.	Standard Deviation.
82	78·957	4·84

The Chinese are thus almost as brachycephalic as the French, and more so than the English.

---

[1] See for a discussion of the point, Welcker, *Schiller's Schädel u. Todtenmaske*, Braunschweig, 1883.

on these skulls to the kindness of Messrs. E. R. Barton and W. H. Peile. They give the following results:—

	No.	Mean.	Standard Deviation.
Men . . .	107	74·725	3·306
Women .	102	74·990	3·367

Thus we see that the women are both more brachycephalic and more variable than the men.

The great divergence between the means of the cephalic indices for the first and second series of English skulls is noteworthy. I find from series of a few hundreds for the living head [1]—

	No.	Mean.	Standard Deviation.
Men . .	150	77·75	2·52
Women .	100	78·75	2·96

There can, I think, be no doubt that English women are thus more variable in cephalic index, but it would appear that there are very considerable divergences in the mean indices for classes, or *for different periods*. For 1102 Cambridge male students—unfortunately there are no results yet available for women students—I find—

	No.	Mean.	Standard Deviation.
Men . . .	1102	79·600	3·033

We are therefore justified in concluding that the English middle and educated classes have a skull-index

[1] From returns of the Anthropometric Committee of the British Association.

of 77 to 78, while the lower and working classes—at least of a few centuries back—have a skull-index of only 74 to 75. This for the problem of evolution is a most significant difference.

French.—I have to thank M. Manouvrier for the statistics on which the following data are based :—

PARISIENS DE L'OUEST

	No.	Mean.	Standard Deviation.
Men	77	79·534	3·274
Women	41	77·923	4·414

PARISIENS DE LA CITÉ

	No.	Mean.	Standard Deviation.
Men	67	79·249	4·456
Women	42	78·001	2·807

We may conclude from both series that Parisian women are less brachycephalic than the men, but just as in the case of the skull capacities the relative variability changes its value if we pass from the West End to the City; see p. 331. In order to test more satisfactorily the relative variability of French men and women, I give data drawn from a large series of skulls in the Paris Catacombs measured by MM. P. Broca and L. Manouvrier, to the latter of whom I am indebted for a transcript of the numbers from the *Registres Crâniométriques* of the Laboratorie d'Anthropologie. The Catacomb skulls were removed from the graveyards between 1792 and 1814, and these graveyards had in many cases been used for several centuries.

	No.	Mean.	Standard Deviation.
Men	735	79·673	4·451
Women	283	78·130	4·220

We are justified therefore in concluding that on the whole Parisian men are more brachycephalic and are more variable in cephalic index than Parisian women. I use the word Parisian, not French, for the French peasant skulls at Munich, fifty-six in number, give a mean of 79·79 and a standard deviation of 3·841, a result slightly nearer to the Parisians of the West, who are less variable than their women.

Italian.—It is interesting to see these results for the French confirmed by the corresponding results for the Italians,—another Romance people. My material was drawn from German museums, the Royal College of Surgeons, and Barnard Davis's *Thesaurus Craniorum.* I find—

	No.	Mean.	Standard Deviation.
Men	110	80·791	4·676
Women	30	80·017	3·636

The high standard deviations of both Italians and Parisians from the Catacombs suggest that, in both cases, we are not dealing with a pure race.

Ancient Romans.—The Italians lead us to the Ancient Romans, and from various sources I have drawn the measurements of forty-three Roman skulls dug up in Italy. They give—

	No.	Mean.	Standard Deviation.
Men . .	31	78·09	3·823
Women .	12	78·67	3·369

These results are not in complete agreement with those for the Romano-Britons (p. 364), who will be found, like the French and Italians, to have their women less brachycephalic than the men, but on the other hand equally variable.

Dutch.—My statistics were principally drawn from German museums. I find—

	No.	Mean.	Standard Deviation.
Men . . .	25	80·00	3·677
Women . .	19	79·395	4·911

Thus the Dutch women are slightly less brachycephalic, but far more variable than the men.

Germans.—My first statistics are taken from Ranke, *Beiträge zur Anthropologie der Bayern*, Bd. i. They are for the Bavarian peasantry.

	No.	Mean.	Standard Deviation.
Men . . .	100	83·41	3·579
Women . .	100	83·095	2·952

The men are accordingly more brachycephalic and more variable than the women.

A second German series is given in Ranke for "Oberfrankish" skulls from Waischenfeld. It is for a series of 100 skulls in all, and I deduce the following data :—

	No.	Mean.	Standard Deviation.
Men . . .	57	83·91	3·525
Women . .	43	84·60	2·790

Here the women are more brachycephalic than the men, but their relative variability remains much the same. It is clear therefore that so far as cephalic index is concerned the Bavarian peasant, from districts so far apart as Aufkirchen and Bayreuth, is more variable than his wife.

Further the greater variability of the German man in cephalic index is confirmed by the following results deduced from Ecker's measurements in the *Crania Germaniae* on the modern Badensians :—

	No.	Mean.	Standard Deviation.
Men . . .	67	83·82	4·003
Women . .	33	83·39	3·380

Even the greater female brachycephaly of the Franconians is not here maintained.

It is important, however, to notice that we cannot determine from a single head measurement straight off whether other head measurements will have a like degree of relative variability. Thus while the Bavarian peasant is much more variable than his wife as to cephalic index, he is far less variable in skull capacity (see p. 333).

Again, I have worked out the numbers for the horizontal circumference of the Waischenfeld skulls, and find—

	No.	Mean.	Standard Deviation.	Coefficient of Variation.
Men . . .	57	528·84 mm.	14·79 mm.	2·797
Women . .	42	502·69 „	13·94 „	2·773

Thus we see that the relative variability of the two sexes for this measurement of capacity is practically one of equality. Unfortunately I had not the capacity measurements of these skulls to compare with those of the *Alt-Bayerisch* population.

The *Alt-Bayerisch* population give for skull circumference—

	No.	Mean.	Standard Deviation.	Coefficient of Variation.
Men . . .	100	524·35 mm.	15·02 mm.	2·865
Women . .	99	501·40 „	15·65 „	3·095

The women are thus, both relatively and absolutely, more variable than the men in skull circumference, although they are less variable in cephalic index.

Modern Badensians, for which the statistics will be found in Ecker's *Crania Germaniae*, give—

	No.	Mean.	Standard Deviation.	Coefficient of Variation.
Men . . .	63	518·95 mm.	15·733 mm.	3·017
Women . .	33	495·76 „	11·587 „	2·337

Row-Grave skulls principally from Baden (Ecker, *Crania Germaniae*) give—

	No.	Mean.	Standard Deviation.	Coefficient of Variation.
Men . .	20	526·6 mm.	14·03 mm.	2·7
Women . .	18	513·6 ,,	12·40 ,,	2·4

Thus both modern and ancient Baden skulls invert the order of relative variation given by the Bavarian skulls, but the last series is so small as to give a difference of the order of the probable error. It illustrates, however, the general rule that the sexes are more nearly equal in their means and have less variation among the less civilised races.

Another point to be borne in mind in discussing the greater variability of German men in cephalic index, is that the standard deviation, as found from material in *village* churchyards, is much lower than that for a town population, and, owing to endogamy, is not a completely satisfactory test of variability. For example, Weisbach[1] gives the following series for Viennese German women,—a branch of the German family closely related to the Bavarians—unfortunately without the corresponding data for men :—

	No.	Mean.	Standard Deviation.
Women . .	24	82·67	4·196

Here the degree of brachycephaly is much the same, but the variation is much greater than that of the Bavarian peasant women.

If we pass to an anatomical collection for a town population such as that of Munich, we find the standard deviation even still higher, *e.g.*—

[1] *Der deutsche Weiberschädel*, 1865.

	No.	Mean.	Standard Deviation.
Men . . .	56	83·39	5·424

Here again, if we compare Viennese German women with Munich German men, the former sex will be found less variable. The variation in the men is certainly exaggerated. Still I think we may conclude that, as far as statistics are *at present* available, the men of South Germany are more variable in cephalic index than the women. The exact value of the relative variability will depend upon the nature of the population, and there is need of larger numbers being measured before it can be definitely determined. It would be fallacious, however, to argue from greater variability in the cephalic index to greater variability in the head in general (see pp. 328, 343).

American Children.—Here I have only the head-index measured on living children, and not the skull-index. Further, I have only the conclusions based by Mr. Porter on his statistics, and not the raw material to calculate from. He does not give the head-index, but the mean length, mean breadth, and probable deviations for boys and girls. From these the mean index and its standard deviation can be calculated.[1] I have

[1] If the distribution of deviations about the mean be symmetrical, and if the deviations be small as compared with the mean, then the head-index mean, r_m, and the standard deviation, σ_r, can be found from the mean length, l_m, mean breadth, b_m, and their standard deviations, σ_l and σ_b, as follows: Let ϵ be a length deviation, η a breadth deviation, and n the number of observations, then

$$r_m = \frac{1}{n}\text{Sum of }\left(\frac{b_m+\eta}{l_m+\epsilon}\right) = \frac{1}{n}\frac{b_m}{l_m} \times \text{Sum of }\left(1 + \frac{\eta}{b_m} - \frac{\epsilon}{l_m}\right)$$

if we neglect terms of order $(\eta/b_m)^2$ and $(\epsilon/l_m)^2$.

confined my attention to children from six to ten years for reasons given in the case of stature and weight, although the approach of puberty does not nearly so markedly influence variation in the case of the head-index.

	Age.	Number.	Mean.	Standard Deviation.
Boys	6	589	80·32	3·12
Girls	6	607	80·87	3·71
Boys	7	1532	80·86	3·63
Girls	7	1508	81·22	3·73
Boys	8	2038	80·89	3·77
Girls . .	8	2050	81·24	3·62
Boys	9	1974	80·72	3·77
Girls	9	1899	81·09	3·64
Boys	10	1869	80·79	3·59
Girls	10	1796	81·10	3·76

Here the number of children measured is the mean of those given for length of head and width of head by Mr. Porter, which are not quite equal.

We see at once that in the sixth, seventh, and tenth years girls, in the eighth and ninth years boys, are more

Thus
$$r_m = \frac{b_m}{l_m}\left(1 + \frac{\text{Sum of } \eta}{n b_m} - \frac{\text{Sum of } \epsilon}{n l_m}\right),$$
but the sums of the deviations η and ϵ are zero. Hence
$$r_m = b_m/l_m \qquad \qquad \text{(i.)}$$
A little knowledge of the theory of chance shows that
$$\sigma_m = r_m \left\{ \left(\frac{\sigma_l}{l_m}\right)^2 + \left(\frac{\sigma_b}{b_m}\right)^2 - 2\rho \frac{\sigma_l}{l_m}\frac{\sigma_b}{b_m} \right\}^{\frac{1}{2}}. \qquad \text{(ii.),}$$
where ρ is the coefficient of correlation between length and breadth of the head. My best *skull* measurements give ρ for a Teutonic people about ·28. I have used (i.) and (ii.) for my reductions of Mr. Porter's data, putting $\rho = ·28$.

variable in the head-index. The mean standard deviation for girls is 3·69, and for boys 3·58. Thus we see that girls are slightly more variable than boys. They are uniformly more brachycephalic.

Now the years of childhood are essentially the years during which natural selection may be supposed to be most active. Yet for the organs we have taken (weight, stature, head-index, etc.) there is a slightly greater variety for progressive evolution to work upon in girls than in boys. Other organs might, perhaps, give a slight advantage to boys. But, taken as a whole, it appears fairly certain that girls are not more conservative than boys to their type.

Ancient Celtic and Teutonic Races

Swiss.—The material is given by His and Rutimeyer in the *Crania Helvetica*. The same difficulties as we have previously (p. 336) noted, again arise. The mixture of various races would not influence the standard deviation as a test of relative variability, if fairly equal proportions of men and women had been taken in each class. Thus the authors give—

(1) Sion type, Mesocephalic (77·2) . . 16 men, 12 women.
(2) Hohberg type, Hyperdolichocephalic (70·7) 10 ,, 3 ,,
(3) Disentis type, Hyperbrachycephalic (86·5) 19 ,, 8 ,,
(4) "Mixed" types . . . 17 ,, 8 ,,

If, as the authors suppose, these are different racial types, and not collections of extremes from several races mixed together, we ought to have equal proportions of men and women under each type to come to any definite conclusions, but it will be seen at once that the proportions are very badly balanced. Nor can we suppose, if they are not distinct types, that we have got a really random selection, for the several types have been filled up to their present numbers by "selected modern skulls." Taking the material for what it is worth, I find—

	No.	Mean.	Standard Deviation.
Men . . .	62	78·89	6·36
Women . .	36	80·51	5·54

The women are thus far more brachycephalic than the men, and much less variable. The large values of the standard deviations, however, show at once that we are dealing with a mixture, and the data must be considered as of no weight for our present purpose.

Ancient Germans.—From the Row-Graves of the fourth to the sixth centuries in Baden, a number of skulls have been measured by Alexander Ecker in his *Crania Germaniae meridionalis occidentalis*, 1865. From the eighty-three skulls from ancient graves in that work, only forty-four can be taken as Row-Grave skulls with sex fairly well determined. From their measurements I deduce—

	No.	Mean.	Standard Deviation.
Men . . .	24	73·71	2·283
Women . .	20	74·07	2·349

Thus the women are more brachycephalic and more variable than the men. Virchow has already noted that the women of the Wiesbaden Row-Graves are more variable than the men in the shape of their eye-sockets (see his *Beiträge zur physischen Anthropologie der Deutschen*, § 141). This, however, is not in agreement with the conditions existing among the Bavarians (see p. 327, where we have dealt with large numbers as compared with Virchow).

Ancient Gaulish Skulls.—The statistics are given by Thurnam in the work cited on p. 337. I find—

	No.	Mean.	Standard Deviation.
Men . . .	36	78·36	4·44
Women . .	25	75·40	4·31

The men are thus much more brachycephalic and slightly more variable than the women. This agrees with the conclusion we have formed for the modern French.

Long Barrow British.—The statistics are due to Thurnam. A difficulty here occurs about the female skull No. 19 (see p. 69 of Thurnam), which has the remarkable index of 56! Thurnam remarks: "To a small extent, some of the existing narrowness of this calvarium may be due to posthumous distortion." So little weight must be given to these statistics, that if we include this skull we find women more dolichocephalic and more variable than men; if we exclude it, they are more brachycephalic and far less variable; whereas, if we allow a quarter of its deviation from the mean to be due to posthumous distortion, we shall have to conclude that women and men are sensibly equal in index and variation! Yet it is on isolated measurements of this kind that craniologists have too often based some statement as to the relative variability of the sexes.

	No.	Mean.	Standard Deviation.
Men	60	71·77	3·89
Women with skull, 19 . .	21	71·57	4·21
,, without skull, 19 .	20	72·35	2·41
,, allowing for skull, 19	21	71·76	3·54

It is clearly impossible to make any very definite assertion as to the relative variability of the Long Barrow British skulls. We have not sufficient Round Barrow female skulls to form the comparison which would be of interest. The Round Barrow men give for twenty-five skulls a mean of 80·92, and a standard deviation of 3·825. Thus while the variation of the two races is practically the same, one is hyperdolichocephalic in character, and the other brachycephalic.

If we take the whole series of Ancient Britons given in the *Crania Britannica*, we find—

	No.	Mean.	Standard Deviation.
Men . . .	114	77·3	5·51
Women . .	30	76·8	5·42

The men are here very slightly more brachycephalic and more variable than the women, within, indeed, the limits of probable error. The curve for the men, however, shows us pretty clearly that we are dealing with a mixture of races, a fact also evident from the high variation.

Romans and Romano-Britons.—This is the title of a group of skulls included in the *Crania Britannica*. They give the following data:—

	No.	Mean.	Standard Deviation.
Men	36	77·31	3·41
Women	13	76·08	3·45

The men are more brachycephalic than the women, but very slightly less variable.

Friesians.—My statistics are drawn from Virchow, Sasse, and Barnard Davis. I find—

	No.	Mean.	Standard Deviation.
Men	83	77·753	3·573
Women	40	79·025	3·788

Thus the Friesian women are more brachycephalic and more variable than the men.

Anglo-Saxons.—The statistics were taken from the *Crania Britannica*. The data obtained are—

	No.	Mean.	Standard Deviation.
Men	35	75·00	3·135
Women	21	75·05	2·553

The men and women are about equally brachycephalic, but the men are more variable than the women. The close relation of the means in these results to those for the Whitechapel English is to be noted.

Aborigines of Sweden and Denmark.—My statistics are taken from the *Crania Britannica.* I find—

	No.	Mean.	Standard Deviation.
Men . .	35	77·86	3·97
Women .	13	78·15	4·13

The women are thus more brachycephalic and more variable than the men.

Virchow, in his work, *Die Altnordischen Schädel zu Kopenhagen,* gives forty-three skulls belonging to the stone-age from Borreley, Falster, and Möen, without determination of sex. From his measurements I find— mean, 77·27, and standard deviation, 3·66 ; results fairly in accord with the above.

Thurnam (*loc. cit.* p. 337) gives twenty-eight skulls from the chambered long barrows of Falster and Möen, from which I deduce—

	No.	Mean.	Standard Deviation.
Men . . .	20	78·9	3·51
Women . .	8	79·87	3·85

The series is far too small to be of weight, but, so far as it goes, it confirms the above result that the ancient Scandinavian women were more brachycephalic and more variable than the men.

To sum up the results for the ancient Celtic and Teutonic races, we may state that—

(*a*) The ancient Celtic women were less, and the

ancient Teutonic women more, brachycephalic than the men.

(b) There is in neither sex a marked preponderance of variability, and it would be difficult to draw very definite conclusions. The Celtic women appear on the whole to be slightly less, and the Teutonic women slightly more, variable than the men.

Ancient Civilisations

Etruscans.—My statistics are taken from the Leipzig Anthropological Catalogue. I find—

	No.	Mean.	Standard Deviation.
Men . .	84	78·53	3·31
Women .	36	78·21	3·46

The women are very slightly less brachycephalic, and are more variable than the men.

Egyptians.— The measurements were made on mummy skulls, and are published in various parts of the great German Anthropological Catalogue. They give—

	No.	Mean.	Standard Deviation.
Men . . .	336	75·08	3·35
Women . .	173	76·22	3·36

The women are more brachycephalic than the men, but both sexes are sensibly equal in the amount of their variation.

Libyans (?)—The skulls were brought from Egypt

by Professor Flinders Petrie, and the necessary measurements most kindly made for me by Mr. H. Thompson. I find—

	No.	Mean.	Standard Deviation.
Men ..	89	73·16	2·881
Women ..	125	74·56	2·879

We conclude therefore that the women are more brachycephalic than the men, and that both sexes are equally variable.

Peruvians.—The statistics of this race are taken from the Leipzig Anthropological Catalogue. The hyperbrachycephaly of the race appears to be largely due to artificial flattening of the skull, the index being in several cases, not confined to one sex, over 100!

	No.	Mean.	Standard Deviation.
Men ..	47	89·15	8·25
Women ..	23	91·80	8·47

Thus, whether the brachycephaly be in large part artificial or be natural, the women exceed the men in roundheadedness and also in variability.

Summing up our results for the old civilisations, we find women slightly more brachycephalic and slightly more variable than their male comrades.

Lower Races

Aino.—The statistics are taken from the work referred to on p. 302. A lesser number of skulls has been dealt with by Tarentzky, but they were from another island. He finds the women sensibly more brachycephalic than the men (76·1 to 74·5), so far confirming the data below. Not having seen his original paper, I have been unable to compare his results for variation with those of the Japanese craniologist.

	No.	Mean.	Standard Deviation.
Men . .	87	76·53	2·41
Women . .	63	77·72	2·54

The women are thus sensibly more brachycephalic and more variable than the men. In the case of skull capacity, we have seen (p. 340) that the men were very slightly more variable than the women.

Negroes.—I owe my statistics to the same source as those for skull capacities (see p. 340). I find—

	No.	Mean.	Standard Deviation.
Men . . .	54	73·28	2·77
Women . .	23	74·85	3·52

The women are thus more brachycephalic and sensibly more variable than the men.

Panjabi.—These results are calculated from the measurements of Professor Charles referred to on p. 341.

	No.	Mean.	Standard Deviation.
Men . . .	79	70·66	2·985
Women . .	17	72·34	3·749

The women are thus much more brachycephalic and much more variable than the men.

Polynesians. — Barnard Davis, in his *Thesaurus Craniorum*, gives a fairly large series of Kanaka skulls. Unfortunately, they appear to be drawn from rather diverse districts, and the variation is accordingly much larger than we should probably find it to be in a more locally restricted series. I find from Barnard Davis's numbers—

	No.	Mean.	Standard Deviation.
Men . . .	69	79·29	4·325
Women . .	57	80·26	4·261

Thus the women are more brachycephalic and the men more variable. The difference of variability, however, is considerably less than the probable error (about ·37) of the difference of the standard deviations. In other words, if this series stood alone, we should only be justified in saying that men and women were equally variable. The reader must be careful to remember that, throughout the many series treated in this paper, the difference between male and female variability is over and over again less than the probable error of the observations, and that it is only by judging how these differences run in the mass of cases considered, that we shall be able to judge of any preponderating variability in either sex.

Andamanese.—The *locus* of the measurements upon which my calculations are based is given on p. 343. I find—

	No.	Mean.	Standard Deviation.
Men . . .	12	80·567	2·631
Women . .	12	82·725	2·157

Thus the women are much more brachycephalic and less variable than the men.

Aborigines of Australia.—(W. L. H. Duckworth, *Journal of the Anthropological Institute*, vol. xxiii. p. 284, 1894). This is a very small series for women, and accordingly but little weight must be given to it.

	No.	Mean.	Standard Deviation.
Men . . .	29	70·34	2·986
Women . .	5	72·20	2·023

The women are again more brachycephalic than the men, and less variable.

Thus the lower races give us results in sensible accordance with those we have drawn from the data for ancient civilisations, namely, the women are on the whole more brachycephalic and slightly more variable than the men.

If we form a table of the variability in cephalic index of men and women, grouping the races dealt with into the same four classes,—Ancient Civilisations, Lower Races, Ancient Celts and Teutons, Modern Civilisations,—and take the mean values of the standard deviations in each group, we have the following results :—

VARIATION IN CEPHALIC INDEX[1]

Group.	No.	Men.	Women.
Ancient Civilisations. . . .	3	3·18	3·23
Lower Races	5	3·02	3·25
Ancient Celts and Teutons	7	3·47	3·49
Modern Civilisations	11	3·85	3·66
Total Mean		3·51	3·54

This table shows us that the modern civilisations and the ancient races from which they sprung are more variable than the ancient civilisations and the lower races, and this in the case of both sexes. In all the groups, except that of modern civilisations, woman is slightly more variable than man. In the latter group she is less variable. For the mean of the whole twenty-six races included in this table she appears slightly more variable. If the *whole* series of observations be weighted, she appears slightly less variable: see the Table, p. 374.

So far, then, as this important ratio goes, we have on the whole no evidence whatever for a much greater trend to variability in man than in woman. Yet it is an undoubted fact that the brachycephalic populations have ousted the dolichocephalic in the struggle for existence; they are the dominant races of the modern world. In the cephalic index, at least, there appears some evidence of the influence of the struggle for existence, and in this measurement we might hope to find some evidence

[1] All series with a standard deviation greater than five have been excluded as heterogeneous, or as influenced by artificial deformation.

of the greater variability of man, if that indeed be a great biological fact. But we find no certain traces of it whatever. Cephalic index, like skull capacity, and like indeed stature, brain weight, body weight, and profile angle, gives us no indisputable evidence of the variability of man being sensibly greater than that of woman.

General Summary.—In order to render it to some extent possible for the reader to appreciate the general trend of the various statistics given in this paper, I have endeavoured to roughly weight the various observations cited, not with reference to any assumed accuracy on the part of the observer, but solely on the basis of the number of observations recorded in each case. If 25 observations be taken as the unit, then the weights of 25, 100, 225, 400, 625, 900, 1225, 1600, 2025, will be respectively 1, 2, 3, 4, 5, 6, 7, 8, 9. In each case it has been considered sufficient to use the weight corresponding to the number in the above series nearest to the number of the lesser series of measurements. By this means the following table has been deduced for the frequency of each ratio of variations :—

Value of Ratio of Male to Female Variation.	Frequency.	Value of Ratio of Male to Female Variation.	Frequency.
Between		Between	
·60- ·65	5	1·10-1·15	13
·65- ·70	2	1·15-1·20	5
·70- ·75	10	1·20-1·25	16
·75- ·80	34	1·25-1·30	9
·80- ·85	39	1·30-1·35	0
·85- ·90	43	1·35-1·40	6
·90- ·95	82	1·40-1·45	0
·95-1·00	161	1·45-1·50	3
1·00-1·05	89	1·50-1·55	0
1·05-1·10	48	1·55-1·60	3

The mean of the whole series is ·973, with a probable error of the mean of ·007. The "scatter" about this mean of the frequency is given by a standard deviation of ·1337.

Since the mean differs by nearly four times its probable error from unity, we may consider it probable

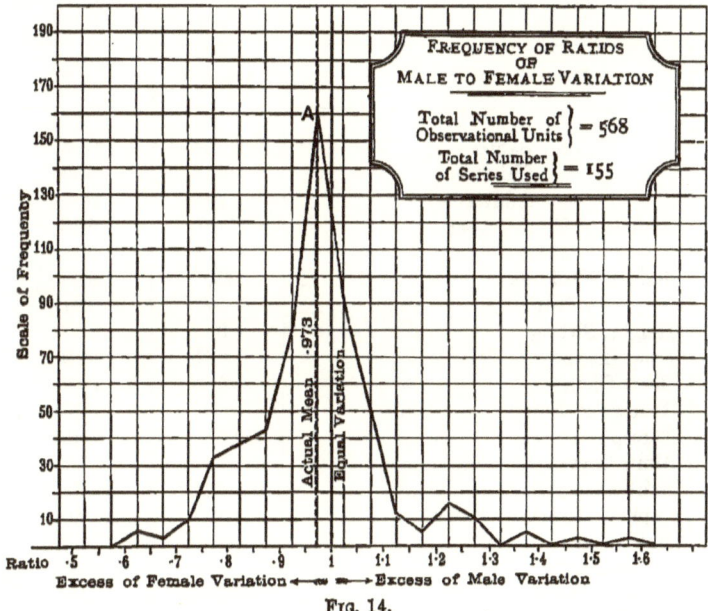

Fig. 14.

that the ratio of male to female variation has a quantity less than unity for its mean value, or that on the average there is a slightly preponderating variation in the female sex evidenced by the present series of measurements. The reader will best realise the clustering of the ratio of male and female variations round the value unity by an examination of the accompanying figure. The slight preponderance which actually exists will be seen to be on the side of woman.

I strongly suspect that this preponderating variability of women is mainly due to a relatively less severe struggle for existence. The following table gives the weighted means of the sexual ratio and the variation ratio for the chief groups of measurements dealt with, and illustrates the general result from a somewhat different point of view :—

Organ or Group of Organs.	Sexual Ratio.[1]	Variation Ratio.[1]
Body Weight, Babies	1·034	1·024
,, Children	1·038	·899
,, Adults	1·193	·899
Weight of Vital Organs	1·130	·886
,, Brain	1·109	·984
Stature, Children	1·007	·988
,, Adults	1·077	·971
Height, Sitting	1·032	1·146
Long Bones	1·086	1·019
Chest Girth	1·024	·951
Squeeze of Hands	1·207	·879
Perceptivity [2]	1·061	·898
Skull Capacity	1·124	1·011
Skull Circumference	1·042	1·082
Cephalic Index	·997	1·046
Head Index	·995	·982
Profile Angle	·994	·765
Alveolar Angle	·994	·790
Eye-Sockets, etc.	·991	1·184
Nose and Palate	1·013	·949

In the above seventeen groups it will be seen that female variability is greater in eleven, and male variability is greater in six. A notable feature is that woman, while more variable in stature, is less variable in height sitting and in long bones, which are the principal com-

[1] Here sexual ratio is the ratio of male to female mean, and variation ratio is the ratio of male to female variation.

[2] Keenness of sight and touch (sensitivity).

ponent parts of stature. It would seem therefore reasonable to hold that the parts of a woman's body are more closely correlated than those of a man's.

So far as the data we have considered extend, the conclusion we must draw from them is that there is no markedly preponderating variability in either sex. The variability of men and women is not very different now from what it was 5000 years ago, and the differences in male and female variability are apparently far less than racial differences in variability, and even less than differences in the same race living under diverse conditions, or indeed at opposite ends of the town.

I am quite aware how small are some of the series dealt with, how few are the races considered, and how isolated the organs in these races, of which the variation has been discussed. But I would ask the reader to remember how sparse is the available material, and how comparatively laborious is the arithmetic. Skulls are to be obtained not by the hundred, but too often only by the ten, or even only by units. I have used as wide a range of material as I could find. When more material is available, and finer methods are applied, then, perhaps, it will be possible to detect a more noteworthy preponderance of variability in the one or other sex. What I would contend for at present, however, is embraced in the following statements:—

(a) A principle, as to the greater variability of the male, has hitherto been often enunciated.

(b) Variability, however, has not hitherto been defined in a quantitative manner that will admit of a real comparison of the variability of the sexes.

(c) There is more than one method of quantitatively measuring variability, but the measure which is really significant for progressive evolution has not hitherto been determined.

(d) This measure, if determined, ought to be applied to normal variation, rather than to pathological characters.

(e) If we accept as a possible or indeed probable measure of significant variation, the so-called coefficient of variation, i.e. the percentage variation, for cases in which the sexual means differ considerably, and the standard deviation for cases in which the means are practically identical, then there is in the material considered in this paper—and it appears to represent more cases of normal variation than have hitherto been treated quantitatively—no evidence of greater male variability, but rather of a slightly greater female variability.

(f) Accordingly, the principle that man is more variable than woman must be put on one side as a pseudo-scientific superstition until it has been demonstrated in a more scientific manner than has hitherto been attempted.

(g) Those writers who find in this principle not only "social and practical consequences of the widest significance," but also an explanation of the peculiar characteristics of "the whole of our human civilisation," are scarcely to be trusted when they deal with the problems of sex.

I would ask the reader to note that I do not proclaim the equal variability of the sexes, but merely assert that the present results show that the greater variability often claimed for man remains as yet a quite unproven principle. The numerous popular writers who have seized this principle as a text upon which to preach various social lessons are, in my opinion, starting from either a dogma or a superstition, and not from a result of genuine scientific research. The "sequacity" exhibited by the multitude of semi-scientific writers on evolution is possibly a sign of the very small capacity for intellectual variation possessed by the literary male.

APPENDIX

I HAVE reprinted this paper notwithstanding its very controversial character, because I am extremely anxious that mechanism, which is the basis of all modern science, should be rightly understood, and not confused—as it apparently is both by Mr. Balfour and Mr. St. George Mivart—with the materialism of a Ludwig Büchner.

SECTARIAN CRITICISM[1]

"He never states his case fairly, and makes wonderful blunders."—Darwin on Mivart, *Life*, iii. p. 148.

THE sectarian critic is one who is so carried away by his own beliefs, or rather the beliefs of his sect, that he, consciously or unconsciously, refuses to those he criticises every characteristic which is peculiar to them. The criticised may time after time have asserted that they hold such and such views; it matters not, the sectarian critic insists that they *shall* hold some opinion which he, the critic, can relieve his own conscience by pulling to pieces. "Is your name Daniel Nathaniel, sir, or Nathaniel Daniel?" there is no other possibility, because the sectary is a deaf and incompetent judge. As he himself accepts his beliefs at the bidding of his ecclesiastical authorities, so the criticised are bound to accept what he in his turn thrusts upon them *nolentes volentes*. Now if I have for years protested against anything in particular—and many may think I have done a good deal of protesting—it has been against the attempt to force any form of materialism upon science. It makes, however, no difference. I must be a materialist, because such is the con-

[1] From the *Fortnightly Review*, November 1895. A rejoinder from Mr. Mivart will also be found in the December number of the same journal.

clusion arrived at by Mr. St. George Mivart.[1] My "idealism is—
no doubt unconsciously " (I am much obliged for the tribute to my
honesty)—"an idealism of parade, to be brought out occasionally
(above all, to confound some intellectualist or advocate of common
sense), but ordinarily to be ignored in favour of practical materialism.
To the vulgar a doctrine is presented which, as understood and
accepted, is truly materialistic, while to opponents of materialism it
is offered in terms of idealism." . . . To prove that I "ordinarily
ignore" idealism, Mr. St. George Mivart quotes two or three
passages, dragged from their context, in my *Grammar of Science*,
and cries, "Ha! see the materialist!" Now, having carefully
explained in that work that phenomena are for us "constructs"
ultimately based on sense-impressions, and that behind the veil of
sense-impression we cannot penetrate and *know*, does Mr. Mivart
expect that every time I use a noun denoting a phenomenon, I
must add: Yes, but it is a "construct"? I am not to use the
word "physical," or speak of a "star," or talk about evolution
being at the basis of human history, although I fully define what I
mean my reader to understand by the word physical, by an
object and by history in my work at large. Mr. Mivart asserts
that the vulgar are hereby ingeniously presented with practical
materialism. I do not know who "the vulgar" may be to whom
he refers, but if he means thereby those professed freethinkers who
have not a scientific training, he has only to examine the pages of
abuse to which I am treated in the second volume of Bonnar's *Life
of Bradlaugh* to ascertain that "the vulgar" by no means mistake
my idealism for any form of practical materialism. Nay, I go so
far as to assert that Mr. St. George Mivart is, "no doubt unconsciously," dishonest when he asserts my materialism and yet
professes to have read my article on "Politics and Science," in
which the following passage occurs:—

> It has been left entirely to an always limited, and now practically
> discredited school—that of Moleschott and Büchner—to "explain" the
> whole universe by "matter" and "force." . . . It must always be impos-
> sible for any one who has the least acquaintance with logical processes to
> deduce an "explanation" of anything by attributing "laws of force" to an
> inexplicable "matter."

I repeat that it is—"no doubt unconsciously"—dishonest of Mr.

[1] See the *Fortnightly Review* for September 1895.

Mivart to profess to have read my *Grammar of Science* and then to suggest that I

Find mental satisfaction in thinking of minute, solid, moving particles as the really essential constituents of all bodies . . . and the sufficient explanation of all the properties they possess.

Or that I, with "the greatest simplicity," fall into the error of "explaining" things by motion at all.

Over and over again in the *Grammar* I assert that an *explanation* is never given by science. That the whole of science is *description*, and that mechanism explains nothing. I further assert that corpuscles, whether atoms or molecules, are *not* real and essential constituents of bodies, but merely mental concepts, and that while we experience change of sensation, motion is itself as conceptual as geometry:—

If, however, the scientist projects the whole of his conceptual machinery into the perceptual world, he throws himself open to the charge of being as dogmatic as either theologian or metaphysician. On the other hand, when he simply postulates the conceptual value of his symbols as a mode of describing past and predicting future perceptual experience, then his position is unassailable, for he asserts nothing as to the *why* of phenomena. But as soon as he does this, matter as that which moves, and force as the cause of motion, disappear into the limbo of self-contradictory notions. What moves is only a geometrical ideal, and it moves only in conception. Why things move thus becomes an idle question, and *how* things are to be *conceived* as moving the true problem of physical science (p. 385).

Now it was perfectly open to Mr. St. George Mivart to argue that this statement is nonsense, but when he asserts that the writer of it is teaching "practical materialism" to "the vulgar,"[1] then he is merely exhibiting that sect bias which cannot get beyond shrieking "Daniel Nathaniel, sir, or Nathaniel Daniel?" What I demand is simply that the word "materialism" shall be used in its legitimate and technical sense, *i.e.* to describe some form of philosophic belief

[1] Perhaps the most amusingly "vulgar" was the member of my Gresham audience, who, hearing the lectures, afterwards rewritten as the *Grammar of Science*, wrote to the then Lord Mayor that I ought to be removed from my post, as I was an infidel, *because* I did not believe in "matter." Yet I think he had more insight than Mr. Mivart exhibits.

which starts from properties asserted to belong to matter—and that it shall not be used as a sectarian word of abuse for any one who differs from the user in his theory of life. Especially is the word out of place, when the chief feature of the philosophy of life to which it is applied consists in the statement that the idea of matter has no place in the field of knowledge, and ought to be excluded from all scientific treatises.[1] This statement may be true or false, but it is mere fatuity to characterise it as "practical materialism." Mr. Mivart is not, however, content with confusion as to materialism, he has never apparently attempted to define metaphysics for himself. He still belongs to the thoughtless crowd, who, if they read words of which they grasp not the meaning, ejaculate : Metaphysics ! Now the *Grammar of Science*, rightly or wrongly, with that I am not now concerned, confines the sphere of knowledge to the world of perceptions and the conceptions drawn from it. It denies the possibility of our knowing what lies behind the perceptual veil. In short, correctly or incorrectly, it repudiates the entire field of metaphysics.[2] Yet Mr. Mivart asserts that its author is a metaphysician *malgré lui !* Again we demand that words shall at least be used—especially by one who claims to be a man of science—with some regard for their customary or accepted senses.

Nor does Mr. Mivart's—"no doubt unconscious"—misstatement of my views end here. He states that I *complain* that " Mr. Balfour has demonstrated that naturalism affords no basis for ethics." Now I never made any complaint at all, nor have I ever allowed that Mr. Balfour has succeeded in demonstrating anything.[3] What I did write was that " Mr. Balfour's demonstration " (hopelessly illogical) "that naturalism affords no basis for ethics . . . will go far . . . to bring the new bigotry into line with the Tory party." That was no complaint ; it was a statement of fact, or rather a prophecy which has been amply fulfilled by the recent elections. In the next place, I never *complained* that the appearance of anarchists of the type of Caserio and Vaillant was attributed to

---

[1] "If our leading scientists either fail to tell us what matter is, or even go so far as to assert that we are probably incapable of knowing, it is surely time to question whether this fetish of the metaphysicians need be preserved in the temple of science,' *Grammar of Science*, p. 295.

[2] See *Grammar of Science*, pp. 87-90.

[3] My criticism of Mr. Balfour's *Foundations of Belief* will be found in the essay on " Reaction !"

teaching such as *my own*, which is what Mr. Mivart causes me to say. What I did do was to point out that reaction had seized even the Liberal journals, for they attributed "to the materialism of science and 'naturalistic' ethics the appearance of criminal anarchists" ("Politics and Science," p. 149). As I in the very same article distinctly repudiated the relation asserted between materialism and science, and as I further repudiate entirely, both for myself and for science, what I can understand of Mr. Balfour's account of naturalistic ethics, it is merely sectarian criticism to alter not only the form but the sense of my words, and suggest that there was any personal reference in the sentence at all. The object of Mr. Mivart is, of course, extremely clear; he wishes to hint that there is after all some relation between criminal anarchists and those who, like myself, have not emulated Mr. Herbert Spencer "in the excellent service he has of late done to rational conservatism."

If the sole criticism which Mr. Mivart is able to pass on the *Grammar of Science* is the nominal one that I am a metaphysician *malgré lui*, who teaches "practical materialism"—for he does not criticise one of the special features of the work—how much feebler still is his reference to my article on Lord Salisbury's Address! He raises only two points. In the first place, he says I am very angry (as a matter of fact amusement was then, as it is now, uppermost in my mind) with Lord Salisbury for saying that we know absolutely nothing about the ether except that it can be made to undulate. I said that that statement was as absurd as the statement would be that we know nothing about planetary matter except that it can gravitate. On the whole, upon second thoughts, I consider that it is rather more absurd, and the statement would possibly be better appreciated by Mr. Mivart if he were a physicist—especially a physicist who looked upon the ether not as an unknown feature of the phenomenal world, but as a conceptual model used to briefly resume a wide range of phenomenal experience. Probably Haeckel, if he considers the ether as God, as Mr. Mivart asserts, knows as little about it as his biological critic. At any rate, "scientific physicists" did not want Lord Salisbury's remarks to save them from falling into the views which Mr. Mivart attributes to Haeckel. I have had occasion to study a good deal of the recent mathematical and physical literature on the ether, and find absolutely none of those "exaggerated notions" "so widely spread" from which Lord Salisbury's remark is to save "persons interested in physics, and, above all, scientific physicists." If Mr. Mivart will study the recent work of J. J. Thomson, Heaviside, and Larmor, he will then be in a better position to judge whether we know nothing about the ether "except that it can be made to undulate." Of course nobody knows what a phenomenal ether is, any more than they know what a phenomenal force or a phenomenal molecule is; but this is not surprising, if, as the present writer holds, ether is a pure concept. To know *how* a thing moves—or, as I should prefer to say, to know what conceptual motions must be attributed to the ideal system in order to efficiently describe phenomena—is the essential problem of physics, and of the *how* of ether-motion we know infinitely more than can possibly be covered by the words used by Lord Salisbury. To revert for a moment to old terminology, we do not know what matter is, but would the phrase "we know nothing about matter except that it can be made to move," in the least express the present condition of molar physics? In the case of both matter and ether the fundamental scientific problem is the *how* of motion, and not the search for a metaphysical basis for those groups of sense-impressions which science describes, and on the whole describes so successfully, by aid of molar and etherial motions.

The next point which Mr. St. George Mivart cites from "Politics and Science" is my criticism of Lord Salisbury's remarks on the problem of the origin of the elements. Mr. Mivart, as usual, tries to confuse the issue by asserting that I suggest that the "chemical elements may have arisen by 'natural selection' after all." Now I did not use the word natural selection in this sense in my paper on "Politics and Science," although I might very well have done so. What I did say of the problem of the elements was, it was highly probable that evolution by physical "selection of stable forms is the key to the solution" ("Politics and Science," p. 156). In the *Grammar of Science*[1] I drew for convenience a distinction between physical and natural selection, although everything "physical" is of course "natural." I made this distinction because I wanted to

---

[1] I stated in the *Grammar* that the idea of physical selection of stable forms is in the first place due to Crookes (p. 423), a fact which Mr. Mivart seems strangely ignorant of, when he speaks of the suggestion as coming from Haeckel or from me!

remind biologists that in the early stages of life what they were accustomed to speak of as natural selection passed over into what might be described as a mere physical selection of stabler compounds. But as a matter of fact, natural selection in its true meaning covers inorganic just as much as organic selection. When Mr. Mivart writes "the essence of natural selection is the *hereditary* transmission of favourable variations," then I simply and flatly say that his statement is absolutely incorrect. Natural Selection in itself has nothing to do with heredity. Darwin's theory of evolution is that of natural selection *combined* with heredity, and Lord Salisbury is better informed than Mr. St. George Mivart since even he speaks of "accidental variations *perpetuated by heredity* under the influence of natural selection."

Natural selection itself merely signifies the selection of variations useful to the individual, or giving it a more stable relation to its environment. It is perfectly compatible with a complete absence of heredity, but natural selection without heredity is, of course, not "Darwinism." Now the word evolution covers not only natural selection, but physical selection, and sexual selection, or any *vera causa* of progressive change in organic or inorganic types. Hence my criticism of Lord Salisbury's statement that nothing was to be got "by muttering the comfortable word evolution," for the problem of the origin of the elements was perfectly justified. His jest about the breeding of elementary atoms, only showed that he had not grasped the really important part which, with a high degree of probability, the physical selection of stabler groupings plays in the evolution of both inorganic and early organic life.

Mr. Mivart then proceeds to ask how prime atoms came to acquire "the characters and qualities necessary for them to be able to congregate and adhere in groups." He professes to have read the *Grammar of Science*, and still asks *me* this question! He is, indeed, a materialist with a vengeance; the prime atom is clearly for him a most real and material entity, and not a mere symbol of description. No doubt his soul is equally vexed by a particle of matter obeying the law of gravitation, but because I accept, with the majority of physicists, that particles are to be considered as gravitating and atoms as attracting, am I called upon to "explain" (a word I entirely repudiate for science), on the penalty of being termed a "denominational scientist" and a slave to "shallow and illogical imaginary phantasms," how Mr. Mivart's materialistic atoms and particles adhere? I have no doubt I shall take poor Mr. Mivart's breath away, and he may even suggest that I am blasphemous, but I assure him that I honestly hold the view, that it is the physicists themselves, and not any "influence from *without*, or powers *within*," that make particles gravitate. Why do we make them gravitate? Simply because up to date no better formula has been found for working the conceptual model by which we describe phenomena.

My two criticisms of Lord Salisbury are the *sole* sentences indicating my "scientific prejudices," which Mr. Mivart cites to justify his statement that I am "a denominational writer, only second in self-confident dogmatism to Haeckel." He might have brought forward far more individual and dogmatic statements from the *Grammar of Science*, but they would not have suited his purpose, for they would have shown that my scientific heterodoxy lay in idealism, not in materialism. As Darwin wrote of Mr. St. George Mivart, nearly a quarter of a century ago, "he meant to be fair, but he was stimulated by theological fervour." That is the real, the true basis of Mr. Mivart's attack—he is "stimulated by theological fervour." That is the reason why he makes such an astounding trinity out of Professor Weismann, Professor Haeckel, and the insignificant *Grammarian*. We agree in one matter, and one matter only,[1] that we are agnostic as to the supersensuous; we decline to admit that the unknowable can be reasoned about. Mr. St. George Mivart talks about a "curious hostility to religion which disfigures my pages." I assure him that I have only respect and sympathy for the man who *believes*, but a supreme contempt for the man who attempts to bolster up his belief by an appeal to pseudo-science. He only exhibits the complete shallowness of what Mr. Balfour would term his *epistemology*; he has never logically thought out for himself a critique of the knowable.

Here it is where the shoe pinches Mr. Mivart. He wants to *reason* about God, immortality, heaven and hell, instead of simply believing what his emotional needs, his religious traditions or his

---

[1] In the *Grammar of Science*, I expressly state my dissent from Haeckel's views on the struggle for existence as applied to man. Both in that work and in the papers on "Socialism and Natural Selection" and on "Politics and Science," I express my dissent from what I can understand of Weismann's views on germ-plasm and panmixia.

ecclesiastical authorities require of him. And he is much moved to find that science cannot legitimately aid him, and that some scientists are prepared to tell him so. My readers "may think me a bigot when I say, after studying Mivart, I was never before so convinced of the *general* . . . truth of the views"[1] contained in my *Grammar of Science*. Let me explain what I mean. The *Grammar* asserts that of such a metaphysical concept as the soul—not based ultimately on sense-impressions—science cannot possibly reason. Mr. St. George Mivart, on p. 432 of his paper, asserts that—

> We are conscious of being a twofold unity; that we are both material, extended substance, and immaterial persistent energy—a body and soul.

Shortly before he speaks of "the force (*sic !*) which energises (*sic /*) in our consciousness" as "a continuously persisting principle," "a simple unity." In other words, he asserts the existence of an immortal and immaterial soul in man, and adds :—

> No certainty we can attain to about any other object can be nearly so certain as is this truth. It is the primary and highest truth of biological science.

Now what is Mr. Mivart's conception of scientific truth? He leaves us in no doubt. He writes on p. 423 :—

> Different, indeed, is the object of science, the one aim of which should be the advancement of truth. To teach what is true with exactitude, to proclaim that which is doubtful to be doubtful, that which is unknown to be unknown, and that which is true and certain to be evident truth—is its one function, compared with the correct fulfilment of which everything else is relatively valueless.

The object of biological science ought accordingly to be to teach its "primary and highest truth"—the existence and immortality of the soul—with exactitude and certainty. How many biologists— and many are devoutly religious men who *believe* in the existence and immortality of the soul—would venture to follow Mr. St. George Mivart in his glib assertion that this doctrine of their faith is capable of scientific demonstration? Yet if Mr. Mivart cannot *demonstrate* it in a manner to convince the majority of scientific biologists,

[1] See Darwin on Mivart, *Life*, vol. iii. p. 144.

who then is the "denominational scientist"? Who then is assuming "the dogmatic tone of a rash student of divinity"? Accordingly I challenge Mr. St. George Mivart to prove that he is a real man of science and not a blind sectary, by producing a demonstration of "this primary and highest truth of biological science"—a proof that will satisfy the professors of biology in our leading Universities, and enable them "to teach what is true with exactitude"—*Ryk ud med Deres bevis, bygmester! Beviset på bordet!* If Mr. St. George Mivart cannot produce a proof that will satisfy the consensus of biological authority, then it is he, not I, that illustrates "denominational science." He has laid down a standard of the exact and true in science; he has propounded a dogma which he says is the highest truth of biological science. I directly challenge him to demonstrate his asserted truth to the satisfaction of undenominational biologists. If he declines my challenge, or fails to produce a valid proof, then, in the words of Darwin again, we can only "conclude with sorrow that though he means to be honourable, he is so bigoted that he cannot act fairly."[1]

[1] Darwin to Wallace on Mivart, *Life*, iii. p. 145.

END OF VOL. I

Printed by R. & R. CLARK, LIMITED, *Edinburgh.*

www.ingramcontent.com/pod-product-compliance
Lightning Source LLC
Chambersburg PA
CBHW020106010526
44115CB00008B/710